Major General Harry Hill Bandholtz:

An Undiplomatic Diary

With an Introduction on Hungary and WWI

by Fritz-Konrad Krüger

Edited by Andrew L. Simon

Copy of the original book courtesy of the Cleveland Public Library Reference Department

Published by Simon Publications, P.O. Box 321, Safety Harbor, FL 34695

Printed by Lightning Print, Inc. La Vergne, TN 37086

Contents

Introduction

by Andrew L. Simon

Major General Harry Hill Bandholtz was America's representative to the Inter-Allied Supreme Command's Military Mission in Hungary at the end of World War I. Before the first world war, Bandholtz was Chief of the American Constabulary in the Philippines from 1907 until 1913. During WWI Bandholtz was the Provost Marshal General in General Pershing's American Expeditionary Forces in France. His organization, 463 officers and 15,912 men, was the world's largest military police command at the time. Directing it was a huge responsibility. Despite his qualifications and experience, his six-month assignment to Budapest was apparently the most frustrating encounter in General Bandholtz's distinguished military career. He, and his French, British and Italian colleagues and their staffs were supposed to supervise the Romanian occupation of Hungary after the end of the heinous but fortunately brief Bolshevist regime in 1919.

Reading Bandholtz's Diary—notes by an unbiased, high-ranking American Military Police officer having full access to information about the conditions in Hungary—one learns the truth about that turbulent period. First of all, the reader realizes that the popular allegations concerning a "White Terror" in Hungary are without foundation.

On September 29, 1919 Bandholtz wrote: "Colonel [Nathan] Horowitz, who is a member of the Committee on Army Organization and who had visited western Hungary, turned in a report on the general conditions there, and in particular concerning the Jewish persecutions. He stated that in his opinion Admiral Horthy's army had done everything within reason to prevent any such persecutions, and that he considered that no more atrocities had been committed than would ordinarily happen under the stress of such circumstances". On November 18, Bandholtz continues: "As a matter fact, the arrests that were made were practically insignificant, and none were made that were not perfectly justifiable."

As the absolutely incorrect historical memory has it, five thousand people were executed and 70 thousand were imprisoned by Admiral Horthy's Nationalist Army. At least one finds these precise numbers in several history books on

1

Hungary published in the 1990's. They symbolize a gross falsification of history, comparable to the denial of the Holocaust. These lies are obviously the products of well organized and uninterrupted Bolshevik and Little Entente propaganda that went on for some 80 years.

Bandholtz writes far more about atrocities by the "Allied" Romanian Army, about the occasional rumors of impending communist uprisings, or terrorist attacks against the new government. For instance, he reports, on December 17, communist infiltrators attempt to blow up the headquarters Horthy and the Inter-Allied Military Mission.

Anti-Hungarian propaganda started early. Bandholtz heard about Hungarian army's pogroms and bloody suppression of communist uprisings in the provinces. Upon finding them untrue, he wrote on January 20, 1920: "these persistent rumors of Bolshevist uprisings and killings in Hungary are due to unfriendly propaganda, but it is hard to tell just who starts it." Today, of course, we know the sources.

About the alleged anti-Semitism in Hungary at the end of the war Bandholtz wrote: "...although all Bolshevists were not Jews nor were all Jews Bolshevists, nevertheless Béla Kun, the Hungarian Bolshevist leader, practically all his lieutenants, and most of his followers, were Jews, and as a result the people of Hungary were simply furious and determined to rid themselves of the Semitic influence" (September 15, 1919)

General Bandholtz's daily contact with the Romanian military and diplomatic personnel for these six months gave him a unique learning experience. He made no secret about his conclusions. On November 11, 1919, he wrote in his Diary: "It is simply impossible to conceive such national depravity as those miserable "Latins" of Southeast Europe are displaying".

Having spent six months in Hungary, General Bandholtz was impressed by the Hungarians. Before his departure he concluded in his Diary:

"Personally I came here rather inclined to condone or extenuate much of the Roumanian procedure, but their outrageous conduct in violation of all international law, decency, and humane considerations, has made me become an advocate of the Hungarian cause. Turning over portions of Hungary with its civilized and refined population will be like turning over Texas and California to the Mexicans. The great Powers of the Allies should hang their heads in shame for what they allowed to take place in this country after an armistice."

It is fortunate that General Bandholtz's personal diary was saved by his widow. Long after the war, she was persuaded by a history professor of Ohio's Wittenberg College, Fritz-Konrad Kruger, to agree to its publication. Kruger wrote an excellent introduction to Bandholtz's work describing in detail Hungary's involvement in World War I, the process that led to Romania's attack on Hungary. He also included copious footnotes into the diary. Together, Kruger's Introduction and Bandholtz's Diary describes a historical panorama of this sorrowful period in Central Europe, the memory of which reverberates even today.

Professor Krüger was a self-effacing person. Aside from stating his professional affiliation with Ohio's Wittenberg College, he didn't make a single reference to himself in the book. His introduction and footnotes are crucial: He explained the diplomatic history of Hungary's participation in W.W.I, from the events that lead to the war through its course, ending with the collapse of the Austro-Hungarian Monarchy. Relying on an excellent collection of references, Krüger described the efforts of the Hungarian government in 1914 to prevent the war, the events that led to Hungary's Bolshevik regime in 1919 and the Romanian invasion.

According to a contemporary copy of *Who is Who in America*, Frederick Konrad Krüger was born in Kottbus, Germany, on June 27, 1887. His parents were Fritz-Johann Krüger and Elizabeth Zippel. He studied at the University of Berlin, then immigrated to the United States in 1907. Graduated at the University of Nebraska in the same year. He obtained his doctorate at the University of Tübingen in 1909. He attended graduate school at Columbia University in 1911. In 1913 he married Gertrude M. Jaeggi, they had two children. He became a naturalized citizen of the U. S. in 1930. He was a fellow and lecturer at the University of California in 1912 -14, professor of political science at Midland College, Fremont, Nebraska; University of Omaha, Nebraska, 1919 - 23; Wittenberg College, Springfield, Ohio, from 1923. Guest professor at the University of Göttingen, 1927-28; University of Berlin, 1934 -35. He wrote *The Government and Politics of the German Empire,* and contributed articles on the German government to the *Encyclopedia Americana*. While a professor of Wittenberg College, he wrote this book in 1932, It was published originally by Columbia University Press under the title: General Harry Hill Bandholtz, U. S. Army: *An Undiplomatic Diary.* The current text is based on this earlier publication but was thoroughly reedited. Some material that came to light later was added, for example the story of the clandestine Slovak Peace Delegation that visited General Bandholtz in Budapest.

3

The grateful Hungarian nation placed a statue of General Bandholtz right in front of the American Embassy in Budapest. It was removed during the years of communism following WW2. After the collapse of Communism, the statue was reinstalled. Bandholtz's *Undiplomatic Diary* was out of print for over 60 years. The true story of the rape of Hungary in 1919, described by the American general was all but forgotten, replaced by fables concocted by Hungary's enemies. Republishing this work was long overdue.

Andrew L. Simon

Professor Emeritus

The University of Akron

Hungary and World War I.

by Fritz-Konrad Krüger

A integral part of the Austro-Hungarian monarchy, Hungary participated in the World War on the side of the Central European Powers. It is now a well-established fact that her Prime Minister, Count Stephen Tisza, was the only leading statesman of the Dual Empire who opposed the fateful ultimatum to Serbia, the rejection of which led to the outbreak of the World War.[1]

---

1   Proof of this Statement is, above all, found in the collection of official Austro-Hungarian diplomatic documents, *Östreich-Ungarns Aussenpolitik von der Bosnischen Krise, 1908, bis zum Kriegsausbruch, 1914; Diplomatische Aktenstücke des Österreich-Ungarischen Ministeriums des Äusseren;* Ausgewählt von Ludwig Bittner, Alfred Francis Pribram, Heinrich Srbik und Hans Uebersberger, Wien und Leipzig, 1930, Vol. VIII. Of special importance is the report of Tisza to Kaiser Franz Joseph on July 8, 1914 (pp. 371-73). In addition, see statements on pages 343-51 and 448. Count Ottokar Czernin says in his *Im Weltkriege*, Berlin, 1919 (p.16): Several months after the outbreak of war I had a long conversation with the Hungarian prime minister, Count Tisza, about all these questions. He, Tisza himself was positively against the sharp Ultimatum since he had foreseen a war and he had not wanted it. It is one of the most popular errors when to-day Tisza is designated as a "warmonger". Compare with Czernin's opinion that of Oscar Jászi in his *Dissolution of the Hapsburg Monarchy*. Chicago, 1959, p.408: "It must be noted that his [Tisza's] resistance to the catastrophe-policy of Vienna was very platonic and lukewarm"; and p. 409, "He helped to make the ultimatum unacceptable to Serbia." Jonescu's opinion, as expressed in *Some Personal Impressions*, New York, 1920 (p.183), that "Count Tisza was the prime mover in unchaining the conflict," and that "he provoked the universal carnage," is unwarranted by the facts. Likewise E. Beneš was mistaken when he wrote in 1917: "When the Crown Council in July, 1914, decided on the declaration of war against Serbia, Tisza and the Magyar nobility gave the decisive vote." See, on the other

In March, 1914, Tisza wrote a memorandum in which he advocated a peaceful policy of readjustment in the Balkans. In this document he proposed the strengthening of Bulgaria against Serbia in order to attach the former country to Austria-Hungary. Furthermore, he advised a careful treatment of Roumania for the purpose of winning back, if possible, this country which had lately been alienated from the Central Powers, or, in the event of the failure of this attempt, to threaten her from two sides. In procedure he favored a "politique de longue main." Immediate war with Serbia he considered a "fatal mistake," one which might provoke a world war.[2] This memoir was laid before Count Berchtold and Emperor Franz Joseph. Both approved it. Later on—at the time of his visit to Vienna (October 26, 1913)—Emperor William II accepted in general the proposed Balkan policy of Austria-Hungary. Before any action could be taken in conformity with this memorandum, the assassination of Archduke Franz Ferdinand took place at Sarajevo on June 28.

Three days later Count Tisza wrote a letter to Franz Joseph recommending the maintenance of peace and, in the council of the Austro-Hungarian ministers on the seventh of July, he again advised moderation and strong *diplomatic*, rather than military, action. This position he again stated the next day in a letter to Franz Joseph, and he maintained it throughout the fateful month of July.

hand, Sidney Bradshaw Fay's *Origins of the World War*, New York, 1928, Vol.11, p. 188 *passim;* and the symposium of Harry Elmer Barnes, Count Berchtold, Count Hoyos, von Wiesner, von Jagow, and Zimmermann in *Current History*, July, 1928, pp. 619-36, on the question: *Did Germany Incite Austria?* Also Harry Elmer Barnes' *Genesis of the World War*, New York, 1927, pp. 178-80 and 247; A. Weber's "Graf Tisza und die Kriegserklaerung an Serbien," in *Die Kriegsschuldfrage,* Berlin, 3. Jahrgang, Nov. 12, 1925, pp. 818-26; and Rodolfo Mosca's *Problemi politici 1'Ungheria contemporanea*, Bologna, 1927, pp.27 ff.

2   The German text of this memorandum may be found in Wilhelm Fraknói's *Die ungarische Regierung und die Entstehung des Weltkrieges*, Vienna, 1919. An English translation of the original Hungarian, as given by Professor Henrik Marczali, is contained in the *American Historical Review*, Jan.. 1924, XXIX, 303-10, in an article entitled "Papers of Count Tisza, 1914-1918," pp.101-15. See also Pierre Renouvin's *Immediate Origins of the War*, translated from the French by T. C. Hume, New Haven, 1928, pp.37 and 55-56.

However, on the twenty-eighth of July, when war against Serbia broke out, Tisza immediately and unreservedly supported the cause of Austria~Hungary and her ally.[3]

His ultimate support of the cause of Austria-Hungary and the Central Powers may be explained in various ways. He was not a friend of the assassinated Archduke Franz Ferdinand or of his policies, for it was well known that the Archduke was quite sympathetic to the desire for more extensive rights for the Transylvanian Roumanians and that he had certain plans for the federalization of Austria-Hungary at the expense of Hungary. However, when the unfortunate Archduke fell by the hand of a fanatic assassin, Tisza, always chivalrous and noble in thought, was greatly shocked and incensed at the complicity of the Serbian government, whose hands were obviously not clean. The whole Hungarian nation, which has throughout its history been distinguished by a somewhat feudal fealty to its legally recognized leaders, shared Tisza's feelings. It was indignant over this outrage, the last of a chain of political assassinations which had characterized the history of Serbia, in marked contrast with Hungary's record, which in this respect, was absolutely clean. Of course, Tisza realized that the aspirations of the Serbian "Black Hand," which was back of the crime at Sarajevo, were directed towards the creation of a Greater Serbia, which meant the severance of Croatia from Hungary and probably the complete dismemberment of the Dual Monarchy. He also regarded the semiofficial Serbian conspiracy and the official policy of Serbia, encouraged as it was by Russia, as merely links in the policy of encirclement, directed by the Entente against the Central Powers. In a letter to his niece, written on August 26, 1914, he expressed this opinion in the following words:

'My conscience is dear. Already the noose with which they would have strangled us at a favorable moment, unless we cut it now, had been thrown around our necks. We could not do otherwise; but it agonized me, that we had to do as we did'.[4]

When Tisza, therefore, was assured that an ultimatum to Serbia was unavoidable and that Germany was supporting the policy of the Ballplatz, he acquiesced in the majority decision and from then on fulfilled his duty in a most loyal way.

---

3   See S. B. Fay's *Origins of the World War*, Vol.11, "Berchtold's Efforts to Convert Tisza," pp.224-36, "The Conversion of Tisza," pp.239-43.

For two reasons I have dwelt at some length on the position of the responsible leader of Hungary in connection with the outbreak of the World War. First, because it seems to me that, in the light of these and other post-war disclosures, some rectifications of the incredibly harsh and dangerously foolish Peace Treaty of Trianon should be considered, in the interest of Hungary and humanity;[5] second, because in many respects Count Tisza is the personification of his nation, especially of its ruling class, with its virtues and some of its shortcomings. He was, on the one hand, proud, cultured, loyal, strong in adversity, intensely patriotic, honest, courageous; on the other, haughty, contemptuous of the plebs, autocratic, and supernationalistic.[6]

Once more before the end of the War did Tisza raise his voice in protest against the policies of the Central Powers, when he opposed the declaration of unrestricted submarine warfare, which, he feared, would give President Wilson the opportunity of bringing the United States into the War and thus of saving England from threatened disaster.[7] He opposed unrestricted submarine warfare because he felt sure that America's entrance in the War would mean the defeat of the Central Powers and the destruction of Austria-Hungary.

4 Cited from S. B. Fay's *Origins of the World War*, p.241.

5 The outstanding non-Hungarian advocate of such a revision is Lord Rothermere. See his article in the *Daily Mail* of June 24, 1921. It appeared in German translation in the *Pester Lloyd* of June 24, 1927, and was reprinted in *Europäische Gesprache*, Berlin, Oct., 19117. Charles à Court Repington says in his diary, *After the War*, Boston, 1922, p.168: "It is pathetic how all the Magyars confide in the legendary justice of England and in her power to put matters right. I tell them all that the mass of our people were too much preoccupied with affairs more vital to them to worry about little Hungary, and that I felt sure that few outside the official classes knew of the measure meted out to her and what it all implied."

6 To characterize as a "deluded Don Quixote" this realistic and powerful personality, to whom posing was absolutely foreign, indicates either bad judgment or poor taste. Dr. O. Jászi, in *Revolution and Counter-Revolution in Hungary*, London, 1924, p.4.

7 I wish to state explicitly that I am presenting Tisza's opinion, not my own. The latter I have expressed in *Deutsche Stimmen*, April 9, 1922, in an article entitled "Woodrow Wilson-Tumulty versus Graf Bernstorff."

On May 23, 1917, Count Tisza resigned his position as Prime Minister of Hungary, which position he had held since 1913. Shortly afterwards he left for the battle front.

On October 17, 1918, the announcement was made in the Hungarian Parliament that the War was lost and that Hungary would be transformed into an independent state in an Austrio-Hungarian Federation.[8] Two days later the last Prime Minister of old Hungary, Alexander Wekerle, presented his resignation, and on October 25 Count Michael Károlyi reorganized a National Council. From now on events of the greatest importance followed in quick succession. Between October 30 and November 1 a revolution occurred in Budapest, during which Michael Károlyi was entrusted by the National Council with the formation of a cabinet and given dictatorial powers, Tisza was assassinated on October 31, and on November 1 Emperor-King Karl was forced by Károlyi to retire from his governmental duties.[9] On November 3 General Diaz, representing the Allies, signed at Padua an armistice with Austria-Hungary, and the Hungarian soldiers soon began to return home. But Károlyi, thinking that he could secure more considerate treatment for Hungary from the French Commander in Chief on the southern front, General Franchet d'Espérey, went to Belgrade on November 13 to obtain from the latter new armistice terms.

Károlyi believed himself entitled to friendly treatment by the Allies because he had always been an advocate of Western European political democracy. During the War he had been a leader of the Hungarian defeatists, who had been more interested in over throwing the aristocratic government at home than in the safety or victory of their fatherland. Dr. Oscar Jászi, Minister of Nationalities in the Károlyi government,[10] has expressed in these words the hopes held by the Károlyi followers:

We had confidence in the democratic and pacifist quality of public opinion in the Entente states and especially in the policy of President Wilson, a policy which

---

8   This statement, as well as many other documents concerning post-war Hungary, may be found in Malbone W. Graham's *New Governments of Central Europe*, New York, 1924, pp. 538-601.

9   It is to be remembered that Károlyi had accepted his position as Prime Minister from the hands of Emperor-King Karl. Karl did not formally abdicate.

stood higher than any mere nationalism. - We were convinced that the conquering Allies would show the utmost good will to her [Hungary's] pacifist and anti-militarist government, and especially Károlyi, who had so often stood with unexampled courage for the policy of the Entente; we were sure that they would apply the plebiscitary principle on which they had so often laid stress, and that if we had to suffer losses of territory it would still be possible, with the aid of just and liberal commercial treaties, to assure the undisturbed continuance of communication with the lost area.[11]

These fantastic ideologists, Michael Károlyi, the Don Quixote mounted on the Rosinante of the Fourteen Points, and Jászi, his Sancho Panza, were quickly disillusioned. To use the bitter words of Dr. Jászi:

The bright promise of Wilson's League of Nations, the just peace and the right of self-determination and the plebiscite, in which the Hungarian people had placed their trust, burst like soap bubbles. We saw ourselves not only defeated, broken and plundered, but, a much crueler wound to public feeling, bluffed and swindled.[12]

10 Oscar Jászi was an official in the Ministry of Agriculture under the old regime. He resigned because he disagreed with the government. Founder of the Hungarian Sociological Society and editor of its organ, *The Twentieth Century*, he was associated with the movements for land reform, universal suffrage, and cultural autonomy for the minorities in Hungary. On the eve of the world war, he founded the so-called Radical Party, a pacifistic and liberal-socialistic group. After the outbreak of the October revolution, Dr. Jászi entered the Károlyi cabinet. Shortly before the collapse of the Károlyi regime, he resigned to become professor of sociology at Budapest, a position which he held until compelled by the Bolsheviks to give it up. Since 1919, he has lived as a voluntary exile, first in Vienna and later in the United States, where he now holds a professorship in political science. [Later he taught at Oberlin. Ed.] Dr. Jászi's book, mentioned before, is the most responsible and the ablest explanation and defense of the Károlyi regime yet published. Michael Károlyi has thus far written only the first volume of his story, entitled *Against the Whole World*. This volume does not contain his account of the Hungarian revolution.

11 Oscar Jászi, *ibid.*, p.37. In view of this and of other statements, as well as of the actions of the Károlyi cabinet, we can hardly believe Jászi when he says (page 3): "Nor was I blind at any time to the Janus-headed policy of the Entente."

General Franchet d'Espérey was a typical French militarist, as a victor, arrogant and merciless. He received the Károlyi delegation with studied brutality. When the radical Socialist member of the delegation, the President of the Council of Soldiers and Workers, Mr. C. S. Csernyák, who had been selected to impress the General with the change of heart of the Hungarian government, was introduced to him, he remarked contemptuously, "Well, have you come to this already?"[13]

As a result of the military convention concluded with Franchet d'Espérey without the specific sanction of the Allied Supreme Council, a line of demarcation was laid down foreshadowing the territorial provisions of the future peace. This convention transferred a large slice of Hungarian territory to the Serbs and Roumanians, who immediately began to occupy it. It was expressly stated that the Hungarian police and civil administrations were to be continued. This agreement was violated. The inhabitants of the occupied area were forced to take the oath of allegiance and were even pressed into military service. The Czechs, who had not been included in the military convention, were authorized by the Supreme Council to occupy Slovakia, and they not only carried out this mandate, but notified the Hungarians that they would proceed beyond the fixed line of demarcation.

On December 1, 1918, the Roumanians of Transylvania declared their secession from Hungary and on December 27 they were formally annexed by Roumania.

In vain did the Hungarian government protest against the Czech invasion of Northern Hungary as a violation of the Belgrade Convention. The Allies merely ratified the action of the Czechs *post hoc* and fixed new frontiers for Hungary, information as to which were on March 20 communicated to the Hungarians by the French Lieutenant-Colonel Vyx, the chief of he Inter-Allied Military Mission in Budapest.[14] Thereupon Károlyi immediately resigned.

On November 16, 1918, Hungary had been proclaimed republic by Michael Károlyi, who on January 16,1919, had been appointed its Provisional President.

12 0. Jászi, *ibid.*, pp.56-57; also p. 40: "We were doomed by the very internationalism which was the basis of our whole policy."

13 "Êtes-vous tombé si bas?"

We have seen how unsuccessful Károlyi was in his dealings with the Allies, misjudging completely their motives and miscalculating their aims. He had permitted Hungary to become stripped of all means of self-defence.[15] Naively he had relied on a sense of justice and fairness in Hungary's enemies, and now no one could tell when and where their desire for more territory would stop.

Economic conditions had become extremely bad. The food blockade of the Allies had continued after the Armistice, causing unspeakable misery in the large cities of Hungary.

Under these circumstances it is no wonder that the radical element in the government got the upper hand and gradually replaced the Liberals and moderate Socialists. Furthermore, the Károlyists must be charged with ignorance of the dangers of Bolshevism, an ignorance resulting from a combination of their naive liberal doctrinarianism and their hatred of the old régime. Thus Jászi informs us:

I was in agreement with those who held that no limit should be set to the Bolshevist propaganda as long as it used, no matter how recklessly or with what demagogy, the normal means of political controversy; I agreed that the Bolshevists must be respected as the pioneers of a great unrealizable idea.[16] . . It was generally felt that this government was no longer able to save the October Revolution; and if a choice

14 Vyx, like Franchet d'Espérey, was a typical militarist who offended the Hungarians unnecessarily by the form in which he handed his orders to them. This is contrary to the statement expressed by Jérome and Jean Tharaud, *When Israel is King*, New York, 1924, p.144. Translated from he French: *Quand Israel est roi*, Paris, 1921, by Lady Whitehead. These French writers are Hungarophiles and try to explain away the bad treatment which the Hungarians received from the French. The diary of General Bandholtz is ample evidence of the futility of such efforts. The Hungarian opinion is expressed in the following words: "Taking advantage on his position, Colonel Vyx has trodden on our self-respect. He has treated the Eastern bulwark of Europe as the French officers treat the savages in their own colonies." Cécile Tormay, *An Outlaw's Diary: The Commune,* New York, 1924, p. 39.

15 See J. and J. Tharaud, op. cit., p.144. The first measure of the Károlyi government had been to demobilize the army. Béla Linder, the War Minister, had said that "he did not wish to see soldiers."

16 O. Jászi, op. cit., p.86.

had to be made between White and Red counter-Revolution the Red was preferred.[17]

Károlyi was in despair and felt extremely bitter against the Allies, who had rewarded so cruelly the services he had rendered them and the trust he had put in their professed ideals. He furthermore was a vain political amateur,[18] an over ambitious hazard player, who was willing to risk his country's welfare to satisfy his passions, with a terrible result to Hungary and great danger to civilization. This explains why he finally decided to turn over the government to the Communists, with the words:

'Our Western orientation, our policy of reliance on Wilson, has been definitely wrecked. We must have a fresh orientation, which will ensure us the sympathies of the Labor International.'[19]

The new government, a combination of radical Socialists and Communists, with the latter in control, was established on March 21. It set up a Soviet Republic and affiliated itself immediately with the Third International.[20] Its nominal president was the bricklayer Garbai, but the real power was Béla Kun,[21] a capable, shrewd,

17 0. Jászi, ibid., p.88.

18 It seems to me that his vanity can be implied from the statements in Jászi's book (p.63): "Károlyi rewarded and overvalued men who brought news and material which bore out his pet ideas and convictions." The incompetence of Károlyi and his colleagues can be seen from the words of Dr. Jászi: "It proved impossible to control the course of events." Like the apprentice in Goethe's poem, Der Zauberer, these leaders could not control the ghosts whom they had summoned and were duly overpowered by them.

19 In a speech before the Council of Ministers, end of March. Quoted by Jászi, p.94.

20 The dictatorship of the Proletariat was formally declared on March 22.

21 Previous to the war, Béla Kun had been an obscure newspaper reporter and secretary of a worker's mutual benefit society, in which capacity he had misappropriated a small sum of money and was about to be hailed into court, when the war broke out and prosecution was halted.

and unscrupulous young Jew, who had been captured by the Russians during the War, and who had become an ardent admirer of Lenin and his teachings. Converted to Bolshevism, he was employed by the expert propagandist, Radek, for the spreading of communistic propaganda among the prisoners of war.

A few weeks after Károlyi's revolution, Béla Kun returned secretly to Budapest and, lavishly supported by the Moscow government, carried on extensive propaganda in Hungary. On February 22 he and other Communist leaders were arrested by the Károlyi government but, at the instigation of its radical wing, he was released on March 21.

Knowing the intense patriotism of the non-Bolshevik Hungarians, he appealed to all Hungarians to unite against the "imperialistic aggressors." In a wireless message to the workers of the world, he stated: "The reply of the Hungarian people to the ultimatum of the Entente demanding the immediate and final surrender of Hungarian territory to the Roumanian oligarchy, is the proclamation of the Dictatorship of the Proletariat!"

On April 20 Soviet Hungary declared war on the invading armies of the Czechs, Roumanians and Serbs. At first the Communists were successful against the Czechs, and on June 7, receiving a distress signal from the French general at Pressburg [now Bratislava], the so-called "Big Four" issued an ultimatum to Béla Kun promising him provisional recognition of his government, provided he withdrew his troops from Slovakia.

During all this time the Soviet leaders in Budapest had been trying to establish firmly their rule in Hungary, and to bring about the socialization of all means of production. To take revenge on the hated bourgeoisie, and to crush all attempts at counter-revolution, a bloody terror was established, both in Budapest and in the rest of the country, under the direction of Tibor Számuelly, Cserny, Korvin, László, and others.[22] The men who carried on the Red régime in Hungary are described as follows by Dr. Oscar Szöllösy, Councilor in the Royal Hungarian Ministry of Justice:

Lenin's well-known axiom to the effect that in revolutions for every honest-minded man (unfortunately) are to be found hundreds of criminals, can scarcely be applied to Hungarian Bolshevism.- Criminologists of long standing who lived through the horror of the Red regime in Hungary, which lasted from March 21st to the end of July, 1919, could testify, even without the decisions of the court of laws, that the leading spirits of the "Soviet Republic" (with the exception of a few fanatics)

14

consisted of common criminals, to the greater part of whom may be applied with perfect aptness the definition of Anatole France, "encore bête et déjà homme."[23]

In general the policy of the Soviets followed Béla Kun's dictum: "I do not admit the distinction between the moral and the immoral; the only distinction I know is the distinction between that which serves the proletariat and that which harms it."

The explanation of the temporarily apathetic acceptance on the part of the majority of the Hungarian people of the rule of a handful of Communists, may be expressed by the two words, despair and hunger.[24]

The main reasons for the downfall of the Bolshevik government lie in the abandonment of Béla Kun by the Supreme Council,[25] the counter-revolution of

22 See the graphic description of the rule of the Red Terror by the well.
known Hungarian writer Cécile Tormay, in *An Outlaw's Diary*, New York, 1924; also the popular pamphlet *From Behind the Veil, the Story of Hungarian Bolshevism*, Budapest, 1920. The author of this interesting pamphlet is Karl Huszár, as Count Paul Teleki states in *The Evolution of Hungary and its Place in European History*, New York, 1923, p.138. On the other hand, Dr. Jászi always explains, excuses, and minimizes the Red Terror, in contrast to the so-called White Terror. Korvin-Klein, for instance, is called a martyr. According to the Hungarian Ministry of Justice, 585 persons were publicly executed by the Bolshevists.

23 Reprinted from the *Anglo-Hungarian Review*, in the *Appendix* (pp. 215 ff.) to Cecile Tormay's *Outlaw's Diary*.

24 The blockade of the Allies was not raised until March, 1919. - "The "Bolshevism is a horrible caricature of state management. War is its father, famine its mother, despair its godfather": Ottokar Czernin: *Im Weltkriege*, Berlin, 1919. "The bewildering fact of military defeat threw the older and established classes of Hungary, together with the bourgeoisie, into a state of torpid lethargy.": Stephen Bethlen, "Hungary in the New Europe," in *Foreign Affairs,* Dec., 1924, Vol.111, No.2, p. 432.

25 The Entente officially broke with the Soviet government of Hungary on July 16.

the bourgeoisie and the nobility,[26] and the stubborn passive resistance of the peasantry, who showed a determined hostility to the economic and antireligious ideas of communism and who starved Budapest, the citadel of Bolshevism, into submission by boycotting the city.

In vain did Béla Kun try once more to appeal to Hungarian patriotism, for the benefit of international Bolshevism, by sending a workers' army against the Roumanians. It was utterly routed. The Roumanians pursued the defeated Bolshevists. Their rule collapsed, Béla Kun and some of his companions fled to Austria, while others were captured and punished.

On July 31 the Roumanians, after having pillaged and devastated the country through which they had marched, entered Budapest, where a social- democratic government under Peidl had then been established.[27]

On the sixth of August the Peidl government was replaced through a *coup d'etat* by an extreme nationalist-clerical government under Prime Minister Stephen Friedrich. The new government desired to put on the throne Archduke Joseph, who, before Emperor-King Karl's withdrawal, it is alleged, had been entrusted by him with the power of appointing Prime Ministers.

The invasion of Hungary, the sacking of the country, and the seizure of Budapest had taken place in defiance of the order of the Supreme Council.[28] The Roumanian adventure was being eagerly watched by Hungary's other neighbors and by Italy, who were all anxious to help themselves in Hungary or elsewhere, in case the Supreme Council should acquiesce in the *fait accompli*. In addition, the prestige of the future League of Nations was at stake, for if Roumania could defy the principal powers of this future association, it would be an object of ridicule even before it was born.[29]

Therefore the Supreme Council sent a message, signed by Clemenceau, to the Hungarians, through its military representative at Budapest, the Italian Lieuenant Colonel Romanelli:

26 It was organized in May at Arad, then held by the Roumanians. In June it was transferred to Szeged. Its leader was Julius Károlyi. He was joined by Count Stephen Bethlen, who had worked for the counter- revolution in Vienna. Horthy organized the Army of Loyal Veterans of the World War.

Hungary shall carry out the terms of the Armistice and respect the frontiers traced by the Supreme Council,[30] and we will protect you from the Roumanians, who have no authority from us. We are sending forthwith an Inter-Allied Military Mission to superintend the disarmament and to see that the Roumanian troops withdraw.

In accordance with this decision, four generals, representing the four chief Allies, were appointed to head the Military Mission to Hungary, viz.:

General Bandholtz of the United States Army,
General Gorton of the British Army,
General Graziani of the French Army,
General Mombelli of the Italian Army.

27 The statement made by Professor William Bennet Munro, in *The Governments of Europe,* revised ed., New York, 1931 (p.794), to the effect that "with the aid of the Roumanian troops this soviet administration was ousted and a national government restored," is somewhat misleading. The Roumanians were as hostile to the Hungarian national government as to the Bolshevik government, but they desired to weaken the latter through the former. The Hungarian feeling in this matter is given in the words of Cécile Tormay: "what a terrible position is ours: The invaders fill us with horror, and yet we await them eagerly: we look to assassins to save us from our hangmen."

28 Charles Vopicka, a Czech by birth and naturally Slavophil, who was then minister of the United States at Bucharest, tells us that he did not join his colleagues at Bucharest in their advice to the Roumanians not to take possession of the new line of demarcation until they were given permission by the Peace Conference to do so. On the contrary, he incited the Roumanians indirectly to go ahead (p.301). Since the Allies did not reply to their request, the Roumanians went to war. Thereupon Vopicka telegraphed to Paris asking the Peace Commission to force Béla Kun to retreat, and to call the Czechs, Jugo-Slavs, and Roumanians up against him in case he did not obey. *Secrets of the Balkans.*

29 This point is well brought out by Frank H. Simonds in the article 'Hungary, the Balkans and the League," in *The American Review of Reviews*, Sept., 1919, which, with the article, "The European Reaction,"

Here the narrative of General H. H. Bandholtz begins. He was commissioned on August 6, 1919; started for Budapest in an automobile with the then Director of Food Supplies, Herbert Hoover; arrived in the capital of Hungary on August 10 and stayed there six months, until his mission was ended. He left Hungary with the Hungarian Peace Delegation on February 10, 1920.

FRITZ-KONRAD KRÜGER

Late Professor of Political Science

Wittenberg College, Springfield, Ohio

November, 1932

in the issue of October, 1919, is an interesting and, in general, well-informed journalistic commentary of the situation then existing in Hungary.

30 On June 13, 1919

Preliminaries to Bandholtz's Arrival in Hungary

Supreme Council's Instructions to the Inter-Allied Military Mission to Hungary.

It will be the object of the Mission:

1st: To get into communication with the Hungarian Government with a view to insuring the observation of the armistice and rendering the disarming effective.

To this end it will be obliged:

(a) To fix the *maximum number* of effectives of the Hungarian army to be maintained under arms, with the sole object of insuring order in the interior:

(b) To proceed to the disarming of all the demobilized urn tb and to the dissolution of the depôts or mobilizing centers:

(c) To insure the surrender to the Allies of the arms, munitions and war material in excess of the material necessary for the units kept under arms; to include the material coming from the Mackensen Army:

(d) To regulate, in accord with the Allied commands, the distribution of this various material among the Allied Powers interested, taking into account the military effort furnished by each, and the present war situation:

(e) To stop immediately the production of the arsenals and the war manufactures:

2nd: To make a report on the present condition of this matter and its probable outcome:

3rd: To establish liaison with the Commander in Chief of the Roumanian and Serbian armies, in order:

(a) To prevent on the part of the victorious armies all measures which would tend to excite the national sentiment in Hungary or which in any way might prolong the troubled situation in this country and retard the conclusion of peace:

(b) To determine according to the situation of the moment the effectiveness and the emplacements of the Roumanian and Serbian troops that it will be necessary to maintain on Hungarian soil to guarantee order and the execution of the armistice:

(c) To regulate with the Roumanian and Serbian commands the withdrawal of the excess Roumanian and Serbian troops:

The Mission is informed for its further instruction:

1st: That the frontiers of Hungary having been defined already by the Conference and communicated directly to all the Governments concerned, it is the policy of the Conference to withdraw all foreign troops from this country, avoiding all unnecessary delay. It must be noted that the Roumanians have promised to withdraw their armies as soon as the disarming of the Hungarians is accomplished, and in accord with the armistice terms:

2nd: That orders have been given to raise the blockade against Hungary and to proceed to the immediate importation of food stuffs of the most urgent nature:

3rd: That the maintenance of these new conditions will depend on the conduct of the Hungarian Government toward the Allied and Associated Powers:

4th: That these Powers have not the least desire to interfere in the interior affairs of the Hungarian nation concerning the choice of their government, but that at the same time they cannot treat with any government which they cannot trust to carry out fairly its international obligations.

....

Appointment of General Bandholtz to the Inter-Allied Military Mission

American Commission To Negotiate Peace, Paris,

August 6, 1919

Brigadier General H. H. Bandholtz, U.S. A.,

Paris, France.

By direction of the American Commissioners I have to inform you that you have been named the American representative on the Inter-Allied Military Mission to

Hungary, established by the Supreme Council of the Peace Conference. A copy of the instructions to the Mission as agreed upon by he Council is enclosed herewith for your information and guidance.

I am, Sir,

Your obedient servant

[signed]

Diplomatic Secretary

....

General Headquarters

American Expeditionary Forces, France, August 9th, 1919

Special Orders No.210

[Extract]

10. Brigadier General Harry H. Bandholtz, U. S. Army, is relieved from assignment as Provost General, A. E. F., and will report to the Assistant Secretary of State, American Commission to Negotiate Peace, Hotel Crillon, Paris, for duty.

By Command of General Pershing:

James G. Harbord

Official:

Chief of Staff

Robert C. Davis

Adjutant General.

....

Bureau of Accounts,

Department of State, Washington, D. C. March 23, 1920

H. H. Bandholtz,

Brig. General, U.S. A.

American Military Representative in Hungary.

Dear General:

I wish to acknowledge receipt of your final account dated February 17, 1920, for expenditures amounting to $2,536.68.

I enclose herewith a copy of the above account which I have approved as suggested by you.

I wish to state that your accounts have been checked and approved as submitted by you, and that there is no balance due to or from you.

Thanking you for the prompt and properly prepared accounts; I am,

Respectfully yours,

H. R. Young Disbursing Officer,

American Commission to Negotiate Peace.

An Undiplomatic Diary

by Major General Harry Hill Bandholtz

Footnotes by Fritz-Konrad Krüger

August, 1919

August 7, 1919.

Captain Gore, with myself and two orderlies, left Paris at 9.10 P.M. in Mr. Hoover's private car. Colonel Loree, my aide, Lieutenant Hamilton, and the rest of the detachment, remained in Paris and are to follow with the least possible delay. My other aide, Lieutenant Montgomery, was left in Paris with my Cadillac limousine and chauffeur, as my permanent liaison with the Supreme Council.

August 8, 1919.

This morning we found ourselves just across the Swiss border, where we were held up for five hours while they were deciding whether or not our party, some of whom had no passports, could cross Switzerland. In any event they insisted that we wear civilian clothing. I therefore borrowed a blue coat of Mr. Hoover, a lurid purple tie from his stenographer, and a golf cap from somebody else, completing my demobilization by removing my spurs. Captain Gore did likewise, after which they decided we could proceed in uniform, under charge of a Swiss policeman, to the Austrian border. We arrived at the town of Buchs, very near the frontier line, about six o'clock, where we were joined by Captain Gregory, Mr. Hoover's representative in this part of the world, and where, after an hour, we were allowed to proceed on our way.

August 9, 1919.

This morning we found ourselves in the town of Linz, Austria, and from there proceeded to Prague, where we arrived about two o'clock in the afternoon, Here Captain Gore and myself took a drive all over the city, which is most interesting and full of antiquities. We had a very good dinner at the Municipal Restaurant, and at nine o'clock joined Captain Gregory in his car, Mr. Hoover proceeding to Warsaw, and our train being headed towards Vienna.

August 10, 1919.

We arrived at Vienna about noon, lunched at the Hotel Bristol, and then had a long talk with Admiral Troubridge of the British Navy, who is in command of the Danube River, and Mr. James, the American representative on the Danube Commission, both of whom gave me valuable information as to the situation in Hungary. In the afternoon Captain Gore and I took an automobile ride all over the city of Vienna, and at 9.10 P.M. I left with Captain Gregory for Budapest. I had previously sent a telegram to Colonel Yates, the American Military Attaché at Roumanian Headquarters, stating that I was leaving Vienna, that I hoped to arrive early the following morning in Budapest, and that I expected the Roumanian Commander to facilitate my progress and work, in every way within his power.

August 11, 1919.

We arrived in Budapest at daylight and were met at the station by Colonel Yates and Lieutenant-Colonel Causey, who represents the Peace Conference, in charge of railroads. From the station we went to the Hotel Ritz where I opened an office in Room 17. Shortly thereafter I was called upon by General Gorton, the British representative on the Inter-Allied Military Mission. General Gorton and I planned a campaign, and word was sent to the Roumanian General Holban[1] that I would be at the Ritz Hotel at 4.30 that afternoon. He took the hint, called and was given some fatherly advice, At 5.30 in the afternoon the Archduke Joseph[2], the temporary president of the Hungarian Republic, asked to see me and came into the room scared nearly to death, holding in his hand what purported to be an ultimatum from the Roumanian government requiring an answer by 6 o'clock, which meant within one-half hour. The ultimatum was to the effect that Hungary must yield to all Roumanian demands, giving up all of her war material and supplies of whatever nature, agree to back Roumania in taking away the Bánát country[3] from the Jugo-Slavs, and, finally, that she must consent to political union with Roumania, with the King of Roumania as ruler of Hungary, along the same lines as the former Austro-Hungarian monarchy. He was told not to be afraid, and looking at me and trembling, he replied-"I am not afraid; I am a soldier just like you," which left-handed compliment was passed by without remark. He asked what he should do in regard to the ultimatum and was informed that in view of the fact that it had not been presented by the Roumanian Plenipotentiary he could send word to the sender to go plumb to Hell. This relieved the strain on the Archducal physiognomy to a great extent, and he retired in good order. After his departure I proceeded to the Royal Palace, which is on the Buda side of the river, and selected the best large suite in the building for Headquarters of the American Mission; and then suggested to General Gorton that he go over and take what was left for the British Mission. Later in the evening General Mombelli, the Italian representative, arrived, called upon General Gorton and myself, and agreed to the plans I had outlined as to the organization of the Mission.

August 12, 1919.

The French General not having yet arrived, Generals Gorton, Mombelli, and myself met in my office in the Ritz Hotel and organized the Inter-Allied Military Mission on the basis of having daily rotation of chairmanship instead of allowing seniority to govern in the case, thereby securing national equality in the Mission. It was also agreed to make English the official language of the Mission. At the afternoon session, M. Constantine Diamandi[4], the Roumanian Plenipotentiary, or High Commissioner to the Peace Conference, was introduced to the session of the Mission. In view of the fact that it was decided to run the rotation of chairmanship in alphabetical sequence, the American representative, myself, presided at this first meeting. M. Diamandi was read the instructions of the

1   General Holban, who is frequently mentioned unfavorably by General Bandholtz, committed suicide on the eve of the investigation ordered by the Roumanian government after Sir George Clerk had come to look into the situation.

2   Archduke Joseph was a distant relative of the late Emperor-King Karl. He was born in 1872. During the world war he had commanded first a division and later an army corps on the Italian front and had been a popular and capable military leader. He had always considered him-self specifically a Hungarian. During the Károlyi and Bolshevik re-gimes he remained in Hungary, living quietly on his estate under the name of Joseph Hapsburg. On Aug. 6, 1919, he resumed the position of Nádor, or Regent allegedly conferred upon him by Emperor-King Karl. After he was forced by the Allies to resign, he returned to private life and from then on took little part in public affairs.

3   Part of the Bánát was given to Jugo-Slavia by the Peace conference. The Roumanians claimed that it should belong to them and felt very bitter towards the Jugo-Slavs.

Supreme Council to the Military Mission, and asked if Roumania recognized them as valid and was prepared to follow the suggestions of the Mission. He replied that he could give no answer until he had communicated with his government. It was then intimated to him that much time had already been lost and it was expected that the Roumanian Government would proceed to comply immediately with the wishes of the Mission. On two different occasions he waxed furious, jumped up from his chair and started to leave the room, but, finding that his progress was not impeded, he calmed down and returned to his chair. He finally left apparently self-mollified, and promised to give us a reply as soon as possible.

Colonel Loree arrived this afternoon with a detachment of twenty-two men, and joined us at the Hotel Ritz, the detachment being sent to the Hotel Bristol.

August 13, 1919.

General Graziani, the French representative, arrived last night, but was not seen until. this morning. He had come with the full intention of presiding over and dominating the Mission. He had prepared a message to be sent to each of the other Inter-Allied Generals, to report to him at Hotel Bristol at 10 o'clock this date, but it was suggested to him that he send no such message to the American representative as it might cause difficulty. He, therefore, came to our regular meeting room and introduced himself. Through the medium of General Mombelli, there was explained to him in French the plan under which the Commission had been organized prior to his arrival. He could not conceal his chagrin, and explained that he considered that seniority should govern in the question of chairmanship, adding that he had all kinds of that article to show, and that his government had undoubtedly expected him to be presiding officer. I told him that neither my government nor any other government had notified their representatives of anything of the kind, and that in my opinion it was not right that accidental individual seniority should outweigh the question of national equality in representation. He reluctantly agreed to the proposition, stating, however, that he

4   Diamandi, or Diamandy, was Roumanian Minister in Rome from 1911 to 1913. From there he was transferred to St. Petersburg, where he remained during the world war. Later on he was Roumanian Minister to France. Before the world war he was considered friendly towards the Triple Alliance. See the report of the German Ambassador in Rome, von Flotow, to Bethmann-Hollweg, Nov.13, 1913. "Die Grosse Politik der Europäischen Kabinette," 1871-1914, Berlin, 1926, Vol. 39, p. 456.

must inform his Government that he was not to be permanent presiding officer. This, of course, was acceded to. Immediately thereafter M.. Diamandi, accompanied by General Mardarescu, the Commander in Chief of the Roumanian army, and General Holban, the Roumanian commander in Budapest, appeared before the Mission. General Gorton, the British representative, was President of the Day. They agreed to take steps immediately to alleviate the suffering from famine in the city of Budapest, and stated that they desired to coöperate with us as being allies. When they left, M. Diamandi asked if he could see me in the afternoon, was told he could do so, came at 3 o'clock and expressed supreme regret for his display of anger on the day previous, alleging that he thought I was prejudiced against the Roumanians. He told me, incidentally, that the Roumanian government was prepared to accept as valid the instructions of the Military Mission from the Supreme Council for the Peace Conference.

August 14, 1919.

General Graziani, the French representative, was chairman this date. M. Diamandi, in view of his conversation with me on the preceding day and in view of the fact that he had made similar remarks to General Mombelli, was asked to appear before the Mission, and upon appearing was asked if Roumania was prepared to accept as valid the instructions of the Military Mission. He immediately resumed his policy of sparring for wind and replied that he was of the personal opinion that Roumania would acknowledge the Mission as the authorized representative of the Supreme Council, but that he could not as yet give the answer of his government.

In the afternoon all the members of the Mission went over to the Royal Palace, were shown the offices selected by the American and the British representatives, and took what was best of that left. Afterwards there was a short meeting at which I presented a memorandum requiring prompt action on the part of Roumania in complying with the instructions of the Military Mission. Part of it was immediately adopted and copies sent to the Roumanian commander.

Lieutenant Hamilton arrived about midnight this date.

August 15, 1919.

At 8 o'clock this morning, I found the Hungarian Foreign Minister and two others in my office stating that they had understood that I had authorized Captain Gregory to tell them that on account of the overthrow of the Socialist government in Hungary and the practical reestablishment of the Hapsburg dynasty by the assumption of the reins of government by the Archduke Joseph, there were in progress revolutions in both England and America, and to state that the Supreme Council could not stand for a moment for the continuation of the Archduke in power. They were old that Captain Gregory had been given no such authority and, furthermore, that he had said nothing of the kind. They were told, however, that the Supreme Council could not accept or acknowledge the *de facto* Hungarian government as sufficiently permanent in character to justify making a treaty of peace, and that he Peace Conference was most desirous of having a permanent popular government established in Hungary.

The Mission met at 10.30 A.M., with General Mombelli in the chair. The Archduke burst into the meeting, followed by his Foreign Minister, to submit a list of his new cabinet. As it seemed to be becoming a daily practice of the Archduke to come to the Commission for pap of some kind or another, I stepped over to General Mombelli and told him quietly that I must insist that the Mission continue with its session, instead of having its time taken up with Archducal oratory. His Highness was then invited to leave, and the Mission proceeded with its session. The Hungarian Minister of War was called in, and made a report on the former and present police organization of the city of Budapest. He was followed by the Roumanian General, Holban, who agreed to turn over to the Hungarians 6,000 arms for organizing a Municipal Police Force. When questioned, he stated that he at this time had 10,000 men in the city proper and 5,000 in the outskirts. He was told to make the reverse arrangement -to place 10,000 in the outskirts, and to place his 5,000 along the perimeter of the city proper, which he agreed to do. He admitted that, although there were at present 1,800 Hungarian police in Budapest, they had arms for only 600.

There was received this night from the American Mission in Paris a long telegram containing the Roumanian reply to the Supreme Council's ultimatum, and the reply of the Supreme Council to the same, to the effect that the Roumanian papers were interpreted as meaning a yielding on the part of Roumania to the demands of the Peace Conference.

August 16, 1919.

I established my office this date in the Royal Palace, in the room which had been used by the Empress.

It being my turn to preside at the meeting of the Mission, I read to my associates the telegram from the Supreme Council, submitting to them likewise the draft of a

28

paper which I proposed to place immediately before the Roumanian Commander in Chief. This was agreed to, and the latter, accompanied by General Mardarescu and his Chief of Staff, appeared before the Mission at 4.30. The text of the paper handed them was as follows:

1: (a) Cease at once requisitioning or taking possession of any supplies or property of whatever nature except in zones authorized by this Mission, and then only of such supplies as may be necessary for the Roumanian Army, and that this Mission be informed as to the kind of supplies which will be considered necessary.

(b) The Roumanian Commander in Chief to furnish without delay a map clearly showing the requisition zones, and also indicating thereon the disposition of his troops.

(c) Return at once to its owners all private property now in the possession of the Roumanians, such as automobiles, horses, carriages, or any other property of which the ownership is vested in individuals.

(d) To arrange for the gradual return to the Hungarian Government of the railroad, post and telegraph systems.

(e) Make no further requisitions of buildings, stores or real property and evacuate as rapidly as possible all schools, colleges, and buildings of like character.

(f) Cease at once all shipments of rolling stock or Hungarian property of any kind whatsoever, to or towards Roumania, and stop and return to Budapest any rolling stock or property already en route or held at outside stations.

(g) Limit supervision over public or private affairs in the city to such extent as may be approved by this Mission.

2: The Roumanian government to furnish this Mission not later than August twenty-third a complete list of all war material, railway or agricultural material, live stock or property of any kind whatsoever that has been taken possession of in Hungary by Roumanian forces.

The Roumanians received this, agreeing to carry out instructions, and formally acknowledged the Inter-Allied Military Mission as being the authorized representative in Hungary of the Supreme Council of the Peace Conference. While at the meeting they were told that not even Roumanian contact patrols could push on towards Szeged, and that they must not extend their occupation of

Hungary. They were also given a few more bitter pills which they swallowed with apparent complacency. I wired the American Mission in Paris this evening that in my opinion the Roumanians were doing their utmost to delay matters in order to complete the loot of Hungary[5] and that as far as I could see their progress up to date in complying with the Supreme Council's desires, was negative rather than positive.

This evening Colonel Loree, Captain Gore, Lieutenant Hamilton and myself moved to our new quarters, the residence of Count Edelsheim, where we have most

5 This is the first mention of the looting of Hungary by the Roumanians. Other examples are found on pages 38,43, 46, 112, 113, 212, etc (according to the original edition).

The following are some opinions of writers familiar with this aspect of Roumanian occupation of Hungary.

"The story of the pillaging by the Roumanian army in Hungary is Homeric. It equals anything of the kind done in the war.-A member of the English Mission, sent into the East of Hungary to investigate the facts, said epigrammatically, that the Roumanians had not even left the nails in the boards!"-John Foster Bass, *The Peace Tangle*, New York, 1920, p.193.

"The Roumanian invasion was more like an old-time Highland cattle foray than a war."-L. Haden Guest, *The Struggle for Power in Europe*, London, 1921, p.195.

"The Magyars detest the Roumanians on account of their looting during the occupation following the Béla Kun régime.-They are accused of having stolen everything movable - plate, pictures, carpets, linen, furniture, even down to the cloth of billiard tables. They took the best thoroughbreds and let them die in the train for want of food. They took twelve hundred locomotives and left the Hungarians only four hundred. In my hotel Béla Kun had done five million crowns' worth of damage. The Roumanians did seven million worth. They took literally everything, and the rooms are still without telephones as a result of their brigandage. This, of course, is all the Hungarian account of what happened."-Charles à Court Repington, *After the War*, Boston, 1912, p.165.

commodious and almost palatial quarters, with a new Hungarian chef and butler. The Count, the Countess and their daughter occupy the rear portion of the building and give us complete sway over the dining room, the breakfast rooms, the parlors, our bedrooms, etc., and have only the entrance in common with us.

August 17, 1919.

Even E. J. Dillon, the most ardent defender of Roumanian interests, says: "They [the Roumanians] seized rolling stock, cattle, agricultural implements, and other property of the kind that had been stolen from their people and sent the booty home without much ado." *The Inside Story of the Peace Conference*, p.230. How far his statement is correct is left to the reader to judge from the facts given in this diary. Dillon calls the action of the Roumanians "wholesale egotism."

"Hungary has suffered a Roumanian occupation, which was worse almost than the revolutions of Bolshevism."-Francesco Nitti, *The Wreck of Europe*, Indianapolis, 1912, p.171.

Louis K. Birinyi, *The Tragedy of Hungary*, Cleveland, 1924. Especially Chapter XX, "Hungary Fleeced during the Armistice." It is somewhat rhetorical and not always accurate. This is particularly true of his account of the occupation of Budapest by Horthy's troops and the evacuation of Budapest.

On the other hand Cecil John Charles Street, in *Hungary and Democracy,* London, 1923, states "To Roumania was assigned the task of restoring order, and in her execution of it she displayed an ability and a restraint which will forever redound to her credit" (p.200). Mr. Street makes it appear as if the aim of the Roumanians in invading Hungary with their "well disciplined forces" was principally to save the world from Bolshevism. From Street and Jászi is taken the account of Hungary by C. Deslisle Burns, 1918-1928, *A Short History of the World*, New York, 1928. Consequently it is entirely one-sided.

We may also refer to the statement in the standard short history of Roumania by N. Jorga, *A History of Roumania*. Translated from the second edition by Joseph McCabe, London, 1925. "For several months the capital of Hungary was in possession of the Roumanians,

The Mission met this morning at 10.30 A.M., with General Gorton presiding. Yesterday afternoon we had sent word that we desired to have the Prime Minister[6] and the Food Minister report to us at our meeting, but instead, the entire ministry came—less any Food Minister. They explained that the position of Food Minister was at present vacant, that they

ad had four different Food Ministers during the past week or ten days, and that they were now seeking one who could speak correctly all known languages. They were told we did not care for a polyglotic minister, but wanted one with some nerve and intelligence, who could fill the job and use an interpreter. They were also told that we expected the Hungarians and Roumanians to collaborate and accomplish something, instead of spending all their time and the Mission's time over mutual recriminations. I prepared a letter to the Roumanian Commander in Chief, which was adopted by the Mission, directing him, beginning tomorrow, to submit daily a report of the progress made by the Roumanians in complying with the instructions received by them from the Mission.

and a day will come when the baseless charges which are made against the commander of the army will be judged at their proper value. Light is already breaking, in fact, upon these unjust charges" (p.263). Charles Upson Clark, *Greater Roumania*, New York, 1922. Mr. Clark was an American newspaper correspondent. He is a great friend of Roumania. His views are admittedly one-sided. He says: "Relying in general on Rotimanian sources, I shall try to check them up so as not to give too partial an account" (p.242). Of special interest for us is Chapter XIX, "The Roumanians in Budapest." In this chapter he makes the statement that he is "trying to get at the truth - with a strong Roumanian bias, I admit, but anxious to do justice on all sides" (p. 257). "Doubtless few situations have ever combined more complex factors than did Budapest under the Roumanians. - No historian will ever clear them up fully" (p.258).

6   Mr. Stephen Friedrich had originally been a democratic Republican and an ardent personal follower of Michael Károlyi. During the Bolshevik terror he changed his opinions completely and became one of the most active counter-revolutionists and an anti-Semitic nationalist. He is still a member of Parliament and considers himself now a Fascist.

August 18, 1919.

To go back into the original history of the situation[7]: Shortly after the establishment of the Republic of Hungary in succession to the kingdom as part of the Dual Monarchy of Austro-Hungary, the bolshevists under Béla Kun obtained possession of the control of the Government and started a Reign of Terror. They painted red the windows and many of the statues of the magnificent Parliament buildings, and could have painted the roof had their supply of red paint not been exhausted. They arrested and executed hundreds and even thousands, confiscated for distribution everything of value, turned out a currency called white money on account of its color and to distinguish from the blue-colored currency existing prior to that time, and in general started to run things along the same lines as the Bolshevists in Russia. In order to keep up the national spirit, they started a war against the Czecho-Slovaks and beat them. They started another war against the Roumanians and were driving them back when, about the first of August, the Roumanians assumed the offensive, invaded Hungary and marched without opposition into and took possession of Budapest. Promptly after their arrival, the Soviet government was overturned by fifty gendarmes and the Archduke Joseph, a cousin of the Emperor Karl, appointed Governor[8], which position he still holds. The Roumanians on their part immediately began to loot Hungary, removing all automobiles, locomotives, cars and other rolling stock, took possession of and shipped to Roumania all the arms, munitions, and war material they could find, and then proceeded also to clean the country Out of private automobiles, farm implements, cattle, horses, clothing, sugar, coal, salt, and in fact everything of value; and even after they were notified by the Supreme Council of the Peace Conference to cease such requisitioning, they continued and are still continuing their depredations. They have taken possession of all branches of the government, all railroad, telegraph, telephone and postal systems, and at this date have all Hungary completely terrorized and at their feet. Their arrogance, however, has taken a turn and they are no longer treating the Military Mission with the same practical contempt as in the beginning.

Our offices located in the Royal Palace are gorgeous in extreme. This magnificent building must have cost millions to erect and furnish, and no pains or expense were spared. The walls of each room are covered with the same cloth with which

---

7   Cf. Introduction by Fritz-Conrad Kruger.

8   Obviously a mistake on the part of General Bandholtz.

the furniture of the room is upholstered, except the magnificent ball rooms, the walls of which are solid marble, and the details of which beggar description.

At this morning's session, Horthy[9]. It is the same title with which two other Hungarians have been previously honored, John Hunyadi in the fifteenth, and Louis Kossuth in the nineteenth century, who had been Admiral of the Austro-Hungarian Navy, stated he was prepared to reorganize a Hungarian Army and have an effective force ready within four days after he was given permission to proceed. The Roumanians have as yet made no report of any progress in complying with instructions from this Mission.

Last night Colonel Loree and I dined with Admiral Troubridge of the British Navy, and General Gorton.

At this afternoon's session, there was quite a fight between the American and the Italian representatives over the question of having the Roumanian Commander himself attend our sessions or be represented by an authorized staff officer. General Mombelli insisted that this should be done by correspondence, the matter laid out in detail in a letter, and then sent to the Roumanian Commander in Chief, to await his reply. I told him, in view of the fact that all such letters had then to be translated either from English to French or French to English, and that no subject could be fully covered and explained in a communication, that I must insist that the Roumanian government be suitably represented at our Mission when we so desired. He said that it was very hard to require an army commander to stop his other most important work to attend a session. I replied that at present the Roumanian-Hungarian question was the most serious in Europe, that each of our governments had sent a general, accompanied by his staff and a detachment, to devote all their time to this question, and that I did not give a damn whether it were the Roumanian Commander in Chief or the Roumanian King, and I insisted that

9 Nicholas Horthy de Nagybánya. Born in 1868, belonged to an old family of the landed gentry. He entered the Austro-Hungarian navy. During
the World war he distinguished himself greatly and at the end of it was
appointed Commander in Chief of the Austro-Hungarian fleet. He
helped to organize the anti-Bolshevik counter-revolution and was made
Commander in Chief of the army of the new government. On March 1,
1920, he was chosen Governor or Regent, which position he held until
October 15, 1944, when he was arrested by the Germans. He died in
Estoril, Portugal in 1957.

they be subject to call when needed. A letter was sent to the Roumanian Commander in Chief requesting him to come or be represented at tomorrow morning's session.

August 19, 1919.

At this morning's session, matters were much more quiet, although the Roumanians, as usual, won a point by sending as their representative an officer who was authorized to give information on only two points, namely the question of food supply and the question of the organization of the Municipal police of Budapest. General Holban, the Roumanian Commander of Budapest and vicinity, is the representative and apparently knows as much about the military game as does an Igorrote about manicuring. On the fifteenth, when he was before the Mission, he stated that he had 10,000 troops in the city and 5,000 in the suburbs. Today he insisted that he had only 5,000 all told. When called upon to explain his map relative to requisition zones, he could not explain it at all and admitted that he could not turn out a map that would be intelligible. The Serbian plenipotentiary showed up and presented his credentials to the Mission. He rejoices in the euphonious cognomen of Lazar Baitch. It was decided in the future to have morning sessions of the Mission, leaving the afternoons to the members for catching up with their work and making personal investigations. I then notified the Mission that I must insist that General Mardarescu, the Roumanian Commander in Chief, be himself directed to appear before the Mission tomorrow at 11 o'clock. This time there was no dissenting vote. Despite all their promises and instructions the Roumanians are continuing with their wholesale pillaging of Hungary and the Hungarians.

It is not possible to describe conditions in a city or country occupied by an enemy, but judging from conditions in Budapest and Hungary while occupied by the Roumanians, we Americans should promptly take every measure possible to avoid any such catastrophe. Universal training should be adopted without further parley.

Last night Colonel Loree, Captain Gore and Lieutenant Hamilton, Captain Weiss, who is a Hungarian by birth and speaks the language perfectly and whom I have asked to be attached to my office here, and myself called upon Count Edelsheim, his wife and daughter. They told us of the terrors of the Bolshevist régime. The house is filled with beautiful antique furniture and a most peculiar mixture of paintings, ranging from choice antiquities to rotten moderns. Our chef, having cooked for hotels in both London and Paris, is living up to his reputation, but our butler in his previous condition of servitude had undoubtedly been a hostler, and knows more about shoveling in fodder than he does about waiting on the table.

August 20, 1919.

This morning's session, at which I presided, was one of the most interesting that we have had. In the beginning there was considerable discussion about our Board of Claims and Complaints. Then the Hungarian Minister of War was introduced and submitted a verbal proposition for the reorganization of the Hungarian Army. He was told to reduce the same to writing and submit it with the least practicable delay. A complaint has been received that the Hungarians have been making wholesale arrests and committing abuses in certain districts which had been assigned by the Peace Conference to Austria, and it was decided to ask the Supreme Council to give a correct definition of the present geographical limits of Hungary. Next, our old friend Diamandi came in with the Roumanian Commander in Chief, General Mardarescu, and a new star in the Roumanian constellation in the person of a General Rudeanu. General Mardarescu was put on the carpet and told in unmistakable terms that it was up to him to report what had been done in complying with the request from the Mission of August 16, 1919. He resorted to all sorts of evasions and circumlocutions, which may have been intentional or may have been due to his grade of intelligence, which appears to be about that of a comatose caribou. He finally agreed to be a good boy and carry out our instructions. Our friend Diamandi insisted that in the future, whenever we discuss matters of importance with a Hungarian official, the Roumanian government should be represented. His proposition was laid on the table and he received no reply, as we propose to use our own judgment in regard to such matters.

In the afternoon General Rudeanu, with Colonel Yates of our Army, called upon me at my office in the Royal Palace, and practically asked that we let bygones be bygones, stating that he is prepared to turn over a new leaf from now on. He appears to be possessed of almost human intelligence and it is hoped that some progress will now be made.

Later, General Pétain, who is a younger brother of the French Field Marshal of that name, called upon me at the office and spent an hour trying either to deter mine my exact attitude as regards the Roumanians, or to influence me in their favor[10].

August 21, 1919.

At this morning's session a complaint was submitted by the Roumanian government that the Archduke had been declaring martial law in certain places in Hungary and that they could not tolerate this as it was considered an infringement upon their prerogatives. Additional complaints were also received about acts of violence and other abuses committed by Hungarians in territory which had been given to Austria by the Peace Conference[11]. Last night a telegram from the Supreme Council was received intimating that they were not satisfied with a Hapsburg as governor of Hungary. In view of all the foregoing, it was decided to send for our friend the Archduke and his Prime Minister and tell them where to get off. This was done. They promptly arrived and the Archduke was notified that he must immediately revoke his declaration of martial law in any place in Hungary. He and his Prime Minister obsequiously acquiesced and promised to revoke the order immediately. The Prime Minister was then invited to tarry in the antechamber while a little private conversation was addressed to the Archduke, which in effect was that it was our opinion that a government which could act in such an idiotic manner as his had been acting could inspire confidence in nobody, and he was then given the coup de grâce by being told that we considered it our duty to inform His Highness that the mere fact that the head of a state is a Hapsburg diminishes the possibility of feeling confidence in an administration, which furthermore had been established by a coup d'état during a foreign occupation. He maintained that he was the people's choice and practically the only available Moses to lead them out of their present political wilderness. He was informed that on this subject there was a great difference of opinion. At this the Archduke waxed furious, stated that his giving up the reins of government would mean a return to Bolshevism, and dashed madly out of he room without shaking hands with anybody.

The Roumanian General, Rudeanu, and the Roumanian High Commissioner Diamandi were then sent for, and the situation explained to them in order that hey might take the necessary precautionary measures.

10 See other pro-Roumanian actions of the French on pp. 32, 35, 57, 79,105,110, 125,331(of the original edition).

11 The Ödenburg or Sopron district, the so-called Burgenland, in the western part of Hungary.

August 22, 1919.

Last night we entertained at our quarters General Rudeanu and M. Diamandi. They were given champagne and wine *ad libitum* but fought shy of it, apparently fearing there was a scheme on foot or inducing garrulity on their part. Being their host, I allowed no official matters to come up for discussion.

At this morning's session of the Mission, General Mombelli informed us that our old friend, the Archduke, called on him last night and stated that he was in such a twitter at our meeting yesterday that he could hardly speak, and went on to complain that we did not understand that he, as a Hapsburg, was working only or the best interests of Hungary, that he was remaining bravely at his post only to lead his country until the elections, when the wishes of his countrymen would be sacred to him. He failed to add, however, that it would be no fault of his if any Hungarians were left to dare vote against him. He then asked whether our talk to him yesterday was inspired from Paris or was on our own initiative. He was told that gave him just two guesses. He then stated that he thought it was probably inspired from Vienna[12], and was told that, as a supposedly intelligent human being, it was up to him to make his own interpretation.

We unanimously agreed that the Roumanians must immediately aid the Hungarians to organize a police force of 6,000 men in Budapest and that we would take up the reorganization[13] of the Hungarian Army on a working basis of 30,000 men. Everything seems to indicate that the Bolshevists have about 100,000 arms still hidden and we have decided to make the Roumanians, aided and abetted by the Hungarians, get hold of these arms and place them at our disposal. We decided furthermore to tell the Roumanian Commander in Chief hat he would be "skinned" for being off limits whenever he came west of the Danube except at Budapest. Our gallant Roumanian allies turned in a complaint about the Czecho-Slovaks invading a portion of Hungary, and it was suggested that the Czecho-Slovaks had damn sight better ground for complaint of the Roumanians for having done the same thing. I called the attention of the Mission to the fact that our noble allies were still playing the same game and that no report of progress had yet been made. I insisted that there be incorporated in our telegram to the Supreme Council information to that effect. We then discussed the present political situation in Hungary, upon which we were required to make a report, and I have attached hereto my memorandum on that subject which was then submitted.

The question of claims and complaints is so serious and becoming so complicated that I stated that Colonel Loree could no longer be spared for that exclusive work, and it was decided to lay the matter before the Supreme Council, requesting that a suitable number of officers with proper equipment be sent to Hungary for that purpose.

Memorandum on the Hungarian Political Situation

"To consider the present political situation one must start in at least with the assumption of the reins of government by the Archduke Joseph.

12 While the Hungarians were returning to monarchial institutions and showed no dislike for the Hapsburg dynasty, the government of Austria was decidedly socialistic-republican and violently anti-Hapsburg.

13 This is the first statement in the Diary pertaining to the important question of the reorganization of the Hungarian police or gendarmerie, which, on Sept. 5, the Inter-Allied Military Mission put into the hands of colonel Yates, U.S. Army. The Roumanians tried to prevent such a re-organization. References to their policy in this respect may be found in statements of Sept. 1, 2, 18, 22, 24, 29, Oct. 3, and 6. Upon completion of the work Colonel Yates was, on Nov.19, officially congratulated by the Inter-Allied Military Mission.

It was undoubtedly the firmness of the Inter-Allied Military Mission which brought about the desired result, and not the good offices of Mr. Vopicka. Charles J. Vopicka was U.S. Envoy Extraordinary and Minister Plenipotentiary to Roumania, Bulgaria, and Serbia. In his book, *Secrets of the Balkans*, New York, 1921, he assumes some credit for the compliance of the Roumanians with the demands of the Allies.

"Polk," he says, "told me what was demanded by the Allies from Roumania, and stated that unless she complied with this request, the Allies would sever relations. I first spoke to the Roumanian members of the Peace Commission in Paris, and then I sent telegrams to the Roumanian Prime Minister. Within ten days the Roumanian government complied with the first request of the Commission, to supply 10,000 gendarmes in Hungary with arms and ammunition, and also complied with the other things which were required, with the exception that they refused to sign the treaty between Roumania and Austria" (p. 306).

Taking advantage of the fact that the Socialist government had been started but a few days and that an enemy was in possession of the city, a coup d'état was pulled off by about fifty gendarmes with the accessory passivity of the Roumanians. The Archduke himself has shown that when it comes to diplomacy, political matters and the administration of a government, he is still a babe in swaddling clothes. This is demonstrated by the seriousness with which he took an anonymous ultimatum, and by the various ridiculous administrative stunts he has pulled off. He is probably, when all is considered, quite popular in Hungary, but his popularity is neither so extensive nor so deep-rooted as he seems to imagine. It is believed that he has been misled by his intimates, who have lured him into believing that he is the almost unanimous choice of the people of Hungary. However, either independently, or influenced by his advisers, he is believed to have been taking measures to perpetuate his office by declaring martial law with the announced intention of arresting Bolshevists. This is undoubtedly a transparent camouflage to conceal the real intention of disposing of all political opponents and of assuring his ultimate election.

The Hungarians had barely disentangled themselves from the meshes of Bolshevism when the present weak régime came into existence. It would be a calamity if either Bolshevists or the Hapsburgs were allowed to control Hungary. To prevent this, it is important that some strong man of real popularity and influence among all classes be placed in charge and given every assistance in reorganizing a semi-permanent government. To restore a Hapsburg at this time, when it is in the memory of everybody that that unfortunate dynasty was the intentional or unintentional cause of the World War, would seriously afflict all the Allies and would give an impulse to Bolshevism,

In brief, the Hungarian political situation is believed to be critical, but not beyond remedy. If the Roumanian government will shift its gear from first to second, up to third, and do it's best to facilitate the organization of a government and the creation of a police force and an army of suitable size, and to arrange for gradual but prompt withdrawal behind its own recognized boundary, it is believed the present deplorable condition in Hungary can soon be brought to an end."

Before adjourning, a telegram was received from the Supreme Council authorizing the Mission to send detachments wherever necessary to prevent the Roumanians from getting their Hungarian loot over into Roumania, and it was decided to wire the Supreme Council that this would not be feasible either with the means at our disposal or with any force that could arrive in time for the purpose. It was furthermore recommended that additional officers be sent to watch over he points of egress and take inventory of what the Roumanians were making away with.

In the afternoon, after sending a telegram to the American Commission posting them to date on the situation, I took a car and investigated a few of the complaints concerning Roumanian seizures, etc., and found them to be true. I then called upon General Rudeanu, told him I had found his people were removing 4,000 telephone instruments from private houses and were about to take the remaining half of the supplies of the Ministry of Posts and Telegraphs, which hey had not taken in first requisition; that they were seizing the few remaining Hungarian breeding stallions; that they had sent word to the Ministry of Agriculture to deliver to them all maps, instruments, etc.; and that I could give him only too many instances of like character. I told him that his government had repeatedly promised to carry out the Mission's instructions, but that I had been here twelve days, during which the Roumanians had continued their seizures and had not returned a single thing despite their repeated promises. I added that we were all most anxious to coöperate, but that I should like for once to telegraph my superiors that the Roumanians had shown any indication of an intention to play the game according to the rule. He replied that in my place he would feel as I did, that he would confer with his colleagues tonight, and would tomorrow let us know whether or not the Roumanian government really intended to stop requisitioning and return any property already seized. All of this looks like an admission that they had all along intended to pursue the even tenor of their way regardless of the wishes of the Supreme Council.

In the evening Count von Edelsheim called upon us and continued his stories of Bolshevist atrocities.

August 23, 1919.

At this morning's session, after disposing of several routine matters, the Mission prepared to receive M. Diamandi and General Rudeanu, who had faithfully promised to be in the antechamber at 11.30. As a matter of fact, they were only twenty minutes late, which is the closest any Roumanian has yet come to keeping his promise with us[14]. Diamandi seated himself with his unctious diplomatic smile, and stated that he had received advices from his government at Bucharest, and first proceeded to regale us with information that was already six days old and which we had read to him ourselves at one of our sessions. He was politely informed of the fact and then proceeded to other matters, prefacing his remarks by the usual statement that the Roumanian government desired to work in complete accord with its allies, but that we must consider the deplorable transportation conditions in Roumania and the fact that the Roumanians found here in Hungary many supplies taken from their own country, in proof of which he displayed two first-aid packets, two iodine tubes, and one or two other matters with the Roumanian mark. We were overwhelmed with this incontrovertible evidence, but in time sufficiently recovered to let him proceed, which he did by

---

14 I found an amusing laconic footnote by Lieutenant-Colonel Repington in his *After the War, A Diary*, Boston, 1922. "Roumanians are not re-markable for keeping promises or appointments" (p. 327).

adding that all Roumanian property found in Hungary must naturally be subject to unqualified seizure, that the seizures would be limited to what was actually necessary for the Roumanian forces, but that this government must insist that they pick up an additional 30 per cent to replace articles taken from Roumania during the German invasion; that formerly Roumania had had 1,000 locomotives whereas they now had only 6o; that they would be very glad to pay for all private automobiles and other property seized in Hungary, but must insist on doing so with their government bonds along the same lines as the Central Powers had done in Roumania. Then he wished to know, in case Roumania did not take things from Hungary, who would guarantee that the Roumanians got their proper share, and he added that it certainly would be much better to leave all such property in the hands of faithful and truthful allies like the Roumanians, than to leave it with the Hungarians, who were known never to keep their promises. He would probably have gone on indefinitely with similar sophistical persiflage, had I not intervened and stated that on three separate occasions our truthful allies, the Roumanians, had faithfully promised to carry out our instructions, but that up to the present time there was no tangible proof that a single one of the promises had been kept. Certain it was that they were continuing their requisitions and more boldly than ever, that no property had yet been returned, that they had submitted no reports as promised, and that I personally must insist on some proof of the perfect accord that I had heard so much about. M. Diamandi stated that he could say nothing more than was contained in his instructions, and any question whatever that was put up to him would need to be referred to Bucharest for decision, the natural inference being that he could never answer a question inside of about five days. Our little friend Diamandi has always been in the diplomatic service, having served at Rome, Vienna, Paris, and Berlin. He was Roumanian minister to Petrograd when the Boishevist régime started, during which he was arrested by the Bolshevists, and I shall never forgive them for having afterwards released him. He typifies perfectly the Roumanian policy of procrastination with a view of absolutely draining Hungary before it can be stopped.

While the Roumanians were present, a telegram was received from M. Clemenceau, which, after repeating the opinion held by the Supreme Council of our friend, the Archduke, wound up by insisting that "Archie" resign *tout de suite*. The Roumanians were informed of this, gave evidence of great glee, and it is believed sent word to "Archie" as soon as they left the building. In any event, the first thing that was brought up at our afternoon session was how to handle his Royal Highness. Finally we drafted a letter to him, in which was enclosed a copy of a telegram received from the Supreme Council, stating that:

"The Allied and Associated Powers have been further considering the information, derived from your report and from other sources, as to recent events in Budapest. Their conclusions are as follows:

They are most anxious to conclude a durable peace with the Hungarian people but feel that this cannot be done while the present Hungarian government is in power. That government has been brought into existence, not by the will of the people, but by a coup d'état, carried out by a small body of police during the occupation of a foreign army. It has at its head a member of the House of Hapsburg whose policy and ambition are largely responsible for the calamities from which the world is suffering and will long suffer. A peace negotiated by such a government is not likely to be lasting nor can the Allied and Associated Governments give it the economic support which Hungary so sorely needs.

If it be replied that the Archduke Joseph is prepared, before approaching the Allied and Associated Governments, to submit his claim to the test of popular election, we must reply that this procedure cannot be a satisfactory election if carried out under the auspices of an administration which the Archduke himself controls. The difficulties in obtaining by election a faithful reflection of the popular will are, in the present unhappy state of Hungary, of the most serious kind. They would be overwhelming if the election were carried out under Hapsburg influences. Even if the assembly elected under such circumstances were really representative, no one would think so. In the interest of European peace, therefore, the Allied and Associated Governments must insist that the present claimant to the leadership of the Hungarian state should resign and that a government in which all parties are represented should appeal to the Hungarian people. The Allied and Associated Powers would be prepared to negotiate with any government which possessed the confidence of an assembly so elected."

After dispatching the letter to the Archduke, we took up the Roumanian situation, and it was decided, in view of Diamandi's statement that in case he were called he could add nothing to what he had already said, there would be no use in sending for him. I therefore insisted that a telegram be sent from us to the Supreme Council, informing them of all of M. Diamandi's statements and adding that in our opinion so far as the Roumanians were concerned the time of this Mission had been wasted, and that it would be useless to continue its relations with Roumanian officials who apparently were determined to carry on a reprehensible policy of procrastination, and who had repeatedly broken their solemn promises. General Graziani said he would draft this telegram at once, provided he could take a recess of about an hour. When he returned with his draft it contained only the bald statement in regard to M. Diamandi's remarks. I insisted that my reference to our waste of time be incorporated in the telegram. Thereupon I was asked to draft the telegram. I complied with this request and handed the telegram to Lieutenant-Colonel Romanelli, General Mombelli's secretary. He made a very good French translation of it, arid it was then handed to General Graziani's aide to add to the telegram. Just as we were leaving, I saw this aide hand General Mombelli my draft, Colonel Romanelli's translation, and another slip of paper, and asked him what the third paper was. He said that it was for the purpose of putting part of Romanelli's translation into better French. I insisted on seeing that part. He showed it to me, and then General Mombelli said that, as handed to him, it was understood that this new slip of paper was to replace entirely Colonel Romanelli's translation. At this I thumped the table two or three times and said that I absolutely insisted that the statement in regard to the futility of hoping for anything from the Roumanians be incorporated. This was then agreed to. Evidently our French colleague was trying to play a skin game and got caught at it.

At 8 o'clock the Hungarian Minister of Foreign Affairs showed up with a letter containing the resignation of the Archduke[15] and the entire Ministry. He also stated that everything was now in the hands of the Inter-Allied Military Mission. We then sent for the Prime Minister and told him that this Mission did not mix in the internal affairs of Hungary, except to such an extent as it might be definitely instructed by the Supreme Council; that the notice to the Archduke was sent as directed by our superiors, but that it was not within our province to organize a new government. We added that it was the duty of the members of the present cabinet to continue temporarily in office until a new government could be organized, which we hoped would be within a few days. General Rudeanu, our Roumanian liaison officer, was sent for and informed of the Archduke's resignation.

August 24, 1919.

For the first time since my arrival at Budapest, there was no session of the Mission today. This resulted from the almost piteous appeals of both the French and the Italian representatives to have a day off.

About 10 o'clock I was called upon by two representatives of the British press, and I gave them the dope in regard to the official demise of our friend, the Archduke, and filled them full to overflowing with complaints and proofs in regard to the rapacity of our gallant Roumanian allies[16].

I then prepared and sent a long telegram to the American Mission, to the effect that yesterday our suave friend Diamandi, accompanied by General Rudeanu, had called upon Admiral Troubridge, apparently on the verge of tears because we had

---

15 His proclamation on leaving the government may be found in Malbone W. Graham, *New Governments of Central Europe*, New York, 1924, p.583.

not sent for them the day before. They both intimated that probably their usefulness in Budapest was over, in which they were just about right. The rotund and diplomatic Diamandi was undoubtedly thus affected because he had been sent here to pull off a coup in the shape of forcing Hungary to make a separate peace with Roumania practically amounting to annexation, which coup had been demolished by a bomb in the shape of the Supreme Council's handing the Archduke his hat and telling him not to be in a hurry. I also received word that on the twenty-first the Crown Prince of Roumania, as the future King of Hungary, received a number of kowtowing Hungarian aristocrats.

The day before yesterday I sent Colonel Yates, formerly of the Thirtieth Infantry, U. S. A., and now American attaché at Bucharest, to investigate conditions in Hungary west of the Danube. On his return today he reported that Admiral Horthy had about 8,000 well- disciplined, well-trained, and well-armed troops, including machine guns and nineteen field guns under his command.

16 Public opinion in the principal Allied countries and in the United States concerning the situation in Hungary was divided. On page 748 of the *New International Year Book* for 1919, New York, 1920, we find the following summary: "A portion of the American press complained that in France among the official class as well as among the Italian representatives there was a tendency to blame the United States and to a less degree Great Britain for what was considered the harsh treatment of Roumania. As Italian and French representatives on the Supreme Council had approved its action, there seemed to be no color to these accusations, but in the French and Italian press there was a disposition to find excuses for Roumania in every instance, and to oppose any effort toward keeping her within bounds." In this same article, *War of the Nations*, may he found a moderate and critical explanation of the Roumanian viewpoint by a French journalist. The commentary on the disregard of the Allied demands by Roumania was very severe in the United States. Read also the articles by Frank H. Simonds, "Hungary, the Balkans, and the League," in *The American Review of Reviews*, Sept., 1919, and in the October issue of the same Review, "The European Reaction." Another summarizing article is contained in the *Literary Digest*, April 23, 1919, "Roumania's Invasion of Hungary." Dillon says, in the book previously referred to, that the French papers applauded the action of the Roumanians, and also the English; but he gives no example of the latter. In fact, liberal public opinion in England was absolutely opposed to it.

I also wired the American Mission in regard to the incident of last night, when our dapper French colleague tried to put one over on the American and British representatives by not including all that should have been included in the telegram to the Supreme Council. General Gorton, the British representative, read over and concurred in all of my telegram, asked me to say so, and to add that he requested that a copy be furnished the British Mission.

Upon leaving the Palace about 1.30, I was met by a delegation of about 200 Hungarians who said that they were small landholders and wished to see the Inter-Allied Military Mission in regard to their proper representation on the government. I told their spokesman and interpreter that the Mission could do nothing in regard to this, as we did not meddle with internal affairs, but that in case they desired to send any petition to the Supreme Council of the Peace Conference and would present the same in writing tomorrow, I would submit it to the Mission for consideration.

This morning I found on my desk two magnificent bouquets of purple orchids, and I am getting so accustomed to the Royal Palace life and surroundings that it will be pretty difficult to come down to the life of an ordinary American citizen.

August 25, 1919.

Yesterday afternoon, accompanied by Colonel Loree and Lieutenant Hamilton, I visited and inspected the State Railway shops, and found that the Roumanians were gutting the place strictly in accord with the Hungarian reports. In a neighboring freight yard there were 120 freight cars loaded with machinery and material, and in the yard of the shops there were 15 cars, likewise loaded and more than 25 others partly loaded or in the process of being loaded. I then went through the machine shops and saw many places where machinery had just been removed and others where it was in the process of being removed. The workmen stated that the Roumanians had been busy there, despite the fact that it was Sunday, until 4 o'clock in the afternoon, and that they were obliging the Hungarians to do all the work connected with taking out the machinery.

In the evening, at about 9.50, we heard a racket outside of our window, but we did not pay much attention to it at the time because a discussion of Roumanians and Hungarians, none of whom understands the others, usually sounds like a ladies' tea party. This morning I found out, however, that the trouble was all caused by a Roumanian patrol of one officer and eight or ten men who had arrested a British Bluejacket and had declined to examine his pass. One of my men, thinking the rumpus was all due to the fact that the Roumanians did not understand the

Britisher, went to try to explain in German, and met the fate of the peacemaker. He was pricked by a bayonet wielded by a Roumanian soldier. At this, becoming disgusted with the role of peace maker, he yelled to the American soldiers and British sailors across the street. They came tearing to the rescue of their comrade who was promptly abandoned by the Roumanians.

The Mission met at the usual hour, *i.e.*, 9.30, this morning, but there was nothing of great importance. This was mainly due to the fact that the Archduke was now out of the way, and also to our decision to have no more transactions with the Roumanian officials, on account of their lying propensities.

Our officer who had been sent to the bridge over the Theiss [River Tisza], reported that the bridge could not be completed inside of three weeks and that it would take about the same time to complete any of the other bridges.

During the morning a delegation, claiming to represent 600,000 industrial workers, asked to see the Mission, and when they announced that they desired to insist upon suitable representation in the new government, they were told that this Mission could not mix in the internal affairs of Hungary.

August 26, 1919.

Yesterday afternoon a verbose but rather stiff telegram came to me, containing the text of an ultimatum from the Supreme Council to the Roumanian government. I told them in unmistakable terms that in case they persisted in looting Hungary, alleging as an excuse that they were simply reimbursing themselves for what they had lost during Mackensen's invasion, it was all bosh; that they must abide by the decision of any reparation commission the Peace Conference might appoint; and that in the meantime this Mission of Inter-Allied Generals would be authorized to appoint such a commission temporarily. It was added that in case they did not immediately and affirmatively make a Statement that they would abide by all their past agreements, the Allied and Associated Powers would be obliged to make them pay in full any claims against Transylvania and other portions of Hungary which had been given to Roumania by the Peace Conference. The foregoing telegram was followed up this morning by another one preëmptorily notifying those sons of Ananias, the Roumanians, that drastic measures would immediately be adopted if they would not come to time.

I had drafted a telegram, which was sent in the name of the Mission, stating that in our opinion the Roumanians were looting Hungary as rapidly as possible so that they might suddenly evacuate the country, and at the same time they were disarming everybody and refusing to reorganize the police, and in general that, intentionally or unintentionally, every move they made was in the direction of turning Hungary over to Bolshevism and chaos.

There were several more delegations out in the Palace courtyard today, all representing the so-called Christian Socialists; all clamoring against the Jews, and practically demanding control of the government. One delegation, consisting of four balatant and bellicose females (none of them pretty) and three Bolshevistic-looking males, got into the Council Room, frothed at the mouth in Hungarian, English, and French, and were told that the Mission could not mix in the internal affairs of Hungary.

Major Borrow of the British Army, whom we sent to inspect the Szolnok[17] Bridge, reported that it would take two or three weeks to get that or any other bridge across the Theiss River so that it would support loaded cars, but that he found at the bridge, ready to cross, 150 locomotives, 200 to 300 empty freight cars, 4 aeroplanes on cars, 200 to 300 tank cars and, between Szolnok and Budapest, many hundreds of carloads of merchandise.

For the past three days we have been having fairly warm weather; in fact the warmest that any of us have ever seen in Europe, but at that it was not much over 80 degrees Fahrenheit. Today it has turned cool again, and with the clouds and threatening rain, reminds me more of "Sunny France."

August 27, 1919.

This morning's session of the Mission, with General Graziani, the French representative, in the chair, was very quiet and orderly, all due to the fact that we have very little coming in now on account of our strained relations with the Roumanian Commander in Chief. Each one of the representatives had received a basketful of telegrams, nearly all of which came from the so-called Christian Socialists. This party should be more properly called Anti-Jews, because most of their petitions are devoted to a tirade against their Semitic fellow countrymen. They seem to be a blatant minority, but more thoroughly organized than any of the other parties.

---

17 Szolnok, a river port on the right bank of the Theiss. Population not quite 29,000. An important market and railroad center.

Yesterday afternoon I was called upon by Mr. Lazar Baitch, the Jugo-Slav Plenipotentiary to our Mission. He is built along the line of the blonde and bland Roumanian Diamandi, except as to complexion, which is distinctly brunette. Among other things, he stated that his country greatly feared an Italian, Austrian, Hungarian, and Roumanian combination, which would cut the Jugo-Slavs off from the rest of Europe, and that they, therefore, preferred to see a strong and friendly Hungary. He promised to report to me any developments as rapidly as they came to his attention. Then he came to the main object of his visit, which was to ask that I give him the permanent loan of an automobile. I suggested that he apply first to the Hungarian government, knowing damned well that the Roumanians had swiped all they had.

Later on in the afternoon I learned that the fine Italian hand had attempted to get in its deadly work, even during the Bolshevist régime; that the Italians had then bought the magnificent Hungarian Breeding Farms, which are now being seized by the Roumanians; that they were now as mad as a nest of hornets because they cannot stop the Roumanian seizures, as it would give away their rather reprehensible relations with the Bolshevists. I also learned that the Italian Lieutenant-Colonel Romanelli, who has been in Budapest for some time, is understood to have been sent with a mission to induce the Hungarians to accept the Duke of Savoy as their king. This is rather confirmed by the intense hostility towards Romanelli of the Roumanians, who wanted the Crown Prince Carol to be elected King of Hungary[18], and also that most of the Hungarians are sore on Romanelli.

Yesterday afternoon a British correspondent, named Hamilton, representing a Manchester paper[19], called me up over the telephone and said that the inevitable Archduke, accompanied by his former Prime Minister, Friedrich, who is now supposed to be reorganizing the Hungarian government, butted into the Press Bureau at the Hotel Ritz and announced that M. Clemenceau had sent a telegram to Friedrich directing that three Hungarian plenipotentiaries be sent to the Peace Conference to represent Hungary. Hamilton further stated that Friedrich had publicly announced practically the same thing to delegations in front of his house. All of this is, of course, a damned lie and is the line of propaganda spread to

[18] Compare statement to this effect in the entry of the Diary on Aug. 11.

[19] Obviously the *Manchester Guardian.*

delude the Hungarians into the belief that the Archduke's pet, Friedrich, is *persona grata* with the Peace Conference.

The Roumanians are proceeding merrily with their seizures and general raising of Hell, All this cannot last indefinitely and something is sure to pop up before long.

August 28, 1919.

Yesterday afternoon, accompanied by General Gorton, the British representative, I visited some of the places where reports have been received from Hungarian sources that the Roumanians were making seizures. It is remarkable that, so far as we have been able to verify, not a single Hungarian complaint has been exaggerated. At the warehouse of the Hungarian Discount and Exchange Bank, we found that up to date the Roumanians had seized and removed 2,400 carloads, mainly of provisions and forage, and were daily carting away great quantities. At the Central Depot of the Hungarian Post and Telegraph we found seven cars already loaded, two with shoes and five with carpets and rugs. In this connection, it should be remembered that the Roumanian Commander in Chief said that he had never taken anything that was not absolutely necessary for the use of troops in the field. At this place we also found the Roumanians removing the machinery from the repair shops. At the works of the Ganz-Danubius Company we found the Roumanians busily engaged loading five freight cars with material, under the charge of Lieutenant Vaude Stanescu. At the Hungarian Military Hospital Number I, the Roumanians had ordered all the patients out and there remained only 57 patients in the hospital, whose capacity was 800, and these 57 could not be removed on account of the serious nature of their wounds. Next we visited the Hungarian Central Sanitary Depot and found that under Major C. Georgescu, a medical officer, the Roumanians were absolutely gutting the establishment. In all the places we visited, the manual labor is performed by Hungarian soldiers under Roumanian sentinels.

Last night, accompanied by my aide, Lieutenant Hamilton, I dined with General Graziani, who is billeted in the magnificent home of Count Széchényi. His wife was formerly Gladys Vanderbilt. The other guests were the General Mombelli and his aide-de-camp.

At this morning's session, General Graziani reported that he had received a call from the Hungarian General Soós, Admiral Horthy's Chief of Staff, who said that he would submit to the Mission today his plans for the reorganization of the Hungarian Army. This memorandum was received later and is very excellently prepared and arranged. General Graziani then read a telegram he had received from M. Clemenceau stating that there was no objection on his part to the rotation of the chairmanship in the organization of the Mission. General Mombelli then reported that he had had a call from the Hungarian liaison officer, Colonel Dormándy, who explained that Hungary needed a strong government as quickly as possible, adding that he thought that the Allied Powers should have a force here. General Mombelli reported further that he had had a call from our special *bête noire*, the Roumanian diplomat Diamandi, during which the latter stated that his government could do nothing with the Hungarian government under Friedrich, and that they could not consent to the reorganization of the police under Friedrich because they knew that such an organization would be used for political purposes. M. Diamandi then tried to pump General Mombelli in regard to what information we had received from Paris, but he got no reply.

Yesterday afternoon, when General Gorton and I returned from our inspection trip, we found Heinrich, Minister of Commerce, awaiting us. He wanted to know if the Entente had stated that they wanted Friedrich at the head of the government, and also what the Entente's attitude would be toward a cabinet formed either with or without Friedrich. We gave him the stereotyped reply that we could not mix in the internal affairs of Hungary. Later a newspaperman came in and told me that he had verified the fact that Friedrich was the organizer of the Christian Socialist party and that although this party had never had over 10 per cent of the membership in Parliament, it was now the only party that was organized and the only one, therefore, able to make itself conspicuous. The newspaperman also stated that Friedrich was determined to remain in power, with the idea of ultimately accomplishing the Archduke's election and return to the head of the government. I wired all this information to the American Commission.

On arrival at my quarters a little before 8 o'clock, I found General Gorton awaiting me, and he gave me the substance of another ultimatum of a somewhat anonymous character, delivered through the Roumanian Ardeli, who had sent the first ultimatum to the Archduke. This one was along similar lines and included demands for immediate peace between Hungary and Roumania; the occupation of Hungary by Roumania for one year; the cession of practically all the strategic points, and then the annexation of Hungary to Roumania. This was coded and ciphered and sent to the American Commission in Paris with a request that a copy be sent to the British Commission.

Early this morning I sent another coded and ciphered message to the American Commission, to the effect that the Roumanians certainly could not continue their arrogant and haughty attitude unless backed by someone, and that I believed it was the French and the Italians who were trying to accomplish some kind of political or other union between Roumania, Hungary, Austria, and Italy, with a view to isolating entirely the Jugo-Slavs.

August 29, 1919.

At the meeting this morning, there was the usual discussion and gesticulatory machine gun French on the part of our Latin members, especially after I suggested that the Mission, owing to the attitude of the Roumanians, had accomplished less than nothing since its arrival here, and that we should consider whether or not the time had arrived for notifying the Supreme Council that in our opinion our prolonged stay only subjected us to humiliation from the Roumanians, and our governments to steady loss of prestige with both the Roumanians and the Hungarians. After considerable discussion and playing the fine old game of passing the buck, they invited me to prepare a memorandum on the subject, which I agreed to do.

Last night we had General Mombelli to dinner, and our chef surely did spread himself. He sent in course after course of unknown concoctions, but fortunately all of them came in an inviting manner and tasted good.

This morning I drafted a long memorandum on the subject of the Mission's work in Hungary and sent it by courier to Vienna for transmission to Paris.

August 30, 1919.

At the session of the Mission today, at which General Gorton presided, I submitted a memorandum arranged on the basis of the deadly parallel, prefacing the same as follows:

1. This is the eighteenth day that the entire membership of the Mission has been present in Budapest, and unfortunately it must be said that, but for one or two negligible exceptions, practically nothing has been accomplished by the Mission as regards the carrying out of the instructions given it by the Supreme Council. As this has been entirely due to the action of the Roumanian officials in ignoring the Mission's requests, in declining to accept the Mission's instructions as authoritative, it is believed that the time has come when the case should be plainly laid before the Supreme Council and a statement made that, unless there is an immediate change in the attitude of the Roumanian government, it would be useless for the Mission to attempt to function at Budapest. In substantiation of the foregoing, there are presented in chronological order the more important requests made by the Mission to the Roumanian government, and in a parallel column the action taken on the same.

After this there were arranged in parallel columns the requests made on the Roumanian Commander in Chief by the Inter-Allied Military Mission and the action taken on the same by the Roumanian authorities, and in conclusion I added:

2. It will be seen from the foregoing that this Mission has been unable to make any progress whatever in the performance of the duties expressly assigned to it by the Supreme Council. It is difficult to understand what motive can inspire the Roumanian government in following its long-continued line of conduct, but whether the same is due to deliberate intent, to inefficiency of subordinates, or to any other cause, the result is the same. It is recommended that the Military Mission seriously study this matter and consider whether or not it should immediately telegraph the Supreme Council to the effect that it is the unanimous opinion of the members that a continuation of the Mission in Budapest could result in nothing but humiliation for all of us and a loss of prestige for our governments. We shall lose prestige with the Roumanians because they seem to feel that they can treat us with contempt, and with the Hungarians because they can plainly see the treatment we are receiving from the Roumanians.

There was a unanimous opinion that the Roumanians had done nothing to aid the Mission, but on the contrary had ignored it, but in view of the fact that an ultimatum had recently been sent by the Supreme Council to Roumania, it would be advisable to await action on the same before further stirring up the question.

General Mombelli stated that the Archduke Joseph came around to see him last night and explained that Hungary wanted a real monarchy, and that this was the only form of government suitable for these people. He stated that there was some talk of the return of the Emperor Karl as King of Hungary[20]; that he himself was personally very fond of his cousin Karl, but that he hardly thought that Karl could fill the bill. He then continued that he felt that he (the Archduke Joseph) was popular in all Hungary, that the people were clamoring for him, and that he should be invested with the royal dignity. General Mombelli stated that he allowed the Archduke to talk, but that he gave him no reply beyond stating that all such matters were for the decision of the Supreme Council, and not for this Mission.

Our beloved Roumanian allies are continuing merrily with their requisitions and seizures, and apparently have not the slightest intention of letting up until they have cleaned Hungary out of everything worth taking.

[20] The Allies would never have permitted Karl to be King of Hungary. At the end of March and Oct., 1921, he made two unsuccessful attempts to seize the throne. He died at Madeira on April 1, 1922.

53

August 31, 1919.

Yesterday one of my agents came to see me and reported that he himself had just had a talk with the Prime Minister Friedrich, who said that he had decided to make peace with Roumania on her own terms inside of seventy-two hours, unless something were done in the meantime by the Entente to alleviate the condition. I immediately sent this by enciphered code to Paris. Later in the afternoon I received word that Friedrich had been to see the British Admiral Troubridge, and had repeated to him practically what he had said to my agent, saying that the Hungarian cause was hopeless, the country was prostrate, the Roumanians were pillaging them right and left, and the Entente was doing absolutely nothing. I repeated this also to Paris. Friedrich is apparently a bullheaded brute who is either in the pay of the Archduke or the Roumanians, or both, and who proposes to run things his own way regardless of all others. He is backed by a powerful minority, which is powerful on account of being organized, and his tendencies are decidedly reactionary. It is believed that he proposes to start a reign of white terror which will make Béla Kun's red terror look like a billy goat by the side of an elephant. They have been beating and maltreating Jews in Budapest and now we have definite information that many wealthy and prominent men have been killed in the country. It is not enough for Hungary that the Roumanians are gutting her, but apparently she now insists on cutting her own throat.

I received word today that Lovászy, the former Minister of Foreign Affairs, who was dropped from Friedrich's last cabinet, has now organized a cabinet of his own and proposes to oust Friedrich inside of twenty-four hours[21]. Business is decidedly poor in Hungary, if we do not have from three to five cabinets per week.

The Roumanians are paying not the slightest attention to the last ultimatum sent them and are going right along with their looting, which has become a habit.

On the twenty-fifth, one of my men, going out with two chauffeurs for an automobile, was held by the Roumanians, and no report about it was ever made to me. For three days he went without food or lodging except such as he could pick up himself. His companions were robbed, and when they were all eventually released, because I took the matter up with the Roumanian Commander here, they were short changed when their money was returned, and for their good blue money they

21 This did not materialize.

were given worthless Bolshevist money. I had the man's statement prepared and sent a curt note to the Roumanian Commander in Chief that I wanted to know, not later than September second, what he had done or intended to do in this case. I am not sure that some of the Roumanian conduct is due as much to ignorance and stupidity as it is to hostility.

It is difficult to realize how European money has depreciated. The French franc, which was formerly worth nearly twenty cents and which was ordinarily rated at five for a dollar, is today about worth twelve cents. The Austrian and Hungarian krone, worth formerly a little over twenty-one cents, is today worth about two cents.

September, 1919

September 1, 1919.

Towards one o'clock yesterday afternoon, M. Heinrich called upon General Gorton and myself and showed a proposition for the reorganization of the government of Hungary, stating that he was authorized by Prime Minister Friedrich to get together a tentative cabinet. We told him to have Friedrich's signature attached to a minute of the meeting of the cabinet at which the discussion took place, and bring the same today at 10 A.M. when it could be laid before the Mission and suitable action taken. I then wired Paris so as to keep them in touch with the situation.

At ten o'clock this morning, M. Heinrich showed up exactly as agreed upon and submitted his list of a cabinet which was actually representative of all parties. He likewise delivered to us a copy of the resolution of the cabinet, which was attested by Friedrich. I immediately wired the American Commission of this fact and stated that the conditions attached to the organization of Heinrich's cabinet were: That the Supreme Council recognize and transact business with the new government as being representative of Hungary; that the Roumanians cease disarming and interning Hungarian officers; that the Roumanians evacuate all of Hungary west of the Danube; that the Roumanians cease cleaning out Hungary of supplies; and finally, that in case for any reason Heinrich had to leave the cabinet before the elections, Friedrich would succeed him. I added that the Mission at its session this morning recommended that the Supreme Council do everything reasonable towards recognizing and assisting the new Ministry. About two hours later the Mission's telegram in French was likewise sent off.

I then read General Rudeanu's reply to my letter of the twenty-seventh relative to evacuating immediately Hungary west of the Danube, and in which he was requested to give an answer either affirmatively or negatively. In the characteristic Roumanian style of begging the issue and of circumlocution, Rudeanu's letter was neither affirmative nor negative. I then drafted a reply to the effect that in view of the fact that our letter of the twenty-seventh required a positive answer, and as the Roumanian answer, though not being affirmative was not negative, we must interpret it, on account of the Roumanian Commander in Chief's repeated assurances of a desire to coöperate, as affirmative, and that we would accordingly proceed with the organization of the Hungarian forces west of the Danube. The Mission decided to send my letter.

We also decided to tell the Roumanian Commander in Chief that we were getting damned tired of the fact that they had not yet answered a single one of our questions definitely; that the organization of the Municipal Police of Budapest was of paramount importance; and, in effect, that if the present Commander could not comply with his promises, someone else ought to be put in his place.

The chief of police of the city of Budapest appeared before this Mission and showed that, although he had 3,700 men, the Roumanians had given them nothing in the way of arms beyond the original 600 carbines.

General Soós, the Chief of the Hungarian General Staff, appeared before the Mission and explained his proposed plan for the organization of the Hungarian Army. His intelligence and knowledge of what he wanted to do was in startling contrast to the Roumanian ignorance and stupidity.

Last night we entertained at dinner Admiral Sir Ernest Troubridge, his Chief of Staff, Colonel Stead, and General Gorton. Our chef is steadily improving and turned out a meal that would have done credit to Paris.

During the afternoon we received word that there was an American in one of the neighboring towns who was advising the people to decorate their streets and prepare for the reception of American cavalry, which was about to enter the town. I had two of my men sent out to locate any such American and bring him in if they found him. About one o'clock they showed up with a most nondescript and comic-opera artist. He maintained in excellent German that he was an American soldier belonging to the Seventh Cavalry, that he had spent several years in America -and there it ended. He had on a pair of gray woolen breeches, a coat that looked like a Roumanian soldier's coat, on the collar of which had been sewn a portion of the Stars and Stripes from an American flag handkerchief. His hat was an imitation of a French lieutenant's. We had previously received word that the Roumanians were endeavoring to stage some pictures for the cinematograph and this fellow had undoubtedly been dolled up by them to pass off as an American so that the townspeople would decorate their town. Then a body of Roumanian cavalry would enter and be photographed accordingly. We have the man jugged over in the barracks and propose to do some pumping[1].

September 2, 1919.

General Mombelli presided at today's meeting and very little of consequence took place.

A strong letter was drafted to be sent to the Roumanians, demanding that they immediately complete the organization of the police as promised, and complaining of subterfuge and procrastination. A similar letter was sent in regard to the evacuation of western Hungary.

Colonel Yates arrived last night from Bucharest, and from his report the Roumanians are pretty generally arrogant and haughty over what they consider their tremendous victory over Hungary, completely ignoring the fact that they could never even have touched Hungary had not the Allies first crushed both Germany and Austria-Hungary. All their talk is along the lines of having a Roumanian officer in a coordinate position on the Inter-Allied Military Mission, and demonstrates the fact that they feel that on account of their little private war with Hungary they are entitled to loot the latter absolutely in payment for their last little war, and leave the Allies to get indemnification from a prostrate nation for their share of expenses in the World War.

I have repeatedly telegraphed the American Commission at Paris explaining the necessity of keeping my present detachment until this matter ends, or at least of having substitutes sent, but all my requests and telegrams have so far been ignored.

The Hungarians also get cocky occasionally, and today, through their liaison officer, sent word to us that Austro-German aéroplanes were flying over western Hungary dropping propaganda, inviting the people to join Austria. They stated that they intended to fire on any such aéroplanes that might show up in the future and requested that we have all Allied aéroplanes marked plainly so that they would not be confused with the Austrian planes[2]. They were told to cut out all such monkeyshines or they would be punished.

---

1   Here we have an example of propaganda in the making. About American propaganda, consult George Creel's *How We Advertised America*; about that of Great Britain see Sir Campbell Stuart's *The Secrets of Crew House*. An excellent summary and indictment of propaganda is Arthur Ponsonby's *Falsehood in War Time*, London, 1928. See also the account of the wireless propaganda lie, told in this Diary, Sept.25, 26, and Nov. 13.

September 3, 1919.

Last night we entertained at dinner the Serbian Minister and Plenipotentiary, Doctor Lazar Baitch, and the Serbian Military Attaché, Major Body. Incidentally, the Serbian Plenipotentiary became quite mellow, cuddled up to me and imparted considerable information as to the Serbian point of view. He said in his opinion the Roumanians would stay in Hungary for at least a year, during which time the elections would be held, and that of course they would result as the Roumanians desired, and that they would bring about some sort of political or economic union of Roumania and Hungary, all with a view to the isolation of the Jugo-Slavs[3].

2   This statement refers to propaganda in the Ödenburg or Sopron district. This part of old Hungary, inhabited in the majority by German-Hungarians, was handed over to Austria in the treaty of St. Germain. It has frequently been suggested that this was done in "compensation" for the transfer to Italy of Southern Tyrol - a country entirely inhabited by German people and belonging to German Austria for a thousand years - as well as for the purpose of driving a wedge between Austria and Hungary. No matter how one may look at the transfer of this territory to Austria, the motives of the Allies were low and sordid. The alleged purpose of embittering the Hungarians against the Austrians has been accomplished. The attitude of a majority of the Hungarians in this respect is reflected in the following passage from Cecile Tormay's *An Outlaw's Diary: The Commune,* New York, 1924: "Our quarrel with Austria has lasted for centuries, and she brought us hard times, yet there is no people on earth to whom her fate causes as much pain today as to us. We have fought and fallen together on the battlefield. Now they hang a beggar's satchel round the neck of unfortunate, torn Austria, and out of irony, with devilish cunning, send her to take her share with her own predatory enemies, in the plunder of Hungary, with a piece of land that promises endless revolts and is meant to act as a living wedge to prevent forever an understanding between the two despoiled peoples. It is a devilish plan, the most perfidious part of the terrible Peace Treaty. It pretends to be a present, but it is a curse and a disgrace."

3   As a matter of fact, the opposite happened. The tension between Roumania and Jugo-Slavia over the division of the Bánát subsided, and in April and June, 1921, Roumania signed conventions with Czecho-Slovakia and Jugo-Slavia, which had entered into an alliance on Aug.14, 1920. Thus the so-called Little Entente was created, an alliance directed against Hungary. See A. Y. Toynbee's *Survey of Interna-*

It was my turn this morning to act as President of the Mission, and General Graziani stated that M. Diamandi called on him yesterday not knowing who was President of the Day. Diamandi was apparently much concerned over the probable elections, maintaining that in case they were run under Friedrich's régime, only Friedrich's tools could be elected to office. In leaving, M. Diamandi turned loose his usual threat, that it was about time the Roumanians left the country, in which they found only difficulties.

General Graziani also stated that he had had a visit from the Minister of Foreign Affairs, Count Csáky, who likewise thought he was temporary President. Count Csáky's mission was to inform the Allied Generals that M. Garami had been accused of having received a large sum of money from Béla Kun, which was explained by saying that M. Garami desired to leave the country when Béla Kun was in power, but that the Communists would give him no passports except on condition that he go via Russia to Switzerland and there get in contact with the Italian Socialists. This Garami refused to do, but being of a timorous nature, and on being offered later an opportunity to go to Switzerland, he took seven hundred pounds sterling for the Communists which was delivered in Switzerland without being touched by him. Count Csáky added that in case the investigation should prove to be unsuccessful, M. Garami would be replaced in the cabinet by another Socialist.

It is quite noticeable that the Roumanians in particular habitually make the mistake of thinking that our French colleague, General Graziani, is the President of the Day, which rather strengthens the suspicion that the Roumanians and French are somewhat in touch.

Up to date, I have practically had no car, and we were just getting one in partial shape when it collided in the Palace entrance with Colonel Yates' car and smashed them both up.

To add to the joy of the occasion, there is as yet no word from the American Commission as to whether or not my detachment can remain with me or be replaced by others. Apparently about next week I shall be left flat on my back with six enlisted men to handle the whole American side of the question. As no remarks would do the subject justice, none will be made.

tional Affairs, 1920-23, London, 1926, pp. 287-303.

At the session of the Mission this morning, General Gorton produced a proclamation from the Roumanian authorities, directing that all motor vehicles bear certain numbers, and in general prescribing the regulations for same. It was decided to send a communication to the Roumanian Commander in Chief to the effect that this proclamation had come to the attention of the Inter-Allied Military Mission and, in order to avoid any misunderstandings, it was desired that instructions be issued immediately so as not to cause trouble with the cars of the various members of the Mission, which would bear either the colors or a miniature flag of the nation represented.

General Mombelli stated that he had sent two letters to Roumanian Headquarters, addressed to General Rudeanu, or whoever was acting in his place, and both have been returned, the Roumanians refusing to sign for same.

September 4, 1919.

Last night my little Serbian friend, Doctor Lazar Baitch, called upon me and in his most unctuous and confiding manner imparted the important information that M. Lovászy was now organizing a cabinet to replace the Friedrich cabinet. This was apparently done without any knowledge on Lovászy's part of the Friedrich-Heinrich understanding, and in complete ignorance of the fact that the Mission had telegraphed a list of the Hungarian cabinet for action by the Supreme Council. For some reason or other, the Jugo-Slavs are afraid of the Friedrich régime and are determined to have Lovászy put into office.

Reports are now coming in that the Hungarians in their turn are toying with the truth, and that instead of having less than 10,000 men in their Transdanubian Army under Admiral Horthy, they have practically 38,000 men.

The Inter-Allied Military Mission is altogether too shy on accepting responsibility, has developed to a chronic extent the habit of passing the buck, and seems determined to refer nearly everything to Paris. It would be a fair assumption that the Generals sent down here are presumed to have ordinary human intelligence and to be willing to accept reasonable responsibilities without spouting hot air, going through calisthenic gesticulations, and then referring everything to the Supreme Council. On the other hand, and probably as a result of this passing the buck, the Supreme Council practically pays no attention to whatever is sent them, whether important or otherwise.

Prime Minister Friedrich today submitted a complaint of the attitude of the Roumanian Commander in refusing to allow the publication of proclamations designating September 28, 1919, as election day in all Hungary; the Roumanians reason, and a damned good one, being that as yet the territorial limits of Hungary had not been defined and, furthermore, that the present government had not been recognized as such by the Entente. Friedrich also complained that the Roumanians would not allow his government to execute death sentences, alleging in this case the latter of the two above reasons. It is no wonder that he is peeved at this action, because, if left to carry it out, he would, in a short time and with all appearance of judicial legality, have been able to rid himself of many of his more dangerous opponents.

This day has really been a Friedrich day, because that gentleman capped the climax by sending information to each member of the Mission that, having heard of the atrocities committed by the White Terror, he had decided to take a special train and go out into the country to investigate. In order to prove the sincerity of his intentions, he invited each General either to accompany him or to send a representative, a like invitation being sent to the Roumanian authorities also. Of course any such investigation committee would run up only against prepared cases, but Friedrich's main object would be accomplished, because if he made a triumphal tour of the country accompanied by representatives of all the Powers, the Hungarians would naturally consider such action as tantamount to recognition.

I put through the Mission, at the session today, at which General Gorton presided, arrangements to place Colonel Yates in charge of the organization of the Hungarian Police along the same lines as the organization of the Hungarian Army with a French officer in charge. By this means, I hope we may be able soon to make progress in the police reorganization.

In regard to the case of the Roumanians holding one of my men several days out in the country, and concerning which I wrote and demanded that they state within thirty-six hours what they had done or intended to do in the case, it should be added that for once they came to time, and an apology was received with assurances that the matter would be immediately investigated and satisfactory action taken.

September 5, 1919.

There was very little of importance brought before this morning's session of the Mission, at which General Graziani presided. Letters were sent to the Hungarian cabinet to the effect that this Mission concurred in the Roumanian attitude in regard to the matters presented by M. Friedrich at yesterday's session. A letter was written to the Roumanian Commander in Chief, stating that Colonel H. E. Yates, U.S. A., had been designated by the Mission on a subcommittee for the prompt organization of the police and gendarmerie in Hungary, and requesting that the Roumanian Commander designate some officer as associate to Colonel Yates. A like request will be made to the Hungarians.

Word was received from General Graziani that the Bratiano government in Roumania was about to fall, and that our not overly-bright friend, General Mardarescu, was to be Minister of War in the new cabinet[4].

Incidentally, I notified the Mission that on Monday next three of my officers and 18 men would leave for Paris and that I could not thereafter furnish any guard at the Royal Palace, as I would have only six men left, whom I needed as orderlies and for ordinary duties.

Last night Colonel Loree, Captain Gore, Lieutenant Hamilton and myself went to the Orpheum Theater as guests of Captain Weiss. The performance began at 5.30 and ended at 9 o'clock, after which we were entertained at dinner in the restaurant attached to the Theater. The whole parquet of the theater was filled with small tables at which the audience could be seated and have tea or dinner served to them, thereby combining two pleasures, that of eating and that of seeing the play. The galleries were arranged in boxes, and along the back walls were likewise placed small tables for two, where meals could be served. The performance was a combination of a comic opera, in three acts, and vaudeville. Some of the singing was excellent and, judging from the applause of the audience, the comedians' jokes must have been of like quality. Besides ourselves at the dinner, Captain Weiss had three or four prominent Hungarians and two of the actresses; one of them accompanied by her husband. The other, after remaining about thirty minutes, said that she had an appointment with her lover, who was becoming insistent, and she must beg to be excused. This one was very pretty, and the other one was very bright. The pretty one spoke beautiful Hungarian, but blended her French and German to such an extent that it was almost impossible to follow her line of talk. The brighter one spoke English, in which she carried on flirtations with four different gentlemen at the same time under her husband's nose, as the latter's specialty in languages was limited to Hungarian.

4   Bratiano resigned on Sept. 13. Mardarescu, as well as Mosoiu, were political followers of Bratiano and became later on ministers in his new cabinet.

September 6, 1919.

Last night we entertained General Graziani at dinner.

At today's session of the Mission, General Mombelli presided, and there was practically no business except to write a letter to the Roumanians asking them to explain why they had established practically a state of siege in Budapest without advising us of their intentions.

Yesterday afternoon a telegram came from the American Commission, stating that none of my telegrams in regard to the necessity of retaining my detachment had been seen by any member of the Commission, and Mr. Polk[5] stated that he would do everything possible to arrange matters. Another telegram came, stating that General Connor[6] had authority to extend the time limit in such cases for a month. My detachment will, therefore, remain at least that much longer.

In view of the fact that there is practically nothing doing, I have arranged to go with Captain Gore to Bucharest. Colonel Yates, the American Attaché to the Roumanian capital, will accompany us and act as our guide and mentor. We plan to leave Budapest at 4 o'clock this date and return about the tenth of September.

5   Frank Lyon Polk, Undersecretary of State of the United States. A lawyer by training, he became Counselor of the Department of State on Aug. 30, 1915. This position he held until July 1, 1919, when he assumed the title Undersecretary of State. From Dec. 4, 1918, until July 18, 1919, he served as Acting Secretary of State at Washington, while Lansing was in Paris. On July 17, 1919, he was appointed Commissioner Plenipotentiary of the United States to negotiate peace. From July 28 to Dec. 9, 1919, he was the head of the American delegation at Paris. Obviously he gave General Bandholtz his full support. Charles Vopicka, U. S. Envoy Extraordinary and Minister Plenipotentiary to Roumania, Bulgaria and Serbia, reports that "Mr. Polk was very much dissatisfied with the inactivity of the Roumanian Government. He said that this government promised everything and did nothing." *Secrets of the Balkans*, p.305.

6   General William Durward Connor, U. S. General Staff Officer, Service of Supply, Nov.12, 1918, to May 26, 1919.

September 7, 1919.

Colonel Yates, Captain Gore and myself, accompanied by a Roumanian liaison officer, left Budapest on a special car and by special train about 4.30 yesterday afternoon. Our special car was about half the length of an ordinary American car, but was very well fitted out and had all conveniences except those for cooking. I know I slept on a hair mattress, because the hairs pushed up through the mattress, through the sheets and through my pajamas, and could be very distinctly felt. In addition to this, the mattress undoubtedly had a large and animated population. All of my traveling companions reported like experiences. Last night, while traveling through eastern Hungary, we saw large numbers of cars loaded with stuff, all en route to Roumania. We crossed the Szolnok Bridge, which had been originally a large double-tracked structure, but in the course of recent repairs had been left mostly single-tracked. We traveled through long stretches of level land in Transylvania and late in the afternoon got into the foothills of the Carpathians, and finally at 7.15 we arrived at Sinaja, where the summer palace of the King is located. We went direct to the Palace, and found that they had planned to entertain us all night and as long as we could stay. The summer palace of the King is called "Castel Palisor[7]," and is beautifully located in the Carpathian Mountains about seventy-five miles north of Bucharest. There are really two palaces here; one which was built for the former Queen of Roumania, the celebrated Carmen Sylva[8] and which, although completely furnished, is not occupied by the present King, who instead, with the Royal Family, lives in the palace which was built for him when he was Crown Prince. This is neither so pretentious nor so commodious as the other, but apparently is better adapted to the present needs of the Royal Family. We met His Majesty at dinner about 8.30, and he had me seated at his left. The only other member of the Royal Family present was Prince Nickolai, neither the Queen or any of her daughters appearing during the evening. The King is of medium height with a full-pointed beard, and with a low forehead with the hair starting from not far above the eyes. He speaks English fairly well, although with a peculiar hissing accent.

After dinner, while waiting in the reception room, I talked with the King and other members of his staff, and stated that I hoped to leave early in the morning. His Majesty then asked me if I would not kindly step into his private office for a little conversation, which I did, and he kept me there about an hour and a half during which he went into details of the Roumanian grievances, especially referring to the fact that the Roumanians were considered to be robbers because they were looting Hungary, whereas the Serbs had looted the Bánát and had never been called to account. He also complained that the Serbs had received some of the Danube monitors, whereas Roumania had received nothing. But his main grievance seemed to be due to the "Minorities" clause in the Treaty of Peace[9] which Roumania was to be called upon to sign[10]. I explained to His Majesty that of course the Inter-Allied Military Mission had nothing to do with any such matters; hat furthermore its instructions were explicit and mandatory, and that we could discuss nothing concerning the same. I assured him that Americans had no ill feeling toward Roumania, and had nothing to gain financially or otherwise in treating her badly. The King then insisted that I remain until noon tomorrow, as the Queen desired to meet me. As a matter of fact, he did not have to insist, because our transportation away from Sinaia was entirely at his disposition, and I could not leave until he saw fit to let me go. I was assigned to a very comfortable

7 Or Castel Pelishor.

8 In 1866, Prince Charles of Hohenzollern-Sigmaringen was called to Roumania to govern this country, which had secured its autonomy after the Crimean war in 1856. Roumania's complete independence was recognized in 1878 in the Treaty of Berlin, and in 1881 Charles was crowned King of Roumania. He was married to the noble Princess Elisabeth of Wied, who as a charming writer and poetess was known by the name of Carmen Sylva. Their only child, Marie, died in infancy. Charles died in 1914, shortly after the outbreak of the world war. Being without male issue, his nephew Ferdinand became his successor to the throne. He had in 1893 married Marie, daughter of the late Duke of Saxe-Coburg-Gotha. The membership of the Royal Roumanian family is as follows:

Ferdinand I (b. 1865, d. 1927), m. Marie (b. 1875)

King Carol II (b. 1893), m. Princess Helen of Greece, 1921

Michael (b. 1921)

Elisabeth (b. 1894), m. Crown Prince (now former King) George of Greece, 1921

Marie (b. 1900), m. King Alexander of Jugo-Slavia, 1922

Nicholas (b. 1903)

suite of rooms and was able to get a good bath, sadly needed after a trip in a Roumanian private car.

September 8, 1919.

We reported for breakfast this morning about 8.30, and I met Her Majesty, the Queen, and one of the Royal Princesses. Her Majesty habitually wears the Roumanian peasant costume, which is very becoming, and she is decidedly a handsome woman, showing that she must have been beautiful when younger. The Royal aide-de-camp informed me that I was to sit at breakfast at the left of Madame Lahovary, one of the ladies in waiting. So we entered the dining room in that order.

Ileana (b. 1909) m. Archduke Anton of Austria-Tuscany, 1931

Mircea (b. 1912, d. 1916)On Dec.28, 1925, Carol renounced his right of succession to the throne. On Jan. 4, 1926, his son, Prince Michael, was declared heir to the throne. In 1927 he became King under a re-gency. On June 8, 1930, Carol was again proclaimed King by Act of Parliament and ascended the throne.

9   Treaty of St. Germain with Austria.

10 The problem of the protection of minorities in Europe is not new. The first to receive special protection were religious groups. such as the Christians and Jews under Turkish rule, the Protestants in certain Cath-olic countries, and vice versa.

Article 44 of the Treaty of Berlin of July 13.1878, contained the follow-ing provision in regard to Roumania: "The difference of religious creeds and confessions shall not be alleged against any person as a ground for exclusion or incapacity in matters relating to the enjoyment of civil and political rights, admission to public employments. functions, and honors, or the exercise of the various professions and industries in any localities whatsoever." F. de Martens, *Recueil général des traités*, 2d series, Vol.111, p.345.

In spite of this treaty obligation, the Jewish minority in Roumania con-tinued to be discriminated against as previously.

Even before the war, the treatment of religious, cultural, and racial mi-norities had received the attention of the liberal and socialistic element

However, immediately after entering, the Queen called out from the head of the table, "General, I want you to sit up by me." So I, in fear and trembling, approached the Royal presence and sat on her left, with the King on her right. Without any preliminaries, Her Majesty turned to me and said, "I didn't know whether I wanted to meet you at all-I have heard many things about you." I replied, "Your Majesty, I am not half so bad as I look, nor one-quarter so bad as you seem to think I am." She smiled and said that the King had told her that I wasn't exactly a heathen, so she had decided really to form my acquaintance. We spent a very pleasant time at the breakfast table, in which considerable repartee was indulged in, despite the Royal presences.

all over the world; and during the world war the right of self- determination became one of the powerful slogans. The tenth of the Fourteen Points of President Wilson demanded "the freest opportunity of autonomous development 'for "the peoples of Austria-Hungary." Several drafts of the League of Nations Covenant contained this principle, as applying to all members of the League. In the final version, such a provision was left out, probably because of the tremendous dangers to the imperialism of the victorious Great Powers.

However, it was realized at the Peace Conference that the transfer of large alien populations to new or enlarged states, especially when such people were of a much superior culture, would be a constant source of irritation and would prevent the stabilization of Europe, unless such minorities were protected against undue persecution. Therefore these States - Poland, Czecho-Slovakia, Jugo-Slavia, Greece, and Armenia - were required to sign special treaties guaranteeing certain rights to the minorities living under their rule. Similar provisions are contained in the peace treaties with Austria, Hungary, Bulgaria, and in the defunct treaty of Sèvres with Turkey. Roumania signed a minority treaty very reluctantly on Dec. 9, 1919. Doubtless the pressure of the very influential Jewish element in the United States had a great deal to do with the insistence of Wilson on these treaties, as suggested on page 170 of Fouques-Dupara's book: "Le président Wilson par sentiment libérale, peut-être aussi par sympathy pour un groupement éthnique, dont la puissance électorale ne peut-être négligé, suivit l'exemple de ses illustres devanciers."

All the minority treaties, which, with the exception of those with Armenia and Turkey, are in effect today, are according to their own terms placed under the guardianship of the League of Nations, and

After breakfast we went out into the garden and I told Madame Lahovary that it was very apparent that the Inter-Allied Military Mission did not stand very high in Roumania. She said, "We have always heard that the four generals were very fine." I asked her if she hadn't heard that the American actually wore horns, or at least was somewhat of a devil. She said, hardly that, but that they had heard that the American representative was very difficult to handle.

After a little time in the garden, Captain Gore and myself took a long walk exploring the grounds about both the palaces, did some writing and had lunch about one o'clock. This time the King and Queen, instead of sitting at the end of the table, sat opposite each other at the middle. I was placed on the Queen's right, with the senior Roumanian General[11], who it is understood will be the next prime minister, on her left. His Majesty had the Royal Princess on his right and Madame Lahovary on his left. During the conversation the Queen said that she felt keenly over the fact that Roumania had fought as an ally and was now being treated as an enemy; that all Roumania had been pillaged by the Huns, and why shouldn't they now retaliate and steal from Hungary, saying, "You may call it stealing if you want to, or any other name. I feel that we are perfectly entitled to do what we want to."

cannot be changed except with the consent of the majority of the League Council. The text of he Roumanian Minorities Treaty may be found in *Current History* of March, 1920. Statistics of the different minorities in Roumania and their distribution in the different parts of the country may be found on page 384 of Jacques Fouques-Duparc's *La Protection des minorités de race, de langue et de la religion*, Paris, 1922. See also Marc Vichniak's *La protection des droits des minorités dans les traités internationaux de 1919-1920*, Paris, 1921; and, Leo Epstein's *Der nationale Minderheits- schutz als internationales Rechtsproblem*, Berlin, 1922.

For the treatment of the Hungarian minorities in Roumania, Crecho-Slovakia, and Jugo-Slavia, see Sir Robert Donald's *Tragedy of Trianon*, London, 1928.

The making of the minority treaties may be followed in David Hunter Miller's *My Diary at the Conference of Paris*, Vol. XIII. (The Appeal Printing Co., 1925.) Only forty copies of this valuable set of diaries are in existence. See there especially the letter of Bratiano of May 27, 1919, protesting against the special obligations imposed upon Roumania (p.89). Also he report on July 16, 1919, concerning Roumania.

The King butted into the conversation and said that anyway the Roumanians had taken no food stuffs. As it is bad form to call a king a liar, I simply informed His Majesty that he was badly mistaken, and that I could give him exact facts in regard to thousands of carloads of foodstuffs that had been taken out of Budapest alone. Her Majesty complained also that a Reparation Board had been appointed to investigate and look in Bulgaria for property that she had looted from other countries, and that all the Allies had been represented on this Board except Roumania. She added that similar action had been taken in regard to the German indemnification. It was apparent that all the Roumanians are rankling, whether justly or no, under a sense of injustice, and they insist on stating, and may be believing, that their present war with Hungary is separate and distinct from the big War, and entitles them to first choice of everything in the country.

After leaving the luncheon table, we spent a considerable time in the reception room, during which Her Majesty and I had much conversation usually on general lines and, when I explained to her that we were leaving early that afternoon, she said that now she would retain recollections of a very pleasant gentleman[12], and added that she desired to give me one of her photographs, so that, whenever I felt hard towards the Roumanians, I could look at that, and she hoped it would make me feel more kindly. She then went upstairs herself and soon brought me down an autographed photograph. We then sent for my two orderlies, who were presented to the Queen, and could do nothing but stammer and say, "Yes, Ma'm" and "No, Ma'm."

We finally left Castel Palisor by automobile, with Colonel Yates, at 4.30. The first part of the trip down the mountains was very beautiful, but we soon struck a flat country through the oil Section of Roumania, and arrived in Bucharest at 7.30 P.M., completely covered with dust and pretty well tired out. Colonel Yates went to his quarters, as he is American Military Attaché at Bucharest; Captain Gore went to a hotel with the orderlies, and I went to the American Legation where I was guest of our Chargé d'Affaires, Mr. Schoenfeld.

11 After Bratiano's resignation, a new government was formed, in October, which was headed by General Vaitoanu and consisted of military men and officials. After a short time, general elections were held and a democratic government succeeded. From November, 1919, to March, 1920, Alexander Vaida-Voevod was the head of the government. See n. 34 below.

September 9, 1919.

After a delightful night's rest at the American Legation and a fine American breakfast, I went with Mr. Schoenfeld, and, by appointment, called upon the Prime Minister, M. Bratiano[13], at 9.30 at his home. He received us very pleasantly, and after I had told him that I had come to get in closer personal touch with the Roumanian leaders, feeling that I could thereby more clearly visualize the situation, he launched into his tale of woe, which in more detail was the same as that of the King and Queen, but which included quite a lengthy history of Roumania. He stated first, however, that he was pleased to have an opportunity to meet me as an American, who would probably have influence with the American government,

12 Compare with these words the actual feelings of the Queen, as given in the statement of January 4, 1920.

13 Ionel I. C. Bratiano (or Bratianu), born 1864, died 1928. He was heir to great wealth and power. His father had led the uprising against the Turks in 1848, and had been instrumental in placing King Carol of Hohenzollern-Sigmaringen on the Roumanian throne in 1868. The elder Bratiano became Roumania's first prime minister. Through the control of oil and other mineral resources, the family was immensely wealthy. Originally liberal-minded, the Bratianos later turned to conservatism. Ionel became he successor of his father in the control of the so-called Liberal party. He "as virtually the political dictator or boss of Roumania. whenever popular ndignation over his autocratic régime became too loud, or when there was oo much corruption in his government, he resigned temporarily to make room for some other leader. Unlike Také Jonescu, Bratiano was not originally a pronounced anti-German. Later on, in the course of the world war, he turned towards the Allies.

At the Peace Conference of Paris, he presented very ably Roumania's interests, but he was practically ignored by the so-called Big Four. (Read the account by E. J. Dillon, *The Inside Story of the Peace Conference*, New York, 1920, p.500 passim). He protested vigorously against the minority clauses contained in the treaties of St. Germain and Neuilly, which imposed upon Roumania the obligation of treating her minorities fairly. His reasoning, as presented in his speech at Paris on May 31, 1919, is contained in these pages of the Diary.

and he stated that he deplored the fact that the United States was so far away as to be in pretty general ignorance of Roumania and things Roumanian. He added that it was unfortunate that the American officers sent there after the War had been selected from those who had formerly been in Roumania, and who had not liked the country. He took up the question of Roumanian grievances in general, and in particular inveighed against the "Minorities Clause" in the Treaty, explaining that some fifty years ago, as a result of the pogroms in Russia, a great Jewish migration to Roumania had taken place; that these immigrants belonged entirely to the middle classes, without trades or professions, and came into a country where commerce had hitherto been almost nonexistent. In the Treaty of Berlin of 1878, the Powers had imposed upon Roumania certain conditions in regard to the Jews, but that when Roumania bought over the railroads which had been built by German capital, these restrictions had been removed, and Roumania was left as independent as any other nation. He added that the Jewish question was not the only one concerning the "Minorities"; that they had acquired about one million Transylvanians, as well as many Bulgarians and Slavs, by their recent acquisition of territory, and that he felt it was administratively wrong to have these "Minorities" come into a government without any obligation on their part of assimilating themselves to the new nation, but on the other hand

Mr. R. W. Seton-Watson, a well-known anti-Hungarian, explains the hostile attitude of the leading men at Paris as follows: "If the Paris Conference showed but scanty sympathy for Mr. Bratiano, it was, above all, the result of his rigid and intransigent attitude on every subject of foreign or internal politics. Unfortunately 'liberal' writers in the west often seem unable to distinguish between the Bratiano family and Roumania." (In his London magazine, *The New Europe*, Oct. 2, 1919. In the issue of Sept. 18, 1919, of the same magazine, he said: "As long as he [i.e., Bratiano] remains in office, there is but little prospect of a real understanding between Roumania and the west.")

Bratiano started the prime-ministership, held by him during the time described in the Bandholtz Diary, on Dec.14, 1918, and he resigned on Sept. 13, 1919, as a protest against the minority clauses of the peace treaties. The new elections, held on Oct. 3, gave a large majority to the Peasant Party and the National Democrats. On Dec. 9, 1919, a cabinet of the democratic parties, with Alexander Vaida-Voevod and Dr. Lupu as the outstanding members, came into power. It was forced to resign on March 19, 1920, and a cabinet formed by the leader of the nationalistic People's Party, General Alexander Averescu, took its place.

with a feeling that they were being protected, in any opposition they might make, by the strong powers. He considered it to be the part of wisdom to allow the Jews and others perfect liberty, but that no independent and sovereign state could accept the conditions which were being imposed on Roumania. He complained that General Smuts had been sent on his fruitless errand to Budapest[14] without informing the Roumanians, who could at the time plainly have told the Allies the uselessness of such a procedure. M. Bratiano said in conclusion that he had hoped the war would equalize all nations that had participated among the Allies, although he could understand why countries like Poland and Czecho-Slovakia, just recently emerging from vassalage, should be treated somewhat differently from the others. He excused himself then, stating that his wife was coming by train, that he was obliged to meet her, and asked if he could not see me again in the after-noon. It was arranged that he call at the American Legation at 5 o'clock. This he did, almost on the dot, and without preamble resumed the discussion where he left off. He first explained how Roumania had been guaranteed by Germany all of the territorial acquisition she has acquired, but that nevertheless she joined the Allies, who had failed to keep their promises to her in regard to war material, as well as to the strategic arrangements for launching an attack from Salonika synchronously with the Roumanian offensive. As a result, the Roumanians were obliged to meet forty-two German divisions, and were gradually forced to evacuate their country. After the Armistice, he stated, the Roumanians, when told to stop at their proper boundary, had done so; that they had not attacked the Hungarians, but that they (the Hungarians), after being recalled from their attack on the Czecho-Slovaks, had attacked her, and the result was of course a violation of the Armistice, and therefore the present was an entirely different war from the Great War. He explained that he knew it had been Béla Kun's intention to create an ocean of Bolshevism in eastern Europe, which would afterwards inundate Italy and western Europe, and he felt that Roumania had saved civilization from Bolshevism. He stated that Roumanian action in Hungary was an action similar in every respect to that of every other victorious army. She was short of rolling stock and very naturally took it where she found it; that this rolling stock was indispensable to her life in the coming fall and winter, and that she had no alternative. I then explained to M. Bratiano that any statements I might make were purely personal, although I felt that my colleagues shared my opinion. I then recounted to His Excellency several cases of a total lack

14 In April, 1919, General Smuts arrived in Budapest to examine the situation in Hungary. He remained in his special train, received Béla Kun
and some other members of the Bolshevik government, and left Budapest on the following day.

of coöperation on the part of the Roumanians and also several instances in which they had told the Mission untruths, among which I gave instances of requisitioning supplies not needed for troops in the field, which General Mardarescu had stated was the only cause for requisition. I also called attention to the fact that General Mardarescu had said that the Roumanians were not occupying western Hungary, whereas they were in many of the towns, and had been interning Hungarian officers and officials. I explained to M. Bratiano that above all it was necessary to organize a police force and an army in Hungary, and that the Roumanians should with the least possible delay evacuate western Hungary, Budapest and then eastern Hungary by successive zones, according to the plans of the Inter-Allied Military Mission. His Excellency said he was willing to do all this on one condition, namely, that the Roumanians be secure from Hungarian attack. I replied to him that of course nothing of this could be done until the evacuation began, and that if this took place I would be glad to recommend to my colleagues, who in turn could recommend to the Supreme Council, that the Hungarians be instructed not to attack the Roumanians under such circumstances. This seemed to impress His Excellency favorably, and he said he would be glad to act in accordance with those plans. After mutual expressions of pleasure at our personal acquaintance, we separated after a two-hour conversation. On both occasions after our interviews with M. Bratiano, Mr. Schoenfeld and I went to his office, a stenographer was called in, and he repeated from memory our entire conversation. This was reduced to memorandum form and signed by both of us.

About 11.30 o'clock in the forenoon, accompanied by Colonel Yates, I called upon Lieutenant-General Vaitojano, the Minister of War, and we held a conversation, all of the points of which had been covered in my talk with their Majesties and subsequently in my talk with the Prime Minister.

After lunch, I took Captain Gore, and we explored the city of Bucharest, returning in time to go with Mr. Schoenfeld to tea at the British Embassy. Here I found Mr. Rattigan[15], the British Chargé d'Affaires, and his very charming wife. The relations between the British and the American Chargés d'Affaires are along the same satisfactory lines as those of General Gorton and myself

15 W. F. A. Rattigan, First Secretary of the Legation. Compare with this statement Mr. Rattigan's confidential report and Bandholtz' critique at the end of the Diary.

In the evening, Captain Gore and myself dined at the American Legation and retired early to bed to get in shape for our start tomorrow.

September 10, 1919.

We left Bucharest about 8 although the train was scheduled to leave at 7.30. My private car and the first-class coach assigned to the orderlies and the Roumanian liaison officer, were attached to the Simplon Express, which took six and three-quarter hours to reach Sinaja, the same distance we had covered by automobile two days earlier in three hours. Fortunately on this train we were able to get our meals in a dining car, although, as there was no train corridor, we were obliged to make connections at station stops.

September 11, 1919.

Our special car was detached from the Simplon Express at Arad, and from there we went as a special train across the Szolnok Bridge to Budapest, where we arrived at 12.15. After lunch, I went to the office and found that the American Commission had been very much, and in my opinion, unnecessarily, exercised over my having gone to Bucharest. I found two telegrams -one asking me to delay my departure and the other suggesting that I engage in no diplomatic discussions. I immediately sent them a long code message descriptive of everything that had been said and done, explaining that I had understood when in Paris that I could make a trip to Bucharest whenever I thought it advisable, but nevertheless I regretted having done so without having obtained specific permission. As a matter of fact, the permission probably would not have come and I would not have had a trip which I know resulted in much good. While in Bucharest, Mr. Schoenfeld told me that conditions in Roumania, as far as Americans were concerned, were worse than rotten. Apparently the French who felt that Roumania came within their sphere of influence and in anticipation of possible rivals, had done everything they could to make the Roumanians dislike the Americans. This was frequently referred to in my conversations with the high officials, and Mr. Schoenfeld told me when I left that in all the time he had been in Roumania, he had never seen M. Bratiano so pleasant and affable as he was with me, and that never before had he made a two-hour call. He said that, on the contrary, the gentlemen in question had been most haughty and arrogant towards all Americans[16].

During the afternoon I called upon Generals Gorton, Mombelli, and Graziani, and read them the entire memoranda which had been dictated by Mr. Schoenfeld covering our interview with M. Bratiano.

September 12, 1919.

On account of my previous absence, I was President of the Day at the session this morning, at which the Mission unanimously approved all that I had done in Bucharest. About 10.30, Generals Mardarescu and Holban and M. Diamandi were presented and, after being photographed and cinematographed with them in the courtyard, we returned to the council room for business. I brought up, as urgent, the police question, during which we showed that the officer and gentleman, General Holban, had lied about the arms question. He had originally said that he could easily furnish 4,000 pistols for the Hungarian police, while he now maintained that it would be necessary to get these pistols from the Hungarians. Before finishing this question, our friend Diamandi asked that it be laid on the table to make way for other important matters. He first stated that the Roumanians did not agree with the Mission that nothing should be taken from the museums, adding that Roumania had now Transylvania and was therefore entitled to such portions of the museums as belonged to Transylvania. General Mombelli had quite a little set-to with his rotund Excellency, who then again changed the subject and stated that Roumanians had unearthed a terrible Hungarian conspiracy which, disguised as an anti-Bolshevist proposition, was really also aimed at the Roumanian Army of Occupation. Our hirsute friend Holban then produced a bundle of documents that would have filled a cart, and proceeded to give us the horrible details. The noon hour, however, arrived before he had finished his song and, as we had all been invited to attend the Roumanian review of a division, we adjourned to meet again tomorrow.

We plowed our way through clouds of dust out to the review field, and saw what was supposed to be a division of about 10,000 men. By careful count and close

16 It must be remembered that Bratiano was treated very badly by the Americans in Paris, and particularly by Wilson, whom Dillon accuses of disliking Bratiano personally. No doubt Bratiano's governmental system did not appeal to him. It is well known that Clemenceau also disliked Bratiano.

approximation, I figured that this division was less than 5,000 men and therefore not much larger than an American war-strength infantry regiment. As the distances between the units of this division were so great that it looked as though the review would last all afternoon, I excused myself at 1.30 and left with Colonel Yates and Colonel Loree. I also noted that some units passed in review twice.

During the afternoon, my little friend, the Serbian Envoy Extraordinary and Minister Plenipotentiary, Doctor Lazar Baitch, called upon me, apparently to give me some information, but really to find out what I had been doing in Bucharest. Before leaving, he had given a little more than he had received.

At 8.30, accompanied by Colonel Loree, I attended gorgeous spread at the Hotel Gellért, as the guest of the Roumanian Headquarters. General Mombelli and some of his officers were also in attendance.

September 13, 1919.

It seems good to be back again where fruit has some flavor. The muskmelons of Hungary being delicious, we naturally thought that those of Roumania would be likewise and, as they were exceedingly cheap, we bought from the car window about dozen fine-looking melons which we thought would be a good investment. After opening all twelve, one at time, we discovered that the Roumanian melons are about as juicy as a can of oatmeal, and have the flavor an immature pumpkin. In fact everything Roumanian makes a sad comparison with Hungarian equivalents. The city of Bucharest compared to Budapest would be like a tadpole by the side of a rainbow trout. At the meeting this morning, General Graziani presided, and our Roumanian friends showed up, as usual, about twenty minutes late. The bewhiskered Holban started to make excavations in his mountain of documents in proof of the Hungarian conspiracy, which I endured for about half an hour, and then told the Mission I saw no reason why we should waste our time hearing all proof of something that was already known exist, but which did not prove that there had been any conspiracy directed against the Roumanians. Little Diamandi then put up the proposition that, because Friedrich, the Hungarian Prime Minister, was directly implicated in this affair, they could now handle him as they saw fit; that whether it were a conspiracy or not, the meeting and the organization were certainly in contravention of Roumanian orders and regulations. He wanted to know whether or not the Mission desired to get rid of Friedrich. Apparently the Roumanians do, anyway. He thought it would not do to arrest and make martyrs of any of the ministers, but he could put sentinels over all the offices and prevent their entering, and he desired to know whether or not the Mission wished this done. He said that in view of the imminent departure of the Roumanians from Hungary and the length of time it would take to get a reply from Paris, they must have an immediate affirmative or negative answer. We cleared the council room, said good-bye to our Roumanian guests, and then held a closed meeting. I stated that ever since we had been on this duty, we had tried to get the Roumanians to expedite matters, but never before had they been in any hurry. I added that in view of the fact that they were going to dine with me tonight, and that I was going to dine with General Holban and others tomorrow night, and that the Roumanians were going to dine with the British Monday night, they apparently could not leave before Tuesday, and we could certainly get a telegram to Paris and a reply before that date. I said that invariably when we put anything up to the Roumanians, they said they would have to telegraph to Bucharest and get a reply. I said that their threat of immediate departure was simply a bluff. The Mission was unanimously of the opinion. So we drafted a telegram along these lines be sent to the Supreme Council this date. The Roumanians stated that the Mackensen material, which is located south of Pressburg, instead of consisting of 4,200 carloads, is now understood to consist of 10,000 carloads. It was noted in General Holban's report of the dangerous anti-Bolshevism organization that this organization was composed of 10,000 ex-soldiers and 13,000 civilians, with 600 mixed arms for the whole 23,000, most of the arms being sabers.

September 14, 1919.

I spent all the morning in my office working, but at noon I was interrupted by Colonel Yates, who insisted that I accompany him and a party Hungarian nobility to a lunch on one of the high hills overlooking Budapest, and then go to the races. I went to the lunch and rather enjoyed it because the party of Hungarians, who were the Colonel's guests, could all speak English. I afterwards went for a while it to the races, over a miserable dusty road, and didn't enjoy myself at all.

Last evening I entertained at dinner M. Diamandi, General Mardarescu, General Holban, and General Sorbescu, who is in charge of Roumanian requisitions. We gave them a sumptuous feast, after which they parted, more or less mellow and verging on the affectionate.

September 15, 1919.

At our session this morning, General Mombelli presided and we were not afflicted by the presence of any heel-clicking Roumanians. After discussing the matter, we decided to send a telegram to the Supreme Council to the effect that, despite our repeated and strenuous efforts to start the organization of a police force and an army for the maintenance of order in the interior on the evacuation by the Roumanians, we had been able to accomplish practically nothing, all due to the fact that our so-called allies not only disregarded all of our requests and instructions, but that they constantly were placing stumbling blocks in our way; adding that the Roumanians were giving as a reason for their delay in helping the police their lack of confidence in the government of Prime Minister Friedrich. We also stated that there were strong rumors to the effect that the Roumanians intended to leave Hungary on short notice, in hopes that such disorder would ensue that they would be promptly requested to return.

In the afternoon, three of the new ministers of the Hungarian cabinet called upon me, and I told them all practically the same thing; that they themselves were to blame for the unfortunate condition in which Hungary found herself; that it was all due to the fact that they had allowed Bolshevism to take root and spread over the country for a period of several months; that, if Bolshevism had not been allowed, there would have been no Roumanians; but, as there was no use crying over spilt milk, it was now up to them to make the best of their horrible situation and show the world that, should the Roumanians evacuate precipitately, Hungary was still able to demonstrate that she possessed civilization to an extent that would not admit of her again falling into the abysm of Bolshevism. I also advised them to be careful about allowing their reactionaries to go beyond reasonable limits. I added that though I sympathized with men of education, refinement and means, whose comfortable homes had been taken charge of by a lot of anarchists, and whose families had been confined to one or two rooms and forced live in close contact with a lot of filthy, ignorant and fanatical Bolshevists, this was no reason why they should not handle the situation with decency and decorum.

On Saturday, a Colonel Nathan Horowitz reported me, despite the fact that I had previously telegraphed in code to Paris that it was inadvisable to send an officer of Jewish faith to Hungary at this time. In writing General Bliss about the matter, I explained to him that although all Bolshevists were not Jews nor were all Jews Bolshevists, nevertheless Béla Kun, the Hungarian Bolshevist leader, practically all his lieutenants, and most of his followers, were Jews, and as a result the people of Hungary were simply furious and determined to rid themselves of the Semitic influence.

We have also heard reports about the Hungarians starting pogroms in several places.

The following is a copy of a letter which has been received from General Bliss[17] and which is one of the most encouraging things I have had since arriving here:

AMERICAN COMMISSION TO NEGOTIATE PEACE.

Hotel de Crillon, Paris

My dear Bandholtz: September 4, 1919.

I take advantage of the fact that an officer is leaving here tonight for Trieste and thence to Budapest to send you this hasty line.

First of all I want to tell you how very much pleased the entire Commission here is at the splendid work you have been doing in Budapest. By word of mouth from various sources we have full confirmation of what appears in your own reports, namely, that you have been working in full accord with your British colleague even though the representatives of other nations may not have shown the same spirit of cooperation. We have every reason to think that you are the strong man of the Mission. It is to be regretted, - but it cannot be helped, of course, - that your hard and excellent work has not been more fruitful in making our Roumanian friends work inside the traces. Today (I think) Sir George Clerk, one of Mr. Balfour's personnel, leaves for the purpose of delivering in person to the Roumanian Government a final note of the Allied and Associated Powers. If this is not promptly effective and if the Entente then shows inability or unwillingness to apply further pressure upon the Roumanians, I think it very likely that our Government may relieve you from the Mission of Generals at Budapest, although it may leave you there as an independent observer. We all think that the time has come to make everybody in Europe understand that if they expect further cooperation and assistance from the United States they must play the game properly or we will show them at once that we intend to withdraw completely and leave them to their own resources.

17 General Tasker H. Bliss, one of the leading members of the American Peace Commission at Paris, was a liberal-minded man and opposed to many the harsh and stupid provisions of the peace treaties. The action of the Allies in regard to Hungary was most severely criticized by him. He declared as "politically unwise" the action of the Council of Ten, taken on Feb. 16, 1919, while President Wilson was away, establishing a neutral zone between the Roumanian and the Hungarian Armies, a zone which extended far into territory of solidly Magyar population. He called it an unfair proposal which "caused the Bolshevik revolution" and said that "it cannot he justified morally before the people of the United States." He recommended a peace with Hungary on the principles advocated by Woodrow Wilson on Jan. 8, 1918, and in subsequent addresses, in contrast to one based on the secret treaty concluded between the Allies and the Romanians on Aug. 18, 1916. See: Ray Stannard Baker's *Woodrow Wilson and World Settlement*, New York, 1922-23, three vols. II, 29-30; III, pp. 238-45.

I have been trying to get for you an automobile in anticipation of those which have been ordered to be sent to you from the Morgenthau Mission in Poland. Unfortunately, the American Delegation has none that it can send. All of ours have belonged to the American Army and have been sold to the French, and as rapidly as we have no use for one here it has to be turned in to the latter government. But Captain Smythe, who arrived here yesterday with dispatches from Budapest, told me that your own automobile and chauffeur were, as he understands, here and doing nothing. I asked him to go at once and see the proper officer and tell him that it was most desirable that this be at once made available for you. Captain Smythe said that if he could get it he would himself drive the machine Budapest. In that case I will have time to send you a further and fuller letter.

Meanwhile, I again congratulate you for myself and the American Mission for the excellent work you have been doing in Budapest, I remain

Cordially yours,

(Signed) Tasker H. Bliss

Last night we entertained Baron Jean de Cnobloch, the Envoy Extraordinary and Minister Plenipotentiary of the German-Austrian Republic, at dinner.

During the evening, General Gorton came over and informed me that Baron Perényi had been to see him tell him that he had been approached by the Roumanians with a view of being Prime Minister of a new cabinet, and that they had offered to return to Hungary all the stuff they had removed on condition of certain territorial and other concessions. Baron Perényi was told that he would be a fool to pay attention to any such propositions, that Hungary in the past as her history proved, had suffered far more than at present and had nevertheless risen above her ruins, that it would be foolish for any of them to consider any offer the Roumanians might make, and that he as a man of intelligence ought to know that the Roumanians would not return one-tenth, if any, of what they had taken away. I sent a telegram immediately to the American Commission, advising them of the information we had acquired, and also stating that the evening paper, which is under the control of the Roumanians, had stated that the Friedrich cabinet had fallen and that the Perényi cabinet had taken its place. There was, however, no confirmation of this up to noon today.

September 16, 1919.

General Gorton left this morning to go out and inspect Admiral Horthy's white army at Siófok, so I was President of the Day one day in advance of my turn.

A letter was read from the French postal authorities requesting the Hungarian government to make postal arrangements between the two countries, and this was given to the French representative as being a matter peculiarly his own.

We had many unimportant letters submitted, among them a plea from a bunch of Hungarian suffragettes. This was tabled.

I repeated to the Mission the gist of the conversation I had held yesterday with various cabinet officials, and then read them the report from Major Borrow, the British officer, who is watching the bridge across the Theiss River. He reports that up to date the following as been sent across that river: 684 locomotives, 231 saloon and private cars, 946 passenger coaches, 2,900 empty box and flat cars, 1,300 mixed carloads of grain, cattle, etc., 1,300 carloads of munitions, 298 cannon, 3 autos, 56 aeroplanes, 1,400 oil tanks, 2,000 carloads of railway material and agricultural machinery, 1,435 of war material, 4,350 contents not visible; also many miscellaneous cars, making a total of 17,319 locomotives and cars.

Just as we were adjourning, a Roumanian colonel came in and stated that they had located another depot of Mackensen supplies, and he was authorized to return there with his committee, investigate and make report.

This afternoon M. Diamandi called upon me and showed me a telegram from the Roumanian Prime Minister, stating that His Majesty, the King of Roumania, had conferred upon me the Grand Cross of the Roumanian Crown, and that the same would be rewarded without delay. His Excellency denied the reports that were current, to the effect that the Roumanians were evacuating the country, but told me confidentially that he had decided to give rifles to the municipal police of Budapest.

This afternoon the Hungarian liaison official, M. Pekár, came in to protest against the increasing Roumanian seizures, and I told him if he had any small and valuable articles, he could bring them to my office. In the evening, we had Count von Edeisheim, his wife and daughter to dinner with us, and found them to be very charming. During the month we have occupied their house, we have seen practically nothing of them, although they have lived all the time in the back portion of the building.

September 17, 1919.

This morning I sent for Colonel Horowitz and had one of the head porters, who belongs to the Royal Palace guard, brought in under the charge of having denied admittance to a person who wanted to see Colonel Horowitz, giving as his reason that the latter was a Jew. He tearfully denied this and the matter was dropped.

General Gorton being absent on his inspection trip of Admiral Horthy's army, General Graziani presided at the Mission's session. I first brought up before the Mission the question of having someone sent to identify museum property which the Roumanians desire to remove, and which action had been requested by General Serbescu. The Mission decided that, in view of the fact that the Roumanians had been told to take nothing, there was no reason why a representative should be sent.

I also informed the Mission what M. Diamandi had said yesterday in denial of the reported evacuation of the country by the Roumanians.

General Graziani read a telegram from M. Clemenceau, gain giving us the already oft-repeated instructions not to mix in the internal affairs of Hungary, but directing us to urge upon both Hungarians and Roumanians the necessity of immediately organizing a gendarmerie.

I then submitted to the Mission the Hungarian financial question, which is getting into acute stages, and which shows that our Roumanian allies have business ideas which would do credit to the Buccaneer Morgan. While the Bolshevists were in power, they issued three and one-half billion kronen worth of money, which, on account of its color, has been called white money. Previous to this, the paper currency of all Austro-Hungary was blue in color, so this currency which is still being used in Austria, Hungary, and Czecho-Slovakia, is called blue money. At the present time, one krone of blue money is worth five kronen of white money. Our good friends, the French, looking out for their own interests, obliged the Hungarian government to pay three hundred thousand kronen blue money for the same sum of white money in the hands of French subjects. As a result the Roumanians then promptly came forward with the demand that the Hungarians give them twenty million kronen in blue money for that amount white money. This was finally agreed to, partly because it was hoped thereby to give the Roumanians only blue money with which to make payment whenever they paid at all. As matters resulted, however, this was only an opening wedge, and the Roumanians demand today that they receive immediately fifty million kronen blue money for that sum in white money, and that within three weeks they receive a total of one hundred and fifty million kronen of blue money for that amount of white money. If this is done, they will undoubtedly continue the procedure, because a man could start out with a few kronen of white money and by a rapid succession of changes make himself a millionaire in a few days. We protested to the Roumanian Headquarters against their thievish propensities, and I reported the matter to the American Commission in Paris.

This date Captain Shafroth reported. and I assigned him to duty with Colonel Loree.

This afternoon when returning to the office from lunch, Colonel Loree and I found a whole company of Roumanian soldiers with their guns on their backs, milling up the entrance to the Palace courtyard. Without any preamble, I took my riding crop in hand and, ably seconded by Colonel Loree, we expelled the intruders into the street outside of the Palace entrance. I then inquired if there was a Roumanian officer about, and they said he had gone into the Palace. I chased him up, dragged him up to my office and asked him what the Hell he meant by insulting the Inter-Allied Military Mission by bringing a whole company of armed soldiers into our precincts. He stated at first that he had heard that there were subterranean passages in the Palace which he wished to explore, and later changed that to saying that he had heard of the Palace and wished his soldiers to see it before they left. I told him that Roumanians would hardly expect a company of American, British or French troops to go over to Genral Mardarescu's Headquarters and, without saying a word to him, proceed to explore the premises. I further informed him that he had committed a serious and gross breach of etiquette, and that we couldn't let one Roumanian company in here without letting the whole army come in, which we did not propose to do. He was most abject, in his apologies and beat it.

This afternoon, accompanied by Colonel Yates, I paid calls upon the new Roumanian Commander for Budapest, General Mosoiu, upon General Holban, who just being relieved from command of Budapest; and upon General Serbescu, who has charge of the requisitions. We were so fortunate as to find that General Josoiu was sick in bed and could not be seen, and the other two were out.

This evening we entertained at dinner Colonel Horowitz, of the regular Army, Captain Weiss, who has just been demobilized, and Mr. Zerkowitz, the Hungarian gentleman who has been acting as my guide and mentor as regards relations with Hungarians in the city.

September 18, 1919.

At this morning's session, General Gorton presided, and I related to the Mission my experience of the day before, in having, accompanied by Colonel Loree, assaulted a company of Roumanian infantry with riding crops and driven them out of the Palace courtyard.

A communication was read from the Swiss consul describing the horrible condition of Hungarian prisoners of war left in charge of the Roumanians in their prison camps.

A report was read from the British officer, Major Borrow, which showed that, up to date, 759 locomotives and 18,495 cars had crossed the Theiss River eastward bound, since we had been able to keep track of them. The total cars reported missing by the Hungarians amount to over 31,000. Major Borrow also showed that, within the past week, twenty-one troop trains had crossed the Szolnok Bridge and seventeen troop trains, containing a division of cavalry, had crossed the Csongrád Bridge, all headed towards Roumania. Everything indicates that our noble Roumanian allies intend actually to pull out of all of Hungary except Budapest and a thin line some distance west of the Danube. This will enable them to prevent any reorganization of the Hungarian police or Army, and will carry out their apparent design of leaving Hungary like a beautiful rosy-cheeked apple, but rotten at the core.

Colonel Yates was brought into the Mission, and from a memorandum showed how the Roumanians had practically done nothing along the line of police organization except to turn loose the usual supply of broken promises. Things have all along been in such a rotten condition that no superlatives can do the subject justice. The Mission finally decided to send again for the Roumanian Commander in Chief to appear before us tomorrow at 10 o'clock, to answer affirmatively or negatively a few questions which will be propounded to him.

I received a telegram from the American Commission in Paris, wanting to know if newspaper reports the effect that Italy and Germany were mixed up a deal with Roumania and Hungary were true. I replied that the same rumors had come to my knowledge, but that they were not verified, had not yet been proved to be true, and therefore I had not inflicted them upon my superiors.

Apparently the opera season is on, and I received tickets for the Royal box, to hold twelve occupants, with additional boxes for twenty-four more. They run their shows and operas from 6 in the afternoon till about 8, after which the audience can go to dinner.

A report came in today that a French major had gone to the State Railway's offices and demanded a report in regard to the management and expenses of the railway for the past year. As the Hungarians were not certain whether this was the individual action of the French or the joint action of the Mission, they sent up here to ascertain, and we told them that no such action had been taken by the Mission. I reported the matter to Paris.

At the present rate of Roumanian seizures of cars, this country, with 6,000 kilometers of railroads, will have only 4,500 cars available. As it takes 4,000 a day feed Budapest alone, which contains one-fifth of the population of Hungary, it is not difficult to imagine hat the result will be when winter sets in.

September 19, 1919.

Last night, accompanied by my staff, I attended the opera, occupying the Royal box. As a matter of fact, I had three of these boxes, all of which were turned over to me -myself and staff occupying the center one and soldiers of my detachment occupying the others. After the Opera, Captain Gore and I attended a dinner party at the house of Captain Weiss's brother. There was too much to eat and the rooms were stuffy, so we did not stay overly late.

This morning we had a prolonged and hot session of the Mission, with General Mombelli presiding. He first read a memorandum of questions he proposed to propound to the Roumanians, covering the question of when they were going to evacuate, when they were going to organize the police, and a few other things, which sounded most pre-emptory in character, especially when accompanied by his flashing eyes and resounding fist. As given to us, it was an oriental typhoon, compared to the gentle little zephyr with which he turned it loose on them when they arrived later, which they did at 10.20 A.M., as usual twenty minutes late.

When directly informed that we knew that at least two divisions of Roumanian troops had already left Hungary, General Mardarescu admitted it and went one more, saying that two infantry divisions and one cavalry division had already left; and it was not a case of evacuation of Hungary, but that these troops were being sent to the Bánát, where they were concentrating in considerable force to avoid possible trouble. He said that this was not to be interpreted as a beginning of the Roumanian evacuation, and that whenever they begin to evacuate, he would notify us in regard to same and keep us posted daily.

It was next pointed out to General Mardarescu that, on the twenty-fifth of August, they were requested to evacuate the country west of the Danube and that they replied then that they would take it under immediate consideration, but that so far nothing had been done. General Mardarescu stated that he wanted to be sure the Hungarians would not attack him, and he could not withdraw until he was positive in this respect. This made me *un peu fatigué*, and I told him, that, as a soldier, he should know that the troops that had west of the Danube, scattered as they were, were in far more danger of an attack from the Hungarians than they could possibly be if withdrawn to east side of the Danube and the Budapest bridgehead. General Mombelli then proposed that our committee which is working on the organization of the army, investigate conditions in the zone occupied by Hungarian troops and report upon the same, so that General Mardarescu could know whether or not his organized and valiant army, of which he so loudly boasted, was in danger from about ten thousand poorly-armed Hungarians. It was finally agreed, by both the Mission and the Roumanians, that steps should be taken immediately towards the Organization of a Hungarian army consisting of two divisions and some auxiliary troops, to a total number of 12,500. The police question was then taken up, and considerable discussion ensued. Colonel Yates had insisted on 22,000 police, and the Roumanians were willing to give only 10,000. Finally, however, they agreed to turn over to us, the Inter-Allied Military Mission, 10,000 rifles and 40 machine guns for us to deal out to the police when we saw fit, and with the understanding that a provisional gendarmerie of 10,000 men might be started.

M. Diamandi then brought up the question of Hungarian prisoners of war. He said that they had 27,000 Hungarian prisoners of war, many of whom had been formerly Bolshevists, and whom, of course, they would not care to take back to Roumania with them. He made the point that, in case they were turned over to the Hungarian government, the latter would be given an opportunity to persecute and probably execute great numbers on account of their having belonged to the Bolshevist army, whereas their service had been entirely compulsory. It was decided to discuss this matter at further length later on.

M. Diamandi then stated that the Hungarian government had applied for authority to issue fifty million kronen in small notes, depositing as security an equal sum of large notes. I opposed this on two points: the first being that there was no government as yet recognized, so that the issue would not be legal; and the second being that, even if there were, there would be nothing to prevent their shortly after turning loose the fifty million on deposit and thereby again depreciating the currency. It was decided not to allow the Hungarians to make any such issue.

M. Diamandi showed a telegram from Roumanian headquarters directing him to investigate in the case child mortality, saying that it was understood that e Roumanians had been held responsible for deaths infants in hospitals. I reminded my colleagues of hat had been brought before them at one of our earliest sessions.

M. Diamandi said that they had letters from the hospitals saying that all these reports had been unfounded. It was then proposed to send a committee consisting of a French doctor and an Italian doctor, but I insisted on including an American officer.

M. Diamandi then showed a memorandum stating at several wagon loads of Roumanian documents, seized and removed to Budapest by the Hungarians, were in the cellars of the Palace. It was decided to instigate this.

The question of a probable shortage of cars, resulting from the excessive Roumanian demands, was then ought up and given to the Roumanian officials, who promised to investigate this immediately.

They started to leave us, but I insisted on settling the question about the evacuation of western Hungary, and we actually split on this, the Frenchman and the Italian thinking that this could be discussed later, and General Gorton and myself insisting that it be done at once.

As they started to leave again, a note was brought to me from Colonel Loree to the effect that the Roumanians had demanded that the Hungarians turn over them, before 5 o'clock this afternoon, one hundred millions worth of blue kronen for a like sum of white kronen, threatening to revoke the decree which had placed the two at the rate of five white for one blue, unless this demand was complied with. General Mardarescu stated that the facts were that some time ago the Hungarians offered to replace one hundred million of white money, then in the hands of the Roumanians, by blue money, provided they were allowed to import three hundred million kronen of blue money from Vienna. This was done and they now tried to avoid keeping their bargain.

After they left and we were alone, I told the Mission that I wanted them to understand exactly where they stood on the evacuation question; that I did not and would not agree with them; that I felt sure that they were wrong, although I might be the one in error. I said it had taken the Roumanians since August 25 to arrive at no decision whatever, and now we were giving them another delay for like purpose. I added that we were all supposed to be officers of common sense and experience, and not one of them could look me in the eye and say that there was a particle of danger to the Roumanians, should they evacuate western Hungary, but on the contrary that it would add to their security. They could not do it. I then added that, so far, the Mission had been unanimous, but now we appeared as a divided house before the Roumanians. They then proposed writing a letter to the Roumanians again calling upon them to evacuate western Hungary.

As they looked like licked dogs with their tails stuck between their legs, I let it go at this, and we therefore decided to send our third ultimatum on is subject. This ultimatum business is getting to be quite a habit.

Reports from western Hungary indicate all kinds of atrocities on the part of the Hungarians, who are torturing and butchering the Jews, and having their will on the population. These people down in eastern and central Europe would make Ananias look like George Washington.

In the afternoon I called upon M. Diamandi and, during the conversation, he asked my advice as to what they should do in regard to the Friedrich cabinet. I told him that in my opinion any form of persecution usually resulted in making martyrs of the victims, and at any persecution of Friedrich would result only in his increased popularity.

This evening, Captain Gore and I were entertained dinner by Admiral Sir Ernest T. Troubridge, the her guests being the Roumanian Chief of Staff, Colonel Vasilescu, a fine fellow, and his French wife.

September 20, 1919.

Today being the grand Italian national holiday, General Mombelli appeared all dol led with his various decorations, medals, etc., and our meeting did not last long. As a matter of fact, it never does when I am President of the Day, which I was today.

We first considered several questions which had been left over from yesterday's meeting, including the money question and the handling of prisoners of war. This all brought about a discussion on the present seriousness of the situation, and I insisted that the time had come for us to lay before the Supreme Council in unmistakable terms the necessity for recognizing some form of government in Hungary. My colleagues agreed to this and I drafted a telegram of which the following is the substance:

Unless there is quickly organized in Hungary some government which is recognized by the Entente, the situation will with increasing rapidity, as winter approaches, get worse. The Military Mission cannot carry out plans for the reorganization of the Hungarian gendarmerie and police, for the release of Hungarian prisoners of war, and for the evacuation of Hungary, with a government which has no standing. Furthermore, such a government cannot carry out satisfactory financial transactions, as it properly has no authority to levy or collect taxes; such a government cannot contract for future delivery of fuel and food supplies for the winter, without which disorder and dire suffering are certain to ensue; and such a government cannot make a treaty of peace or perform any of the various functions necessary to a sovereign state. At the present rate of progress, the Roumanians will continue indefinitely with their occupation and attendant looting in which they are daily becoming more expert. The Hungarians, on the other hand, are becoming more and more discouraged and famine, suffering and disorder are approaching. It is recommended that either the Friedrich cabinet be recognized or that explicit instructions be given as to what will be recognized.

The Roumanians are continuing right merrily with their looting, and we have already scheduled over 800 locomotives and 19,000 cars which they have removed.

This morning several letters came in from Roumanian Headquarters, stating that they had located various papers and documents in government offices and in the cellars of the Palace, which had been taken from Roumania by the Austro-Germans, and which they desired to have returned, This was the first time so far that they have proceeded along such polite lines.

September 22, 1919.

At our meeting this morning, the cat came out of the bag with a loud yowl. I again brought up the subject of the Roumanian delay in evacuating Transdanubia and told my Latin colleagues that I considered that their yielding to the Roumanian asinine demand, that they defer any evacuation until was shown that there was no danger from a Hungarian attack, made this Mission responsible for a continuation of the present rotten conditions in western Hungary with all of its consequences; adding that there would be a considerable delay before the committee sent investigate, could report, and asking when the committee would have its report ready. This forced the issue and the French representative admitted that the committee had not yet started and would not start until the twenty-third of September. As the start could have easily been made early in the afternoon of the nineteenth, this will have caused a delay of nearly five days. As reports have been received of engagements been Hungarian and Roumanian patrols, General Gorton mentioned that an officer be sent to remain with the Hungarian Army to avert as much as possible any of these minor engagements and to investigate them immediately and fix the responsibility whenever they occurred. The French member bitterly opposed this, and was carrying on the discussion indefinitely when I proposed that the committee on army organization, of which a French lieutenant colonel is chairman, have charge of this investigation. This he consented to, and then I proposed that the British

91

officer be placed as an additional member on this army committee, and stated that I would furnish an American officer also, and that really the committee should assume an Inter-Allied aspect. He was obliged to swallow this proposition, and eventually the Italian representative stated that he would send an officer also.

Although the occurrence cannot be well described, it gave convincing proof to both General Gorton and myself that the French member was working hand in glove with the Roumanians and was helping them in their policy of delay.

The Italian Colonel Romanelli, who investigated present conditions in Budapest prisons, submitted a report today indicating that they had been simply rotten. Political prisoners had been thrown in with criminals; many of them were badly beaten up, and all the prisons were crowded beyond all reason, with one exception, in which conditions were good. The Hungarians have been called upon to explain why this condition exists and to state how they propose to remedy it.

A Roumanian officer showed up at the Palace this morning, to swipe property from the office of the Minister of Foreign Affairs, and was expelled by Colonel Loree.

The Countess von Edeisheim and her daughter, with a maid, are leaving today for their estate in Czecho-Slovakia, and Captain Gore, not very reluctantly on his part, is in charge of the arrangements for their departure. They had been trying for two weeks to get passports for two servants viséd at the Czecho-Slovakian Ministry, and could not do it. Captain Gore had the thing settled in a few minutes this morning.

Admiral Troubridge reported today that there were only five days' food supplies left in Budapest, and these will not last long at the present rate of Roumanian seizures.

September 23, 1919.

At this morning's session of the Mission, General Graziani presided, and we cleaned out a whole mountain of accumulated unimportant respondence. It is now getting so that both the Roumanians and the Hungarians endeavor to use this Mission as a liaison bureau.

One letter submitted was rather important, in that it was a report from the Hungarian Chief of Police to the fact that the Roumanians had authorized the Socialists to hold meetings on the twenty-fifth, and that the police, being unarmed and almost unorganized, would not be able to handle any serious situation. We decided therefore to notify the Roumanians that it was reported that they had given such permission, and that they would be held responsible for anything that happened.

Yesterday afternoon the Roumanians arrested an undersecretary of the Hungarian War Office because he had delivered to us a memorial addressed by the Ruthenian party of Hungary to the Supreme Council. General Mardarescu has been called upon to explain why he took such action.

Colonel Yates was called before the Mission and explained how despite all the beautiful promises of the Roumanians on the nineteenth to give us 10,000 rifles and 40 machine guns for use of the municipal police, they had, when it came to a show-down, surrounded this munificent gift with such conditions as to make it practically worthless. The Mission instructed Colonel Yates to go to Roumanian Headquarters and tell them that he was ready to inspect the arms they proposed to turn over to us, and then incidentally to bring up the question of the distribution of these arms, and let them know that it was understood that they were under our orders without any Roumanian conditions attached, except that the Roumanians would be informed from time to time of the disposition of these arms.

While before the Mission, Colonel Yates reported this morning that he had learned that the Roumanians were starting to take the fire apparatus out of Budapest, and that he himself had driven away the Roumanian officer in charge of the looting party.

I shall send, in a day or so, recommendations for the D.S.M. for my various colleagues, and shall suggest that we establish an Order of Ali Baba and the Forty Thieves so that our Roumanian friends can also be properly decorated.

This afternoon the Hungarian Minister of Foreign Affairs, Count Somssich, called upon me and, with more bluntness than is characteristic of these people, asked me when the Roumanians were going to leave. I told him that I could give him no more definite information on that point than I could have given six weeks ago; that I did not know. He then said:

"There is apparently nothing else left for us; we will have to make terms with the Roumanians because at the present rate my country will be absolutely ruined, and it behooves us to save as much as we can from the wreck. The Entente either cannot or will not help us, and so far as I can see there is absolutely no alternative but acceding to the Roumanian terms."

I told him that I thought he was very foolish for two reasons: the first being that the Roumanians would demand so much that it would ruin Hungary in perpetuity; and secondly that they, for their part, would not carry out any contract that they made.

He said he realized these facts; that he had been bought up as a gentleman, always hoped to remain a gentleman, but that one had to fight fire with fire, and at when one was dealing with liars and thieves like Roumanians, the only thing to do was to fight them with their own weapons, agree to give practically all they ask for, and then give them nothing. I told him, course, this was rather reprehensible, and that while would not blame him for feeling sore at the way the Hungarians had been neglected and been treated, I was positive that in the long run she would win out and that Roumania would pay dearly for all the pleasures she had derived from looting a fallen enemy.

I asked him how he proposed to negotiate with the Roumanians, and he stated that M. Ardeli, the same gentleman who had acquired the ultimata habit with the Archduke Joseph, was going to see him tomorrow to discuss terms. He finally said that he would listen to the terms, find out just what they were, and let us know, but agree to nothing until he had seen me.

I then asked him if he had been approached at all by the French, and he said no, but that the Hungarians knew that the French were winking at the Roumanians in all they had been doing.

I then asked him if he had had any transactions with the Italians. He said yes, that General Mombelli himself had suggested that the Hungarians come to terms with the Roumanians. He said his reliance was upon the Americans and the British, and that he would be glad to have me talk the matter over with General Gorton. This I did, and we shall now hear what terms M. Ardeli has to offer. Captain Gore and Colonel Loree had planned to go to the opera tonight, but at the last moment did some backsliding and we had a very quiet and satisfactory dinner.

September 24, 1919.

Late yesterday afternoon, Colonel Yates was sent by me to see General Mardarescu in regard to the arming of the Hungarian police. He returned later; said that he had had a talk with General Mardarescu, who told him that they could not establish a depôt for the arms inside of a week or ten days, which means of course that they never intend to furnish any equipment whatever. Later in the evening I called upon General Mardarescu, but the call was essentially social, and no business was discussed. He told me, however, that he was leaving the next night for Bucharest, instead of on Thursday as originally contemplated and he also stated that the French Minister to Roumania had called on him during the afternoon. The question naturally arises then -*what in Hell is the French Minister doing here!*

At the meeting of the Mission this morning, General Mombelli presided and, after dispatching a little routine business, a letter was read from General Mardarescu, stating that he had found it impracticable to establish the arms depôt at Monor and had decided to put it at Czegléd, parenthetically twice as far away; that all the firearms they had, had been shipped to Roumania and, therefore, it would be necessary to ship them back again before being delivered, all of which would take considerable time. He then said the understanding was that the arms would then as needed be turned over to the Hungarians by the Roumanians, assisted by the Entente, but that he must insist that no arms be delivered until he had an accurate report on the number of arms in the possession of the Hungarians, and that all arms in excess of what was absolutely required or the police be turned back to the Roumanians.

I then read Colonel Yates' memorandum of his conversation with General Mardarescu, and I reminded my colleagues that this was just the result that might have been expected from our interview with the Roumanian high officials on the nineteenth, and I recalled to their memories that when I was fighting for the evacuation of western Hungary, Diamandi had made the argument that he thought that for one day we had accomplished a great deal; therefore, why bicker over the evacuation of Transdanubia, adding: "You have already secured 10,000 rifles and 40 machine guns; that certainly is enough for one day." I told my colleagues that the Roumanians were treating us just the same as a teacher would handle a class in kindergarten, and that we deserved it. They asked if I had any suggestions to make, and I said that I certainly had; that I wanted a letter written to General Mardarescu repeating that on the nineteenth we had explained to him, and he had admitted, that the organization of the Hungarian police was an immediate and urgent necessity; that he had promised to have 10,000 arms and 40 machine guns ready by the twenty-third; that these were to be handled by the Entente assisted, if necessary, by the Roumanians; and that now he had broken his promise; that it looked to us as though there was no intention on the part of the Roumanians to help in the organization of the police, and that we should hold them responsible for any disorders or other troubles that might ensue as a result of a lack of properly-armed and organized policemen; and that we would advise the Supreme Council accordingly.

General Graziani suggested that, in addition, we say that if the Roumanians wanted to demonstrate their good intentions, they would now give us two or three thousand rifles. I did a little table thumping and said that I would positively refuse to have anything to do with any such idiotic transaction; that I would not face myself or my country in the position of bickering with the Roumanians for such a paltry trifle, and that I thought it was a disgusting spectacle to see the representatives of France, Italy, Great Britain, and America down on their prayer bones and supplicating the Roumanians for two or three thousand rifles. General Graziani's suggestion was turned down, and the letter was drafted by General Mombelli, as I had suggested. I then telegraphed the American Commission the text of the same.

This afternoon Colonel Yates brought in the Countess Juliska Szirmay, who is a relative of Count von Edelsheim. She craved our protection for her five sisters and her uncle's family on their estate about two hours' automobile drive from here, stating that the Roumanians had threatened to send on the twenty-sixth and remove all their stock. As these people are furnishing us with some supplies, I went myself to General Serbescu and made him write me out a safeguard for their farms.

September 25, 1919.

Last night we entertained at dinner General Mosoiu, who is General Holban's successor in command of Budapest, his Chief of Staff, and Colonel and Mme. Vasilescu. General Mosoiu is a tremendously fat old fellow, but he is a decided improvement over the hirsute Holban.

This morning I presided at the meeting of the Mission. We had but few matters to discuss. First, two communications from Major Body, the Serbian military representative in Budapest, complaining that the Roumanians would not allow him to use his own language, either by telephone or telegraph, in communicating with Belgrade.

A letter was received from M. de Pekár, stating that the Roumanians had now requisitioned 900 of the remaining 4,500 closed cars still in Hungary, and that enforcing that requisition would leave the country in a most serious situation. As this matter had been brought to Minister Diamandi's attention at the meeting on the nineteenth, and he had promised to give it his immediate attention, the Mission authorized me to send him a communication stating that it was not believed that such a thing could have been done with the knowledge and consent of the Roumanian Commander in Chief, and we trusted that remedial action would immediately be taken.

I brought to the attention of the Mission the fact that a company of Roumanian soldiers had taken station in the Royal Riding Hall, right near the entrance to the Royal Palace, and that their commander, upon being interrogated, had stated that he understood he had been sent at the request of the Inter-Allied Military Mission for the purpose of preserving order near the Royal Palace. This was undoubtedly a delicate touch of sarcasm from our Roumanian allies in return for our communication of yesterday, when we told them that their refusal to arm the police would make them responsible for any disorders that might occur. The Mission authorized me to write a communication to the Roumanian commander thanking him for his courtesy and thoughtfulness, asking him to withdraw the guard immediately, telling him that we were perfectly competent to maintain order about our Headquarters, and adding in conclusion that the presence of such a large force might result in friction between them and the Inter-Allied guards.

A report was received from the subcommittee which ad been sent to Admiral Horthy's army to investigate as to the danger of an attack from the same upon the Roumanians, and the result was absolutely what we new it would be. The committee unanimously concurred in the opinion that the Hungarian Army could not in any manner whatever be considered as a menace to the Roumanians, and that there was neither the intention nor the possibility of its attacking the Roumanian forces. The committee found out that Horthy was carrying out to the letter his instructions as regards organization, that even now he could maintain order in Transdanubia whenever the Roumanians evacuated, and that in eight days his entire organization would be practically effected. The Mission authorized me to write to the Roumanian Commander in Chief, repeating the substance of the committee's report, stating that we concurred in the same, asking him immediately to evacuate Transdanubia, and to let us know not later than the twenty-ninth instant his decision in regard to the matter, so that we could notify the Supreme Council. The Minister of Foreign Affairs, Count Somssich, came to see General Gorton and myself and stated that Minister Diamandi himself had been over to the Foreign Office, instead of his go-between, Ardeli; that Diamandi had stated that the Roumanians had all along wanted to leave Hungary, but that the Entente would not let them. Diamandi did not at that time press his terms, but they were discussed and he is preparing them.

Later in the day General Gorton came in with an intercepted wireless message that was being sent by the Roumanians to the Eiffel Tower in Paris, to the effect that yesterday there had been meetings of 150,000 socialist workers; that these meetings were harmonious, well conducted and gotten up in opposition to the Friedrich government, stating that all the workers who attended were most eulogistic of the Roumanians, and expressed their thanks to the Roumanian

Army for having, during the period of its occupation, given them political liberty. General Gorton and I sent a telegram to Paris, stating that such message had been intercepted and to the effect that it was a damned lie.

Captain Andrews, who has been one of Colonel Yates' assistants at Bucharest, arrived today with his bride, en route to the States. Lieutenant-Colonel Causey, who now represents the Food and Railway Missions, is also here, and we entertained Captain and Mrs. Andrews and Colonel Causey at dinner tonight, after which they will leave on the evening train; and I am taking advantage of this, the first opportunity in weeks, for sending off a little mail and my reports to Paris.

September 26, 1919.

At this morning's session of the Mission, General Gorton presided and introduced the question of the intercepted radio from the Roumanians the Eiffel Tower, Paris. It was decided by the Mission to telegraph to the Supreme Council a statement the effect that the workmen's union, instead of turning out 150,000 men at nine different meetings, had turned out less than 20,000, and that one-half of these left before the meetings were through with, and in general that the Roumanian report was a gross exaggeration.

We next received the report of the amount of material shipped by the Roumanians to the east. Up to midnight of September 23-24, and since the last report, 7 train loads of troops with the usual cattle and forage had gone eastward, and our records up to date cover 1,046 locomotives, and over 23,000 mixed cars.

The question of the organization of the subcommittee on army organization was brought up, and it was decided to make that committee permanent, with a representative from each Mission. General Graziani stated that it would be necessary then to relieve Colonel Horowitz by another officer if it was desired to retain Lieutenant-Colonel Berthon as chairman, but I told him that we would waive the rank and leave the committee as it is.

Owing to the small amount of business brought up before the meetings of the Mission, it was decided in the future to have regular meetings on Mondays, Wednesdays and Fridays, and on other dates at the call of any member.

September 27, 1919.

Yesterday afternoon I was called upon by Mrs. Hegeman of New York City and her daughter, the Baroness Virginia Podmaniczky. The ladies just recently arrived from Switzerland and were to be in Budapest a few days to get some clothes and other things together and then to return to Switzerland. They made urgent request for just a little food and a little fuel. I therefore invited them to an informal dinner and also sent them enough to last them until their departure in three days.

Pursuant to our arrangements of yesterday to have meetings only on Mondays, Wednesdays and Fridays, unless called by some one member, there was no meeting today, and I spent most of the forenoon going over the situation downtown. Although the stores do not display much, yet there is far more activity than ever before. The jewelers have nothing of much value but, if you wish to make special arrangements, they will get their better pieces out of hiding and put them on private exhibition, and make special sales. The depreciated value of the krone makes almost anything ridiculously cheap. Colonel Loree this morning bought for the equivalent of $ 30 a large sterling silver cigar box which would hold about twenty-five cigars and one hundred cigarettes. The box had a solid gold rim on the front with a genuine sapphire set therein.

As the American Commission has given me no further intimation as to what is to happen to me, I this date sent them a four word telegram as follows: "Funds exhausted. Instructions requested."

Lieutenant-General Sir Tom Bridges, of the British Army[18], arrived yesterday and will be here for two or three days. I met General Bridges at the Toronto race course in the spring of 1917. We have invited him and Admiral Troubridge to dinner tomorrow night.

September 28, 1919.

I spent most of the morning today working at the office and the afternoon working at the house. In the evening, we entertained at dinner General Bridges, Admiral Troubridge and his son, and Major Foster of the British service. Major Foster is now assisting Colonel Loree on the Claims and Reparations Committee.

General Bridges at dinner mentioned that he understood that General Pershing would not have lasted much longer had the War continued, and he then stated hat he had it from General Foch's Chief of Staff[19] that the American Army was very poorly organized, had called loudly for French divisions to assist them, that supplies were short and, in general, that the American offensive was very poorly managed, if not actually mismanaged. I told General Bridges that I had either been a participant in command of a unit at the beginning of the general offensive, or Provost Marshal General of the American Expeditionary Force, and I did not care who his informant was, that to put it mildly, that gentleman was badly mistaken. General Bridges said that he had known General Graziani and General Mombelli before, and that the latter was considered to be one of the astutest diplomats of the Italian Army, and was always given their more important semi-diplomatic military missions.

September 29, 1919.

At the meeting of the Mission this morning, General Graziani presided. A letter was received from the Roumanians stating that they would agree to begin the evacuation of Transdanubia promptly, that as soon as the Hungarian forces had arrived within thirty kilometers of the cities of Győr, Veszprém and Székes-Fehérvár they would then within forty-eight hours evacuate such cities and retire on a line at a mean distance of thirty-five kilometers from Budapest. They desired to have forty-eight hours advance notice given of the contemplated march of the Hungarians, so that, all told, their movement should begin within four or five days after receiving such notice. We turned this over to the military subcommittee for the arrangement of all the details connected therewith.

Colonel Horowitz, who is a member of the Committee on Army Organization and who had visited western Hungary, turned in a report on the general conditions

18 Lieutenant-General Sir (George) Tom (Molesworth) Bridges. During he world war, he was several times wounded and served with distinction. He was the military member of Balfour's mission to the United States in 1917 and head of the British war mission to the United States in 1918. From 1918 to 1920, he acted as head of the British Mission of the Allied Armies of the Orient

19 General Max Weygand. At the outbreak of the world war, he was colonel and chief of the staff of an army. In 1916, he was made Brigadier General. From the beginning of the war, he served as assistant to Foch, whom he succeeded as the French representative on the Inter-Allied General Staff in 1917. In April, 1918, he resumed his work as Chief of the General Staff under Marshal Foch. This position he held during the remainder of the war. See also October 16 for a repetition of this statement.

there, and in particular concerning the Jewish persecutions. He stated that in his opinion Admiral Horthy's army had done everything within reason to prevent any such persecutions, and that he considered that no more atrocities had been committed than would ordinarily happen under the stress of such circumstances. He stated that a great many rascally Jews under he cloak of their religion had committed crimes, that here really was a great deal of anti-Semitic feeling on account of so many Jews having been Bolshevists, but as to there being a real White Terror, there was nothing of the kind, and this danger was a figment of the imagination of politicians. He stated that Jews and Gentiles alike should unite in maintaining order, and that hey could feel absolutely sure that there was no danger from the Hungarian National Army. It was decided to have this matter published in the local newspapers, in order that it might have a quieting effect upon the excitement of the people of Budapest.

It was also decided to send a letter to the Roumanian headquarters, stating that the Mission desired to have Colonel Yates appointed as supervisor of all police and gendarmerie, requiring the Roumanians, before taking any action against the police, to take it up first with Colonel Yates.

Mrs. Hegeman and her daughter, the Baroness Podmaniczky, called on me a few minutes this afternoon to say good-by.

September 30, 1919.

Last night we had Major Moffat of the American Red Cross informally to dinner. The Major recently arrived here to take charge of Red Cross work in Hungary. He is expecting a train of thirty car-loads of supplies in the near future. This train is supposed to have left Paris over a week ago, but so far has not been heard from.

He is out of patience with the performance of Colonel Anderson, the Red Cross representative in the Balkans, who has devoted all his time and attention to Roumania. It is the common report that Colonel Anderson is very much under the influence of the Queen of Roumania and practically everything sent to the Balkans was distributed as she desired[20]. Certainly there is no more

---

20 On p.275 of the strongly pro-Roumanian book by Charles J. Vopicka, *Secrets of the Balkans,* a picture may be seen showing Queen Marie at the Canteen of the American Red Cross in Jassy with Colonel Henry W.Anderson.

pro-Roumanian advocate in the world than Colonel Anderson, who, however, in his arguments seemed to think that a loud noise was better than logic. In his interview with me yesterday afternoon, he seemed to have undergone a considerable change, and I understand has really given the Roumanians much excellent advice. The next thing is to see whether or not they will follow it.

There was no session of the Mission this date, but I drafted two letters for the President of the Day; one covered the question of the publication of Colonel Horowitz's report on the anti-Semitic agitation in western Hungary, and the other was a recommendation to Roumanian authorities that Colonel Yates be designated as Inter-Allied supervisor of police, gendarmerie and frontier guards.

N. Mavroudis, the Greek Envoy Extraordinary J Minister Plenipotentiary to Serbia, came in to pay respects to me this afternoon, and after the usual effusive compliments and ornate persiflage, wanted to know just what the situation was here and what the Rumanian plans and intentions were[21]. I gave him whatever information I had, which was practically public but which to him seemed to be in the way of news. This afternoon Colonel Loree had difficulty with the Roumanians over the release of a Bolshevist prisoner. Some time they have been having former Bolsheviks, who were known to be murderers and cutthroats, released without trial, undoubtedly as the result of bribery. Two Roumanians went to police headquarters today with the wife of a man who is being held under various charges, including that of torture, and with-any proper papers a Roumanian detective tried to throw a big bluff which was called, and it is trusted he will receive the punishment he deserves.

21 On April 18, 1919, a treaty of amity and friendship had been concluded between Greece and Jugo-Slavia.

October, 1919

October 1, 1919.

At this morning's session, General Mombelli presiding, there was first read a letter from Minister Diamandi, asking that the Mission arrange for the prompt transfer of the Mackensen material to some point in Hungary where it could be divided up and the Roumanians receive their share. I suggested that we write Minister Diamandi that it was in the hands of the Entente, that its distribution was entirely under the jurisdiction of this Mission, and that this matter would be taken up in due course. I then suggested to my colleagues that what the Roumanians ought to have was a letter telling them that we would take up the question of such distribution when they returned the loot that they had already removed from Hungary.

According to a telegram received by General Gorton from the British Commission at Paris, Prime Minister Bratiano has given the Supreme Council representative a beautiful collection of characteristic Roumanian lies in regard to their seizures and requisitions. General Gorton received a telegram stating that Sir George Clerk[1] had been directed to come to Budapest and interview this Mission in order to determine whether it was Bratiano or the four Allied Generals who were lying.

We received two letters from one of my officers, Captain Shafroth, stating that there were certain articles in the Hungarian museums which had been taken, either from Bucharest, or from the portions of Transylvania which belonged to Roumania. He recommend that the books, etc., which had been identified as coming from Bucharest be returned, and that all other articles be held pending the action of the Commission. We received a telegram from the Hungarian town of Drégely, complaining that the Czecho-Slovaks had been posting patrols on all the roads leading to the town, and were allowing nobody to come in or go out, and stating with characteristic Middle-European hyperolism that anarchy and everything else horrible would result on short notice if the situation were not immediately remedied. The President of the Day was accordingly directed to inform the Czecho-Slovakian Minister of the situation and direct him to take the proper measures.

1 See footnote of diary, October 20, 1919.

General Mombelli invited our attention to the fact hat one battalion of Hungarian troops was being formed and was occupying territory which, according to the treaty with Austria, had been given to the latter country. We therefore sent a letter to the Hungarian Authorities to evacuate immediately any portions of territory which had been granted to Austria by the Peace Conference.

Yesterday I received a note from the Countess Szirmay to the effect that the safeguard sent them by the Roumanian General Serbescu and vise'd by him, had been examined by a young Roumanian lieutenant, named Panescu, who said that such paper did not prevent requisitioning by his colonel. I therefore sent Colonel Yates to Roumanian headquarters, and they telephoned out to the colonel of the First Chasseurs directing him to investigate Lieutenant Panescu's conduct and to award the punishment that the case would seem to merit. The Roumanian Chief of Staff, Colonel Vasilescu, sent me two safeguards from the Roumanian headquarters, which I sent out to the Countess with additional information that if Lieutenant Panescu cared to do any more quibbling about technicalities I would myself pay him a visit which he would not enjoy.

Yesterday the Roumanians gave a tremendous dinner at the Hotel Hungaria, to the British officials, during which, I understand, there was much playing of "God Save the King" and much talking about Great Britain as the greatest power on earth and, in general, that the affair was effusively affectionate, and that much champagne flowed. Apparently the Roumanians are trying to cut loose from the French and the Italians.

Yesterday I received a press report to the effect that it was now known that either Clemenceau himself or the French officials had always notified the Roumanians immediately after the dispatch of an ultimatum that such ultimatum could be ignored and that the Supreme Council really did not mean it. All of which is simply in line with the idea General Gorton and I have always maintained in regard to this situation.

October 2, 1919.

Yesterday afternoon Sir George Clerk, the delegate from the Supreme Council, sent to Roumania for the purpose of giving the Roumanian government the last and final ultimatum in regard to the occupation of Hungary, arrived. He spent an hour with the Inter-Allied Military Mission during which he showed himself to be decidedly pro-Roumanian.

He had arrived early during the day, had spent all the forenoon with Minister Diamandi, had been given a tremendous lunch by the Roumanians at noon, could give us only an hour in the afternoon, after which he went to the opera with Minister Diamandi, and was again entertained in the evening by the Roumanians.

His interview with the Mission was in most respects eminently satisfactory. He repeated in substance the same interview with Bratiano that I had had when in Bucharest; to which, however, he added that M. Bratiano insisted on having both banks of the Maros River practically up to Szeged[2] for the purpose of the strategic control of the railroad line. In his reply to M. Bratiano, covering this one particular point, he seemed to show the only gleam of diplomatic intelligence, as he told the Roumanians that he was sure the Allies would not consent to giving any more territory to Roumania; that present boundaries had been investigated and decided upon by a committee of geographical and tactical experts.

He asked the Mission if we thought that after the Roumanian evacuation there could not be made some permanent adjustment between Hungary and Roumania for their future amicable relations. He was told that the unreasonable and ridiculous excesses to which the Roumanians had enforced their requisitions, and in particular their crude and unnecessarily harsh methods of carrying out their seizures, had so embittered the Hungarians that it was not believed they would ever be satisfied until they had retaliated in kind.

It was very comforting to note that the Mission was practically unanimous on all points, and where any slight differences existed as to personal opinion such differences were unimportant.

It was most apparent that Sir George, owing to his prolonged stay at Bucharest, had listened to the siren voice of the enchantress Queen, and had fallen under the spell of Roumanian environment. Her Majesty certainly seems to think that she can control any man whom she meets, and it must be admitted that she has considerable foundation for that opinion. I am inclined to think, however, that she realized that it took more than a signed photograph to cause me to wander from the straight and narrow path of military duty. It is also evident that Sir George has been influenced by Bratiano's sophistry, as he advances the same line

2   Szeged, or Szegedin second town in Hungary, with a population of about 119,000.

of argument as does that distinguished Roumanian Prime Minister. I asked Sir George, at the session of the Mission, if the Roumanians had given him the same song that they had given me, to the effect that they had never seized any foodstuffs in Hungary beyond the actual needs of the Roumanian Army in that country, and he replied that they had. I told him then that any such statement was a lie, using the very word here quoted; that I had personally investigated one case where they had shipped away to Roumania 2,800 carloads, mainly foodstuffs from one group of warehouses in Budapest alone, that they were seizing and removing seed grain and the last head of cattle from many of the farms, especially east of the Theiss River, and that I could give him overwhelming proof of only too many concrete cases.

Early this morning, General Gorton came in to see me, very much disgusted. He said that Sir George Clerk would be here probably only until tomorrow; that he had been wined and dined constantly by the Roumanians; that he himself had asked him to dinner tonight and showed me a note he had received from Sir George regretting that he could not accept because of a previous engagement with some Roumanian. We decided then that we would either get Sir George in deeper, or get him out; so I wrote a formal invitation, inviting him to dine with me tonight, and he promptly accepted.

He promised to be with Colonel Loree from 11 to 1 o'clock, but did not show up until 12, and stayed only for about an hour. At this session, he told Colonel Loree that he had been informed that the Roumanians had shipped back foodstuff to Hungary and were feeding the Hungarians, and was told that nothing of the kind had ever happened. He attempted to justify the seizure of all of the rolling stock, along the same lines as that adopted by the Roumanians, stating that they were taking back only an equivalent of what had been taken from them during the German occupation. He advanced the same old rotten argument that the Roumanian Army in its victorious march upon an enemy's capital had done no more than was customary in time of war, entirely ignoring the fact that there would be no victorious Roumanian Army had not the Entente first smashed the Germanic Powers, and that even then the Roumanians would never have gotten into Hungary had they not unfortunately had the opportunity to sneak in at the time when Hungary and its army were disrupted temporarily by the overthrow of the Bolshevist government.

Yesterday I had invited the family of Count Szirmay to go to the opera and sit in my box, but they had to come so far from the country and were delayed so long en route by the Roumanians, that they did not arrive until the opera was practically finished, and could not, therefore, go to the Opera House at all. As a result, Colonel Loree and I rattled around in the Royal box all alone until the last fifteen minutes, during which we were joined by Colonel Yates. The party eventually arrived and we had them to dinner.

This morning a ceremony took place in my office, during which we decorated a member of the British Mission, Lieutenant Molesworth, with the emblem of the Ancient, Honorable and Puissant Order of the P. E. Club of America.

October 3, 1919.

Last night we entertained at dinner Admiral Troubridge, General Gorton, Sir George Clerk, Mr. Rattigan, the British Chargé d'Affaires at Bucharest, and Admiral Troubridge's son, and Aide. Sir George Clerk looked a little bit shamefaced, but I think was rather glad to have gotten out of the embarrassment that would naturally have resulted from too much appearing in public with the Roumanians. He left early because Mr. Rattigan was obliged, he said, to catch an early train back to Bucharest. He asked if he could resume his conference with Colonel Loree at 9.30 this morning, and was told certainly. But up to 11.30 he had not shown up.

The Roumanians kept on with their lying statements, that all requisitions had ceased on September the sixteenth, but nevertheless they are continuing daily.

Last night I received a telegram from Mr. Polk, stating that he had just had an interview with the Roumanian delegate, M. Misu, and with the Roumanian Colonel Antonescu. The latter had been in Paris for a week conferring with the French, but had just been able to get over to the American Commission. Mr. Polk stated that Antonescu denied all stories of outrages and looting, and was particularly indignant over stories that they had taken hospital supplies. He also gave as the reason for failure to arm 10,000 police, the Fact that the Allies had charge of the Mackensen depôt of supplies and that the police should be armed from the same. Mr. Polk added that Roumania is apparently beginning to feel the pressure of the blockade of the Black Sea, because she could not get in the stores that she had purchased from the French and the Americans, and he added that this blockade would not be raised until the situation was improved. Mr. Polk suggested that a recommendation be sent the Supreme Council, to form a board representing the Inter-Allied Military Mission, with one Roumanian officer, for the purpose of investigating looting and seizures. I received another telegram from him earlier in the evening which was marked "double priority-urgent," wishing to know when Sir George Clerk would be back in Paris. I wired in reply to the latter that Sir George was due to arrive in Paris on Tuesday, and to the main telegram I sent the following answer:

Replying to your No.63, there is only too much proof of Roumanian looting. I myself saw them taking hospital supplies and reported it at the time. They did not loot children's hospitals, but did cut off the usual supply of milk which was equally bad. Concerning Mackensen supplies, please see my telegrams No. sixty-three, sixty-five, sixty-six, and sixty- eight. This depot contained no firearms whatever and only about two thousand carloads of munitions. Roumanian tactics in regard to reorganizing the Hungarian police and army have been constantly obstructive. They seem determined to force Hungary into a separate treaty and, if obliged to evacuate, to leave her ripe for anarchy and Bolshevism so that their return will be requested. Since August 16th there has been a committee of the Mission on claims and complaints of which Colonel Loree is chairman. The Roumanian commander was requested to send a liaison officer, who refused to assist in any investigations, and the Roumanian commander insisted that all claims of any importance should be sent to him for final decision. Under the circumstances, we have gone on investigating and accumulating evidence, which is in as good a shape as possible with facilities at our disposal. Sir George Clerk has been given many data.

In my opinion, the most crying need is to force the Roumanians to carry out the instructions of the Supreme Council as given to them by the Inter-Allied Military Mission. Unless they evacuate Hungary as rapidly as we may require, and in the meantime assist, instead of obstructing, our police and army organization, matters will go from bad to worse. If for the first time they keep a promise and begin the evacuation of Transdanubia tomorrow, the fourth, we shall have made our first step forward.

I also sent a code telegram giving my opinion of Sir George Clerk, which was as follows:

Sir George Clerk spent about an hour with the Mission Wednesday afternoon. He repeated in substance his interview with the Roumanian Prime Minister which was practically the same as my own as to grievances, etc., but being with a diplomat also included demands for more territory on both sides of he Maros River for strategic defense of railroad. He said the Roumanians told him that no food requisitions had been made except for actual use of troops in Hungary. I told him this was untrue and I could give him absolute proof. The Mission was practically unanimous on all points discussed. My personal opinion is that Clerk is under the spell of Roumanian environment and a cooing dove would make a better ultimatum bearer. The Queen thinks she can handle any man she meets and is usually right. Clerk arrived Wednesday morning and, except or an hour with the Mission, he spent the balance of the day conferring with, and being banqueted by, Roumanians. In the evening he went to the opera with Diamandi; declined an invitation tonight to dine with Gorton because of an engagement with a Roumanian. So I asked him and the entire British Mission, and he had to accept. He asked the Mission about the prospects for future amicable relations between Hungary and Roumania, and was told that it was not believed possible, as Roumanian requisition methods and excess had created permanent retaliation sentiment. The Roumanians are devoting themselves almost exclusively to the British. For three consecutive days they have been giving them banquets, but the Admiral and General accepted only one invitation.

October 4, 1919.

Although Sir George Clerk had two appointments with Colonel Loree yesterday, one at 9.30 in the morning and the other at 5 o'clock in the afternoon, he showed up at neither. During the forenoon, he had one of our stenographers, and in the afternoon gave General Gorton a copy of his notes, among which the following appears:

"Cases brought to the notice of the Roumanian authorities such as M. Diamandi, the High Commissioner, or General Mardarescu, Commander in Chief, are indeed dealt with at once by them and an order is immediately issued for investigation, reparation, and if necessary, punishment."

He then adds, further on:

"The Roumanian government, and those responsible for the conduct of its affairs, do realize that Hungary, stripped bare of all necessaries of life, is entirely contrary to the interests of Roumania, and I believe them sincere in their intention to take only what they consider to be their lawful property, stolen from them, and to limit their requisitions to the quantities which they have laid down."

I do not doubt but that Minister Diamandi, General Mardarescu, and others of that ilk, told Sir George just what he set down, and that he believed them. Their statements, however, are untrue. To give a concrete instance: at one of the meetings of the Inter-Allied Military Mission, which was attended by both Minister Diamandi and General Mardarescu, I called their attention to the fact that the Roumanians were seizing and removing articles like Gobelin tapestries, delicate scientific instruments, animals from stock farms, machinery installed in series in large factories, and in general that they were seizing property that had never been taken from them, that was not needed by them at the time, nor were requisitions being made in a proper manner. General Mardarescu stated three times in reply that he had seized only what was necessary for troops in the field. Despite the fact that their attention on this occasion was called to definite cases, no action was taken by either of them in the way of investigation, reparation, or punishment. In particular, I read over the complete list of articles that had been removed rom the Hungarian Directory of Posts, Telegraphs and Telephones, and asked General Mardarescu if he, is a soldier, could tell me that most of the articles seized were needed by his troops in the field. As he could give no direct reply, he invariably circumlocuted and switched to other subjects in which art both he and Diamandi are past masters.

The Roumanians have been most careful to require publication in the Hungarian press of the various banquets, entertainments, etc., given by them to Sir George Clerk, with the evident intention, of course, of impressing the Hungarians with the fact that they stood in with the Supreme Council.

Yesterday afternoon, at General Gorton's suggestion, Sir George saw Prime Minister Friedrich, and I understand that the latter made a most strong presentation of his case, showing how the Roumanians had descend even to petty personal persecution in order to force him to accept their terms.

In my opinion, the Roumanians should be forced by all means to make immediate restitution to the Hungarians of such portion of the seized rolling stock as may be required by the Inter-Allied Military Mission. This would enable the Hungarians, upon Roumanian evacuation, to move their supplies, coal, etc., and would be a great step forward. In addition, it would restore some of the prestige lost by the four great Powers, if it could be shown that the Roumanians had finally been forced to do something. They should also be required to restore draft animals and cattle foodstuffs, certain kinds of machinery, and such other articles as might seem necessary, but the question of rolling stock should be at once insisted upon and forced.

Last night we had a box party in the Royal box at the opera, entertaining Count Szirmay's family, and afterwards we had them at dinner.

October 5, 1919.

This morning reports were received from Colonel Horowitz, U.S. A., and from Major Foster of the British Army, to the effect that the first stage of the evacuation of western Hungary by the Roumanians had been successfully carried through without friction or difficulty worth noting.

Last night Colonel Loree and I attended a dinner as the guests of Mr. Butler of the British Mission, the other guests being Admiral Troubridge, General Gorton, Sir George Clerk, and Sir William Goode. The latter is the representative of the

Supreme Council on the Inter-Allied Food Commission. All of us, during the course of the evening, hammered away at Sir George Clerk, and apparently changed his opinions in regard to his friends, the Roumanians.

Today being Sunday, there was, of course, no meeting, but this afforded opportunity for catching up with back work in the office.

October 6, 1919.

Last night, just after we had risen from one of the excellent meals with which Captain Gore is nourishing us, Colonel Horowitz reported and stated that the Roumanians were at the National Museum with a whole flock of trucks, and proposed to take away many of the works of art.

At a meeting of the Military Mission on October 1, 1919, it was decided that although the Roumanians did claim many articles in the National Museum as belonging to them on account of their present owner-ship of Transylvania, they should have none of these articles until passed upon by our committee, of which Captain Shafroth, U. S. A., is chairman. On the same date the Roumanian Commander in Chief was notified of our decision.

Accompanied by Colonel Loree and one American soldier, I followed Colonel Horowitz back to the Museum, which we found under a strong Roumanian guard. One man tried to stop us, but it did not do him much good, and we went into the building and eventually routed out the Director. It appears that about 6 o'clock in the afternoon, General Serbescu, accompanied by an entourage of officers and civilians, showed up at the Museum convoying fourteen trucks and a detachment of soldiers. He stated that he was authorized by General Mardarescu and High Commissioner Diamandi to take over the objects from Transylvania, and demanded the keys. The Director informed him that the Inter-Allied Military Mission had taken over the Museum and he would not give up the keys. General Serbescu then told him that they would return in the morning and that, if the keys were not produced, they would take the objects by force.

I, therefore, had the Director deliver the key to the storeroom to me and left a paper worded as follows:

"To whom it may concern - As the Inter-Allied Mission is in charge of all the objects in the Hungarian National Museum at Budapest, the key has been taken charge of by the President of the Day, General Bandholtz, the American representative."

This was followed by my signature. I then had Colonel Loree place seals on each of the doors, on which was written:

"This door sealed by Order Inter Allied Military Mission.

H. H. Bandholtz, Pres. of the day.

5 October 1919."

As the Roumanians and all Europeans are fond of rubber-stamp display, and as we had nothing else, we used an American mail-censor stamp, with which we marked each of the seals.

At this morning's session of the Mission, General Mombelli was unfortunately away, having gone to Vienna to meet his wife, but I related to my colleagues my experience of last night and asked whether or not the Mission approved the same, knowing in advance that General Gorton was with me. As there was some little delay before a reply was made, I said that in case the Mission did not care to do so, I personally would take all the responsibility and state that what I had done was done as American representative. At this, General Graziani very gallantly and promptly spoke up and said: "No, I am with my colleague," and that settled it.

I then telegraphed the American Commission in Paris a statement of what had occurred, and wound up with the sentence: "In the meantime the seals are on the doors, and we await developments."

We had another letter today from the Serbian representative, complaining of his treatment by his allies, the Roumanians, and he was told that he should lay his complaint directly before the Roumanians and if they did not act upon it, then he should bring it to us and we would try to force the issue.

Complaints were also received of abuses of Hungarian prisoners by the Roumanians, so it was decided to have our Army Organization Committee investigate and report on such abuses.

A letter was received from the Hungarian Ministry, stating that they had applied to the Roumanians for authority to reopen the mails, to which they had received the reply from General Mardarescu that he had no objection, provided the Hungarians would pay for forty Roumanian censors. This was so ridiculous that it was decided to send a copy of the letter to the Supreme Council.

As the Roumanians are deluging us with statements that they have stopped all requisitions, we are bringing to their attention the more important reported cases, asking them to stop immediately and to make restitution. This morning we had a concrete case of about three million kronen worth of Tokay wine.

Just before adjournment, a letter was received from the Roumanians dated the fourth, in which they acknowledged receipt of the Mission's letter of the first, relative to the objects from Transylvania in the National Museum, and stating that these objects would be seized and that the signers, Mardarescu and Diamandi, would take the responsibility for this action. As it happens, they will now have to take the responsibility for breaking the Mission's seals before they get the objects.

In a burst of generosity, the Roumanians said that they would give one thousand rifles to the police immediately, and then they sent over a colonel to state that there were twelve to fourteen different kinds of makes in the one thousand rifles, that practically none of them were serviceable, and that it would be necessary to return them to Szeged and get others. Of course this will continue indefinitely, and we shall wind up, as usual with the Roumanians, by getting nothing.

Concerning the objects in the Museum, a letter has also been received from the Archbishop of Esztergom and Prince Primus of Hungary stating that these objects were by will placed in his charge on the condition that they form an integral part of a Christian Museum at Esztergom or at Budapest, and protesting against any-one whomsoever interfering with the right of the Roman Catholic Church in this collection.

October 7, 1919.

Colonel Yates returned from Bucharest yesterday afternoon, and Lieutenant Hamilton arrived from Paris late at night, and this morning Lieutenant-Colonel Moore reported for duty with me. He had formerly been in charge of the Courier Service at Paris, so he is well acquainted with the system of railroads through this section of the country, and is a West Pointer of the class of 1903. He came on the same train with Colonel Causey of the Food Commission, who is in Budapest for the day.

Having been invited by General Mosoiu, the Roumanian Commander in Budapest, with all of my staff, to lunch with him at the Hotel Hungaria at noon, seven of us went over and had an American-Roumanian love feast. At the entrance to the Hotel, they had an honor guard drawn up with a band which sounded off with what was supposed to be the "Star Spangled Banner." After we had entered the large dining room, the band came and repeated what was again supposed to be the "Star Spangled Banner," but which was different from the first offense. When we finally left, they sounded off again with the third variety, and also with the Roumanian national anthem.

We opened up the ball with a hot drink, two glasses of which will lay out a full-grown man for about a week. Needless to say, none of us took very much. We then sat down to the usual banquet procedure, which was marked more by sumptuousness than by delicacy. As guest of honor, I sat facing General Mosoiu, who beamed upon me throughout the whole meal with his three-hundred-and-ten-pound smile. As previously stated, however, he is a pretty good old fellow and far above the ordinary Roumanian general, of which there were six specimens present. Colonel Loree sat next to General Serbescu, who, poor devil, is the Director in Chief of Roumanian requisitions, seizures, and thefts. He is really not a bad fellow himself, but has to be fourteen kinds of skunk in the execution of his office. He told Colonel Loree that I had put him between the devil and the deep sea. His orders were to seize the articles in the Museum; that he could not seize them without breaking my seals, and he did not dare to break the seals; so all he could see was disaster approaching in large quantities.

General Mosoiu toasted "Les Etats-Unis," which was responded to with raucous Roumanian shouts. In return, I gave them "The Allies and a lasting friendship," thereby avoiding a direct allusion to any greater Roumania.

On our return from the hotel, when we were crossing the Danube Bridge, we saw a crowd congregated, and proceeded to investigate. It seemed that a Hungarian policeman had tapped a Roumanian soldier in a crowded street car, to warn him that he was in danger. The Roumanian did not understand and promptly pulled a revolver on the policeman, who then reached for his bayonet to defend himself. Seeing this, a Roumanian censor, dressed in civilian clothes, had called up some Roumanian soldiers who promptly responded, and Hell was about to pop. I took the name of the Hungarian policeman, and sent the Roumanian and the Roumanian soldier who had caused the difficulty, in charge of Colonel Loree and Lieutenant Hamilton, to Roumanian Headquarters, where they were turned over, and the situation was explained by Colonel Loree.

October 8, 1919.[3]

Last night we had Lieutenant- Colonel Causey, Lieutenant-Colonel Moore, and Captain Smythe to dinner. Afterwards Colonel Causey returned to Vienna by special train.

At this morning's session, General Graziani presided, and we had no matters of great moment to take up.

Lieutenant-Colonel Berthon, of the Army Organization Committee, reported that some Hungarian officers, during the evacuation of Transdanubia had indulged in considerable talk which was hardly proper under the circumstances, so we decided to communicate with the Hungarian War Department to that effect.

Reports of continuation of Roumanian pillaging between the Danube and the Theiss Rivers were received, and it seems that this pillaging is increasing in intensity, rather than diminishing.

There was received a very peculiar and interesting letter from General Mardarescu, stating that the Roumanians, when entering Budapest, had found several monitors and Vedette boats in the river here; that this matter had been brought to the attention of Admiral Troubridge, who had replied that these boats were the property of the Allies and were awaiting their disposition. The Roumanians, therefore, begged the Inter-Allied Military Mission to intercede in their behalf and see that there were turned over to them, without further delay, two monitors and two Vedette boats. As the matter was one which should be handled entirely by the Danube River Commission and not by our Mission, it was decided to notify the Roumanians accordingly and to transmit their paper to Admiral Troubridge. Just to get a rise out of General Graziani, I suggested that we write to the Roumanians acknowledging receipt of their communication, stating that up to date they had not complied with any of the requests made by this Mission to cease requisitions or anything else, that when they returned to Hungary the property which they had taken and which we had requested, we could consider the matter. In the meantime the boats were in the Danube and as easily accessible to seizure as was all the other property they had taken, the only difference being, of course, that the boats were under British guard. Poor General

3 Date of the Memorandum from Rattigan, British Charge d'Affaires to Roumania to British Foreign Minister Earl Curzon. See text at the end of this Diary together with Bandholtz's comments.

Graziani nearly had a fit of apoplexy when I suggested this. He gave a most audible sigh of relief when I added that probably it might be inadvisable to send such a communication as yet.

Just as we were leaving for lunch, we got word that the Roumanians were down at one of the banks and proposed to seize some funds which, they claimed, had belonged to the Bolshevist government. We accordingly hotfooted over there, but found nobody. Later in the afternoon, we got word that the Roumanians had been to the bank and had taken the funds away, and then we discovered that we had been directed to the wrong bank. Accordingly Colonel Loree and Major Foster of the British Service chased down and hoped that they would be in time to intercept the Roumanian retreat, but they had made a get-away with funds amounting to two million kronen white money, which is four hundred thousand kronen blue money or, reduced to United States currency, sixty thousand dollars. General Gorton and I also went over and found that all the Roumanian high officials were off on a hunting expedition. We therefore sent Colonel Loree and Major Foster over to Roumanian G. H. Q., where they spent the afternoon and left that bunch in fear and trembling.

To show the change of heart on the part of the Roumanians, they volunteered this afternoon to give us at once 10,000 rifles for the police, which proves that they lied in the beginning in saying that the rifles had to be imported from Roumania. The whole thing seems to be turning on the placing of the seals on the Museum, which seals, by the way, are still intact.

October 9, 1919.

Yesterday afternoon I received an inquiry from the American Commission as to the whereabouts of General Jadwin[4], and after I had dictated a telegram saying that he had not been seen or even heard from, word came to me that he had just arrived bringing me two cards, so I spent the evening with him, at his home in the Hotel Ritz, going over common experiences.

4   General Edgar Jadwin of the Engineering Corps of the U.S. Army
      served as director of the light railways and roads for the A. E. F. in
      France, then as director of construction and forestry. In 1919 he was a
      member of the American Mission to Poland, and observer in the
      Ukraine. He died on March 2, 1931.

As indicated in the journal of a previous day, the Roumanians seem to be determined to get revenue from every possible source, including the liberation of Bolshevist prisoners. Last night, some time after midnight, a Hungarian liaison officer brought word that a large number of Roumanian soldiers were at the main prison demanding the release of a Bolshevist prisoner. My secretary, Mr. Fenselau, accompanied by field clerk St. Jacques, was sent over to the prison and found the facts to be as stated. In fact, the Roumanians were about leaving with their prisoner. My men insisted on bringing the matter up directly to the Roumanian high officials, because the officer in charge of the detachment said that they were acting under verbal orders from Colonel Vasilescu. As Colonel Vasilescu is about the squarest Roumanian in the whole service, this looked very fishy, and the fishiness was demonstrated later on when at 2.30 o'clock in the morning neither Colonel Vasilescu nor his wife could be found in the hotel. Our two men hung on to the proposition like a pup to a root, and eventually got word that General Panaitescu, he Chief of Staff, had authorized the return of the prisoner to the jail. I am sending word to Roumanian Headquarters, by Colonel Loree, that if there is any more of this I will personally put an American guard on the prison and allow no Roumanians to enter.

October 10, 1919

Last night I had General Jadwin to dinner at our quarters and invited General Gorton over to meet him.

This morning at 7.45, we all started in automobiles for Vienna. Jadwin and I rode in a limousine and Captain Gore with Jadwin's extra chauffeurs, etc., in a touring car.

When we struck the Hungarian guard station at Gyôr, they did not know whether or not to let us through. They wanted me to go back and see an officer. I told them to bring the officer to see me. Finally after some telephoning, they let us through. At the succeeding Hungarian posts we had no trouble. Subsequently upon arriving in Vienna, I telegraphed Colonel Loree about our difficulty, knowing that he would take it up immediately with the Hungarian War Office so that there would be no delay on our return trip.

When we arrived at Bruck, we ran across the first Austrian guard whom we could not well understand, and as a result they put a soldier on our running board and took us up to some office where they again wanted us to go up and see an officer, and I again refused. We did let one of the chauffeurs go up and he eventually came back with his passport viséd, which they said would be sufficient.

The other car had not caught up with us at Bruck, nor did it again join us because the timing chain was out of gear, and it had to remain there until we afterwards sent the limousine back from Vienna to tow it in. General Jadwin and I arrived at the Hotel Bristol in Vienna at about 3 o'clock, where I stayed as the guest of Lieutenant-Colonel Causey, who is on duty with the American Relief Association.

The American consul, Mr. Halstead, called upon me shortly after arrival, and in the evening we dined at the Bristol as Colonel Causey's guests, but we did not try to go out.

October 11, 1919.

Colonel Raymond Sheldon, for whom I had applied, arrived at Vienna last night, and reported to me this morning. Jadwin and I did a little shopping in the morning, got some French money, changed it into Austrian kronen, and then separated. I spent the rest of the day prowling around Vienna alone.

The Austrian currency has been steadily depreciating, until now it takes ten kronen to make one franc, French money, and it takes about nine francs, French money, to make one dollar of American money. That makes ninety kronen to the dollar. During the day, I received in change some two-heller pieces, which made each piece worth less than one-fortieth of a cent, as it takes one hundred heller to make a krone.

I gave a luncheon party at the Bristol to General Jadwin, Colonel Sheldon, Colonel C. B. Smith, Lieutenant-Colonel Causey, and Captain Gore. Owing to he depreciated currency, a very fine lunch for six cost less than the charge in Paris for an ordinary lunch for one. Colonel Sheldon stated that he was paying thirty-two kronen a day for a fine room with bath. This reduced to United States currency, would be about thirty-five cents.

In the evening we were all guests of Lieutenant-Colonel Causey at dinner at some restaurant near one of the palaces.

October 12, 1919.

I left Vienna this morning about 3.30, the delay being caused by the impossibility of getting gasoline early on Sunday morning. Colonel Sheldon, Captain Gore and I went in the limousine. and on the touring car we loaded all our purchases and supplies, and Colonel Sheldon's baggage.

When we arrived at Bruck, we were again held up by the Austrian outpost. A soldier got on the running board, took us up to the same building, and wanted me to go up and see the officer. I sent word that if he wanted to see me, he could come down. He then sent word that it would not be necessary for me to come up, but only to send my papers. I again told him that if he wanted my papers, he could come down and, as he was rather slow in coming and I understood he objected to the same, we pulled out, made them raise their gates, and proceeded on our way without further difficulty, as the Hungarians did not attempt to stop us.

We arrived at the house in Budapest about 3:0'clock in the afternoon, had lunch, and I put in the rest of the afternoon working at my office in catching up with back work.

In the evening, I went to dinner at General Gorton's, the other guest being the Roumanian General Mosoiu.

October 13, 1919.

At this morning's session of the Mission, at which I presided, there was very much doing.

We started in by having a letter from the British Food Commissioner, Mr. Domaille, complaining that the Roumanians had reduced the food reserve in Budapest to one-third of what it was in September; and another letter from the Hungarian Minister, to the effect that the Roumanian Commander in Budapest would not allow the Food Commissioner to supply the suburbs, containing an estimated population of over 600,000..

There was a complaint from the Hungarian government stating that the Czecho-Slovaks were occupying territory on this side of the Danube opposite the town of Pozsony. As there were no data on hand to determine whether or not this territory belonged to the Czecho-Slovaks, a letter was sent to the Supreme Council asking for a decision.

A complaint was received from the Hungarians that the Roumanians, in the evacuation of Transdanubia, had liberated many Bolshevist prisoners. As this is particularly in line with what they have been doing in the city of Budapest, a letter was sent to the Roumanian Commander in Chief calling his attention to the impropriety of any such conduct and advising him to discontinue it in the future.

A red-hot letter was received from Captain Brunier, the Swiss representative of the International Red Cross, containing conclusions which are embodied in the telegram to the Supreme Council, copied further down. It as decided to send Colonel Sheldon, U. S. A., who had been my second assistant in charge of our prisoners of war in France, accompanied by an Italian doctor, with Captain Brinier to investigate all of the Roumanian prisoner-of-war camps.

A long letter was received from the Hungarian Minister of War, explaining that the conditions in Hungary were so entirely different from those in Austria that the Austrian treaty should not form a basis for a future Hungarian treaty, especially as regards a Hungarian army.

Several other complaints were received and matters worked up to such a climax that I stated to the Mission that, in my opinion, the time had arrived when we should lay the case plainly before the Supreme Council and asked that they either force the Roumanians to evacuate immediately, making much restitution of seized property, or that they relieve the Inter-Allied Military Mission. With very little discussion, it was decided to draw up and send such a telegram, which I did, which reads as follows:

"Cold weather is setting in and a day's delay now more serious than would have been a week's delay two months ago. Inter-Allied Military Mission therefore desires to present the Supreme Council following statements of fact concerning conduct of Roumanians with request for prompt action. They have so thoroughly cleaned out country of rolling stock that there is not enough for transportation of local food and fuel requirements. Their administration has reduced food reserve in Budapest to one-third of what it was in September. According to report of Hungarian Food Minister, they have by unnecessary and cruel restrictions prevented food from going out of Budapest to neighboring suburbs, population of which estimated to be six hundred thousand. It is reported that during evacuation of Transdanubia, they released Bolshevists who had been detained, and in the city of Budapest they have repeatedly, by force and without, written orders taking Bolshevist prisoners out of jails. At Szolnok, where a Committee of this Mission was obtaining information of Roumanian exportation, they have arrested several of the Hungarian railway men who were aiding in our efforts. They have prevented university students from a continuation of their courses. On September 26 their Commander in Chief sent a letter to Mission stating that to cover needs of feeding Hungary, the zone between Danube and Theiss Rivers had been placed at disposition of Hungarian government; that no requisitions would take place in that zone except those necessary for actual feeding of troops; that especially for city of Budapest above zone would be extended to east of Theiss to boundary line fixed by said commander, despite which on October fifth the Roumanian Colonel Rujinschi seized thirty aeroplane motors at Budapest which can hardly be classified as food. On October tenth in Budapest from the firm of Schmitt and Társai they seized and removed machinery which put two thousand laborers out of work. A large number of similar cases with proof are on hand. In reply to letter from Mission that it was desired that objects in National Museum be not disturbed until acted upon by committee, they sent reply that they intended to take those objects and that the signers of letters, Mardarescu and Diamandi, assumed responsibility for such action, this being in effect an insult to nations represented on Inter-Allied Military Mission. That they did not take these objects was due to fact that doors were sealed and signed by the President of the Day at the time and they were afraid to go to extreme of breaking seals. Between five and six o'clock this morning they attempted to arrest Prime Minister Friedrich and did arrest two government officials, as result of which President of the Day in person delivered to General Mardarescu a memorandum from Mission, copy of which was telegraphed Supreme Council this date. They kept their Commander in Chief, General Mardarescu, and High Commissioner Diamandi absent in Bucharest a week, during which no representative was present with whom business could be transacted. Although they in August acknowledged the Inter-Allied Military Mission as representing their superior, they have with comparatively negligible exceptions carried out none of the instructions of this Mission and have always insisted on acting as though Roumania were equal or superior to nations represented on Mission. They have sent misleading reports to Paris placing themselves in attitude of saviors of Hungary and have censored the press in Hungary to such an tent that Hungarians could not refute any false statements. On the nineteenth of September their General Mardarescu wrote to the Mission that he had taken all necessary measures to make treatment of prisoners satisfactory, stating that especially from sanitary viewpoint according to report of his surgeon general conditions were very good. On October eleventh, Mission received communication from International Red Cross representative stating that his investigation at Arad resulted in discovery of conditions so opposed to conventions covering treatment of prisoners of war that he felt this Mission should take some action. His conclusions, which are as follows, concur with all reports concerning same except Roumanian reports:

"I find that these prisoners were not captured on the field of battle but many days after the cessation of hostilities; that the lodgings of the prisoners are unsanitary; that the army which captured them takes no care of them whatever, furnishes them neither food, clothing, medicine, covering, nor anything; that from the date of their captivity, the prisoners have had no funds and that the majority cannot purchase anything for even insufficient nourishment; that doctors are treated contrary to Article IX of Geneva Convention of 1906; that all these men are exposed to serious diseases if they are not promptly aided; that the order given to the Red Cross at Arad to take care of the prisoners' needs is entirely illegal and cannot be based upon any law or international convention."

Doctor Munro of the British Food Commission and the Swiss Captain Brinier of the International Red Cross have just returned from visiting the following towns: Hatvan, Gyöngyös, Miskolcz, Sátoralja-Ujhely, Nyiregyháza, Debreczen, Szolnok, Nagyvárad, Békés-Csaba, Arad, Temesvár, Szeged, all in permanent portion of Hungary, but now occupied by Roumanians, and have submitted signed statement from which following is extracted:

"In all towns occupied by Roumanians we found an oppression so great as to make life unbearable. Murder is common, youths and women flogged, imprisoned without trial, arrested without reason, theft of personal property under name of requisition. Condition of affairs prevails difficult for Western European to realize who has not seen and heard the evidence. People are forced to take oath of allegiance to Roumanian King; if they refuse they are persecuted. Experienced Hungarian Directors of Hospitals have been replaced by inexperienced Roumanian doctors. Roumanian military authorities demand petition for every passport, request for coal or food. Petition must be written in Roumanian language, Roumanian lawyer must be employed, and he charges enormous fees. Station master of Brad and the station master of Kétegyháza have been most fearfully flogged. Last Good Friday Roumanians advanced suddenly to Boros-Sebes and two hundred fifty Hungarian soldiers were taken prisoners. These were killed in most barbarous manner; stripped naked and stabbed with bayonets in way to prolong life as long as possible. Roumanians have established custom-house in every village. Delivery permits can only be obtained by payment of ridiculously large sums. Commerce is impossible. People will soon starve. Deliberately and for no military and political reason apparent the hospitals are not allowed transports for coal and wood which they have already paid for. Very life of hospital hangs on coal. Hospitals will have to close down entirely unless relieved immediately. Results will be disastrous. There will be outbreaks of all sorts of contagious epidemic diseases, such as typhus, typhoid, etc."

An American officer and an Italian doctor, if Roumanians permit, will accompany the International Red Cross representative on a thorough investigation of prisoner-of-war camps. In general Roumanian conduct has been such that this Mission has been almost wholly unable to carry out its instructions and there is apparently no prospect of immediate improvement. It is the unanimous opinion of the Mission that unless the Roumanians immediately evacuate Hungary and make at least partial restitution in particular of rolling stock, machinery and much other property seized, there will result in a very short time extreme suffering from lack of food and fuel and a recrudescence of Bolshevism. This Mission is therefore of the unanimous opinion that either the Roumanians should be forced to evacuate Hungary at once and make restitution as above outlined or that this Mission should be relieved.

After acting upon this, Colonel Loree sent me word that the Roumanians had tried to arrest Prime Minister Friedrich[5] and had arrested at least two Hungarian officials. This action on their part rather got under the skin of all of us and we decided to notify them that in our opinion such action could not be tolerated, and I offered to deliver personally to the Roumanian Commander in Chief a memorandum on the subject. To make sure that there would be no misunderstanding on his part, General Graziani wrote this out in his beautiful French, which afforded me much satisfaction to sign, chase down to Roumanian headquarters, and deliver in person to General Mardarescu. I told him we had received information that he had tried that morning to arrest the Prime Minister of the Hungarian government and that I had the honor to hand him the wishes of the Mission in regard to the conduct of the Roumanians toward the Hungarian government. He turned as pale as he could under his hide, and, as his Chief of Staff

5   Compare Mr. Charles Upson Clark's version of Bandholtz' being deceived by Friedrich in regard to the alleged attempt made by the Roumanians to kidnap him. *Greater Roumania*, New York, 1922, p.267. At the same time the statement concerning Mr. Clark should be kept in mind.

was with him, they discussed the matter for a few minutes in machine-gun Roumanian. His Excellency then told me that it was all a horrible mistake, and that they had never intended it. I told him that I was delighted to hear it, but nevertheless I would leave the memorandum. Then I departed. Thereupon I telegraphed in English the text of the memorandum, to the Supreme Council, which was as follows:

The Mission considers it indispensable that the conduct of affairs by the Hungarian cabinet be not interrupted for a single moment. Therefore in the name of the Supreme Council the Mission demands that the Roumanian authorities leave the members of the Hungarian government entirely alone in the conduct of the affairs of their departments until the Supreme Council has made known its decision.

Drawing up the telegram to the Supreme Council and chasing around after Roumanians took up practically all of my time, and we did not sit down to dinner until nine o'clock, having as our only guest a young Hungarian liaison officer, Lieutenant Széchy, who is attached to the American Mission.

October 14, 1919.

As all day yesterday was taken up with cleaning up accumulation of business, and as result of chasing around with the telegram to the Supreme Council, my whole forenoon was taken up dictating and receiving callers, and the afternoon was similarly occupied. In the evening Colonel Loree and I went as guests at the British "B Mess," which is run by the junior officers. It was certainly a relief to sit down to a dinner where you could talk in your own lingo.

October 15, 1919.

At this morning's session, General Gorton presided, and there was first read a letter from General Mardarescu complaining that British and American officers had been guilty of gross discourtesy toward Roumanian soldiers and had called them pigs. It frequently happens that people do not like to be called by their most appropriate title. In any event our friend, Mardarescu, made a Hell of a howl and demanded all sorts of things. It turned out before we got through that the shoe was on the other foot, and that his pigs had been holding up our officers unnecessarily. His attention was called to this, and he was advised to instruct his soldiers to act more as such and less like animals.

I then turned over to the President of the Day a letter which had been delivered at my office yesterday by the Hungarian Minister of War. Enclosed in this letter was another one from the Roumanian Chief of Staff in which he admitted that three

Roumanian patrols had gone across the neutral zone into Hungarian territory and had been beaten up or otherwise injured. It was demanded by the Roumanian Chief of Staff that the Hungarian Minister of War deliver to the Roumanian Chief of Staff one million two hundred and fifty thousand kronen before noon today, and in the event of failure to do so the food supply of the city of Budapest would be cut off. A letter was written and sent to the Roumanian Commander in Chief, calling his attention to the fact that according to the admission of his own Chief of Staff the Roumanian soldiers were entirely out of bounds, that in case of any difficulties between patrols the matter should be referred to the Army Organization Committee of this Mission, which had a Roumanian member, and that the recommendation of this Committee should be received before any action was taken. It was added that it was not believed that he could be serious in his threat to stop the food supply of two million people on account of the conduct of individuals many miles away.

I then informed the Mission that according to Paragraph 3 (b) of our instructions from the Supreme Council, which empower us to define the lines which occupying troops were to hold, we should notify the Roumanians that it was now time for them to evacuate the city of Budapest. With but little discussion, this was approved and I later drafted the following letter:

"In compliance with the requirements contained in Paragraph 3 (b) of the instructions from the Supreme Council, the Inter-Allied Military Mission has directed me to inform Your Excellency that it is desired that the Royal Roumanian Forces proceed with the evacuation of Hungary and without delay withdraw from the city of Budapest to a line at least fifty kilometers distant."

"Your Excellency will recall that at one of the sessions of this Mission which your Excellency attended it was decided that an infantry division and a cavalry division at thirty kilometers distance would be sufficient for moral effect upon the city, could there be any incipient recrudescence of Bolshevism or any other disturbance."

"The Inter-Allied Military Mission requests of Your Excellency prompt information as to the date upon which the quested withdrawal will take place."

We received a protest from the Roumanians against our proceeding to organize an additional Hungarian division near Szeged, and it was decided to reply to them that this was a matter entirely within the jurisdiction of the Mission. Another letter was received from he Roumanians to the effect that they had heard that Admiral Horthy's army was far in excess of what was authorized and already numbered twenty-five thousand men. They demanded that we check this up at once and that they have a liaison officer at Hungarian headquarters and at each division. We decided that this likewise vas a matter entirely within our jurisdiction, and that he

Army Organization Committee, which had a Roumanian member, was fully capable of handling all such matters.

During the day I received a telegram for delivery to General Gorton, informing him that Sir George Clerk had been designated as Envoy of the Supreme Council at Budapest, and with full powers. Just what this means was beyond us; so I telegraphed the American Mission what was meant by "full powers"-did it mean that Sir George Clerk was to relieve the Military Mission, that the Military Mission was to function under him, or that he was to represent the Supreme Council to act upon matters which we could bring to his attention?

In the afternoon Lieutenant-General Sir Tom Bridges called upon me and we had quite a satisfactory chat.

In regard to the attempted arrest of Prime Minister Friedrich, I have ascertained that the whole affair was undoubtedly a fluke. The Crown Prince of Roumania, whose regiment is but a short distance out of Budapest, and who is about of the same moral fiber as most Crown Princes, was in Budapest on the night of the twelfth, as the guest of General Mosoiu, who commands in the city.

During the table talk, he stated, that when he became King of Hungary he proposed to turn loose the Communists and other political prisoners and that he would do it now but for the fact that that scoundrel, Friedrich, was Prime Minister. It is understood by some that this was taken by Mosoiu as a suggestion to have Friedrich arrested. Other reports are that the Crown Prince himself ordered the arrest. In any event the attempt failed, and I am rather satisfied that Mardarescu's surprise was genuine. It is an example, however, how matters are running in Hungary during Roumanian occupation.

October 16, 1919.

It was remarkable that there were today no reports of Roumanian excesses.

I had luncheon at the Hotel Ritz as the guest of General Bridges of the British Army. With him was also British General Greenly, who is the Attaché to Roumania.

During the conversation, General Bridges repeated me the remarks that he made when he was my guest, the effect that General Weygand, Marshal Foch's chief of Staff, had told him that in the Argonne offensive the American army was badly split up, that were from a hundred thousand to a hundred and fifty thousand stragglers who could not find their organizations; that hardly any supplies were brought up, and in general almost a state of demoralization existed.

I told General Bridges that in view of the fact that was Provost Marshal General at the time and in charge the straggling proposition I could tell him definitely and positively that General Weygand's statement was incorrect. I have written General Pershing informing him of these remarks of General Weygand's.

Of late I have been doing a great deal of adopting, and have several families under my wing. In one case have six young countesses by the name of Szirmay, ranging from twenty-four years for the eldest on down, with about two years' intervals. My staff officers rather like this arrangement.

Last night, considerably to my disgust, I was obliged attend the Grand Opera as General Gorton's guest. He was giving a big party with dinner afterwards in the Országos Casino. Nobody knew what the opera was cause it had a Hungarian name, and the words were Hungarian. It was something about a Jewess, who weighed about two hundred and twenty-five pounds, in love with a little tenor who was six inches shorter and weighed about one twenty-five. During the performance a giant of a cardinal wound up, having the Jewess thrown into a caldron of burning oil where she made a big splash and a red glow. The dinner was not bad, and I finally got home before eleven o'clock. Owing to the attitude of the Roumanians about hours, the opera begins at six o'clock and ends at nine, and each performance consists of a long drawn-out tragedy, with occasional rays of sunshine in the way of a ballet.

October 17, 1919.

At this morning's session, General Graziani presided and we had another report of the invasion of Hungarian territory by Roumanian patrols. Judging from a secret service agent's report of the incidents which occurred at the dinner given to the Crown Prince on the night of the twelfth, the Roumanians intend to put over many of this kind of incursions in order to stir up the Hungarians to something more than passive resistance, so that fines can be imposed on the rest of the country.

A most peculiar letter was received from General Mardarescu, announcing that he proposed to return all the telephone instruments and other apparatus removed from the Hungarian Ministry of War, but he added that this would not take place until the Roumanians were about to evacuate.

A letter was received also from General Mardarescu, complaining that a British officer had gone to the town Gödöllô, forced his way into the château there, and had broken the Roumanian seals on some of the doors. An explanation was demanded. The reply was that Major Foster, a member of Colonel Loree's committee, had gone to the château in question; that there were no seals there whatever; that some doors had been unlocked by the Roumanians themselves, but no seals were broken; and that Major Foster expected an apology from the Roumanian officer that had falsely accused him.

We also received a letter from Colonel Yates, stating at the Roumanians had agreed to accept him as the superior of police and gendarmerie. Everything considered there seems to be a little progress.

October 18, 1919.

Last night about 7 o'clock, a long telegram of about fifteen hundred words was received from the American Commission, with the request that I furnish copies to my colleagues. It contained the last ultimatum of the Supreme Council to the Roumanians. In my opinion if a duck should drop into the Mediterranean Sea, it would have about as much effect on the tide in the Gulf of Mexico as would any such ultimatum on our Roumanian friends. It was as sweet as sugar and honey could make it and of the same type as its numerous predecessors. After reading it over, I went with Captain Gore, about 11 o'clock at night, to General Mombelli's quarters, got him out of bed and translated it to him in my beautiful, fluent, forceful, and rotten French. He seemed to grasp the point, however, and we decided that we would call a meeting of the Mission for the morning.

We accordingly met at 9.30, turned loose all of our interpreters upon the telegram, and eventually absorbed its gentle contents. It started by reminding the Roumanians that there were points at issue between them and the Allies. The first was their demand for both banks of the Maros River, which was diplomatically refused. The second was the question of "Minorities," in which the Supreme Council firmly announced its intention to abide by its original decision, and then wound up by saying in effect that, however, if the Roumanians would only please accept the treaty as it was given them, they could immediately discuss the matter and make any changes for which the Roumanians could give good reasons. The third clause was the Hungarian question, which was subdivided into two parts; the first being the question of requisitions, to which the Supreme Council said it knew very well that the great and glorious Roumanian government never had any intention of seizing anything beyond railroad rolling stock and war material, but that nevertheless there was incontestable evidence that some unruly Roumanian subordinates had gone far in advance of the authorized requisitions and had seized much other property for which the Supreme Council was regretfully forced to hold the Roumanian government itself responsible. It was stated that a Reparations Committee or Commission would be appointed, with Roumanian representation, to go into this matter and adjust it. Then was added one of those little acts called "closing the barn door after the horse stolen"-it was suggested that a Commission be sent the Szolnok and Csongrád Bridges to keep track of exportations from Hungary into Roumania.

The second subdivision was the evacuation of Hungary, and the Supreme Council stated that it would be tickled to death to receive assurances from the Roumanian government that they intended promptly to evacuate Hungary.

There was also another point of the Hungarian question, namely, the constitution of a government. Some time ago our Mission had telegraphed to the Supreme Council recommending that either the Friedrich government be recognized or that specific instructions be given as to what kind of government would be recognized. The reply was another beautiful example of glittering generalities. It was repeated that it was not ought that the Friedrich government was a correct presentation of all Hungarian parties, and that Minister Friedrich should have a member in his cabinet from each party, and that in case he could not do so, the Entente could not make a treaty of peace with his cabinet. In view of the fact that there are at present eighteen different political parties in Hungary, it is apparent that long range theory does not always work.

Later in the morning, the American consul in Vienna, Mr. Halstead, called me up by telephone and gave me a translation from one of the Vienna papers, which was to the effect that the Supreme Council in Paris had received a telegram from the Inter-Allied Military Mission in Budapest in which it was declared that the Roumanians must be forced to leave Hungary; that the Supreme Council agreed with this; that instructions to such effect would immediately be sent forward, and that Sir George Clerk had left on the evening of the sixteenth from Paris for Budapest to hand over such instructions to the Roumanians.

During the session of the Mission, General Gorton stated that he had seen Minister Friedrich at lunch at Admiral Troubridge's, and that the Prime Minister was very much concerned for his personal safety. The General added then that he had seen me and I had agreed to send an American soldier over to stay at Minister Friedrich's house until matters quieted down.

This evening at about 7 o'clock, as I was about to leave the office to dress for dinner, several Hungarian functionaries, wild-eyed and disheveled, rushed into my office to say that the Roumanians, having heard that Sir George Clerk was coming, had decided to arrest Friedrich, and were on their way to make the arrest. I grabbed my riding crop; took the lot in tow, picked up my aide, Lieutenant Hamilton, and one military policeman, and went myself over to the government building, where I personally mounted guard, while Lieutenant Hamilton went and got a corporal and three men. These I posted and left with the idea of having British and American guards alternate in the future. The Roumanian company evidently had heard of this and they stopped in the barracks about three or four blocks away.

This evening Colonel Loree, Captain Gore and myself were invited to dinner by Admiral Troubridge to Sir Maurice de Bunsen[6] and Lady de Bunsen.

October 19, 1919.

This morning, on the way over to my office, I stopped to look over our guard at the government building, and then started for the Palace, and plumb into a Roumanian patrol of about eight. Of course, they understood no English and I no Roumanian, but they evidently understood the sign language of the riding crop and departed from the Palace precincts, escorted by Colonel Loree.

This noon I was obliged to attend a small luncheon party given by General Gorton to Lady Cunningham the Countess Orssich. It was a devil of a nuisance because our courier leaves tomorrow morning and I wanted to finish my memoranda for the American Commission. Anyway I quit early and got back and busy at work.

In the afternoon General Soós came in to see me, and that he understood that the Roumanians were going to evacuate the city of Buda tonight. I told him I though he was mistaken and that only the division which was being relieved by another division, would leave, but in case there was any general evacuation I would let him know, and warned him in any event to be prepared for contingencies.

6   English Ambassador at Vienna, 1913-14. He retired from the diplo-
    matic service in 1919.

This evening we entertained at dinner Mr. Haan, proprietor of the Hotel St. Regis of New York City, his wife and two daughters, one of whom is married to a Hungarian general. Mr. Haan, although now an American citizen, is of Hungarian birth and came with a letter of introduction from Assistant Secretary of State Polk, and also from Lieutenant Littwitz, who as enlisted man was so long my chauffeur with the Twenty-seventh Division. Mr. Haan is bringing over funds to relieve distress in Hungary, but does not wish to appear in the limelight.

October 20, 1919.

The Mission met this morning as usual at 9.30, and it was my turn as President of the Day.

There was read the telegram from the Supreme Council to the effect that Sir George Clerk[7] was coming here purely in a political capacity, that his coming had nothing whatever to do with the duties of the Military Mission, in whom the Supreme Council had the most beautiful and sublime confidence, all of which caused my Latin colleagues a sigh of satisfaction.

General Mombelli then read four letters which had been received from our slippery friend Mardarescu, and which in their order were about as follows:

The astute Roumanian stated that in imposing the fine upon the Hungarian government for the action of the Hungarian National Army towards Roumanian patrols, he was doing only what he considered right and was sure that the Mission would agree to the justice of his demands. A letter was sent him ignoring all of his arguments, but informing him that all matters affecting the conduct of Hungarian and Roumanian patrols, or larger bodies, must be investigated and settled by the Army Organization Committee, which had been appointed by this Mission and which had a Roumanian among its members.

The second letter was a sort of thanks for an apology which had not been given, and covered some unfounded accusations against Major Foster of the British Army.

The third letter was a request that the Roumanians be given free access to the Museums for the purpose of selecting documents and other articles that had been removed from Roumania during the German occupation. He was informed that his delegates could have access to the Museums only when accompanied by Captain Shafroth of the American Army, who was the committee designated for this purpose by the Mission.

The fourth letter was rather curt and to the point. His Roumanian Excellency acknowledged receipt of the Mission's instructions to beat it out of Budapest, and in polite but firm terms told the Mission to go to Hell.

What he said was that the Roumanian Command reserved to itself entire liberty of action in regard to operations, and that it was acting in strict accord with orders from Roumanian General Headquarters. A letter was sent to him in reply, to the effect that the Mission in its original letter had acted in strict accord with its instructions from the Supreme Council, which required it to determine the placements of the Roumanian troops necessary to maintain order on Hungarian soil; that the Mission had been previously recognized by both him and Minister Diamandi, and that the present action could be interpreted only as a decision on the part of the Roumanian General Headquarters to recognize no longer the

7   Sir George Russel Clerk was an English expert on Balkan affairs. In 1913-14 he had been Director of the Oriental Department of the English Foreign Office. "The French government having prudently refused to furnish an envoy" (according to E. J. Dillon's *Inside Story of the Peace Conference*, New York, 1920, p. 2~3), Clerk was sent to Budapest as a special diplomatic representative of the Supreme Council, to deliver the ultimatum to the Roumanians and to bring about the formation of a coalition cabinet in which all the responsible parties of Hungary should be represented (Oct. 15 to Dec. 2, 1919). From General Bandholtz' account, it would appear that he was at first decidedly prejudiced against the Hungarians and inclined to favor the Roumanians. Gradually he modified his viewpoint, undoubtedly strongly influenced by the statements of Generals Bandholtz and Gorton.

Lieutenant Colonel Repington writes in his diary, *After the War* (p.167): "I also gather that Sir George Clerk's intervention here was most happy when all was in disarray. Clerk told them they were not divided on any essential matters and that they should have a coalition government and get on at once. They seem to have followed the advice exactly, and it all worked out, though not fully, till the Socialists were put out and the present lot came in."

On the other hand Professor Jászi's opinion concerning Sir George Clerk Is quite different. He says: "Sir George Clerk, the plenipotentiary representative of the Supreme Council in Hungary, appeared at first

Mission as representing the Supreme Council, which would be notified of this action. There was next read a long letter from the Hungarian authorities in regard to the territory which had been turned over to Austria by the Peace Conference[8], and in regard to which they had as yet received no information. It was decided to forward this paper to the Supreme Council for its information.

Mr. Butler, of the British Food Commission, submitted a letter showing that the food conditions in Budapest were from day to day getting more rotten and, in order to give Sir George Clerk something to do on his arrival, it was decided to give him this letter to take up with the Roumanians.

I then read a statement to my colleagues telling them what I knew about Roumanian movements, and to the effect that two divisions and one regiment were

> to be working this direction [i.e., democracy], seeking a solution in which the socialist and progressive movement would have played the leading part. He was kept informed by Socialists, Democrats and Pacifists as to the steps which needed to be taken. I know that various memorials were submitted to him indicating the clear path of peaceful settlement on democratic lines.

> The Entente, he was told, . . . should at once disarm the White officer's army, replacing it for the time by a reliable Entente force of 10,000 to 20,000 men, until the new Hungarian government had succeeded in organizing a reliable army from peasants and workmen" (p. 154). "Sir George Clerk, at first showed a good deal of sympathy with these plans, but not for long; he changed his attitude in a very few days. He had dined and hunted with the nobles until in the end he had completely assimilated the mentality of the Hungarian ancien régime. He was, moreover, he was so disgusted with Hungarian conditions that he wanted to get out of this Balkan chaos as soon as possible, and was only concerned to produce some sort of order, real or apparent. In the end he obtained the assent of the leaders of the armed bands, the chiefs of the coffee-house cliques, and the Socialists who had remained in the country, to a patched-up compromise" (vid., universal suffrage and a plebiscite on the form of the state, p. 155).

> This viewpoint of Professor Jászi is criticized by R. W. Seton-Watson in sympathetic preface to the book of the former writer. He says: "while, however, it is easy to understand the bitterness with which Dr. Jászi writes of the Entente, it is necessary to enter a certain caveat against

already headed eastward in the direction of Szolnok, that most of the Roumanian troops west of the Danube were being transferred to the east bank, and that other changes were taking place in Budapest. It was decided to inform his Excellency Mardarescu that he had promised this Mission to keep it posted in regard to any evacuation movements, and that we considered that he should have notified us of all of the movements referred to.

I next informed the Mission that I had received a verbal message from Colonel Sheldon to the effect that he had been hampered in all his movements as far as possible by the Roumanians; that at Arad, which place he had reached only through the assistance of the French commander at Szeged, he found that a Roumanian general had hastened to the scene and tried to remedy, but unsuccessfully, the situation. The International Red Cross had been forced to give each man a blanket, the windows had been boarded up, and the Hungarian officers had been taken out and forced to bathe in the open in cold water, as a result of which there were two serious cases of sickness, with more in prospect. The Colonel's report went at some length into the way the Roumanians were handling the wives and relatives of officers, who came there in their behalf. The women would show up with a written release of an officer, and the Roumanians would take this paper and tell them to come the next day. They would report the next day and then be told that no such paper had even been received, but were informed that if they would sleep that night with some Roumanian, matters could be straightened out the next day. Some of the women had yielded and others had been violated. A letter was therefore written to General Mardarescu stating that in the opinion of the Mission, the situation at Arad, which had first been described by the Swiss Captain Brinier, was so serious as to require immediate action, and he was informed that the Mission desired him to enter into

what he says of Sir George Clerk's mission to Budapest.... To blame him for not bringing about a settlement of the acute party discords from which Hungary was in suffering, is really not quite reasonable; and it should be remembered that it was he who compelled the government to uphold universal suffrage, as one of those achievements of the October Revolution which it would not justifiable to reverse. He thereby provided for the first time a basis for popular representation in Hungary," Seton-Watson speaks very highly of George Clerk in his magazine, *The New Europe*, Sept. 11, 1919, p. 210. He calls him a well-known Slavophil. was coming her was coming her

8   The so-called Ödenburg (Sopron) district. See footnote earlier.

133

arrangements with the Hungarian government for liberating the officer prisoners of war at once.

October 21, 1919.

Last night General Gorton and I were entertained by Colonel Yates and Lieutenant-Colonel Moore at their mess. The house was beastly cold and they had only one fire going, so that they were obliged to shove the dining-room table into their parlor and when he dinner was through, shove it out again. Everywhere have heard complaints of the cold, and unless something is done very soon to help out the coal supply, the situation will be serious. Colonel Loree has taken up he matter personally, and is pushing it in every way possible, but the Coal Commission makes the ridiculous argument that they cannot do anything unless a peace treaty is effected with Hungary. Of course the cold weather will hang off until that peace treaty is effected. The reasoning of some of our statesmen is about on par with that of a five-year-old child.

Sometime this morning we received a telephonic inquiry from the Roumanians as to whether or not there was a session this date, and they were told that there was not. I took up the question with General Gorton and insisted that in view of the snubs that both Mardarescu and Diamandi had given the Mission, we should decline to receive them, and he agreed with me. We propose at the next session to insist that the Roumanians submit all their business to this Mission in writing and that they be not received until the Mission has been acknowledged by them as representative of the Supreme Council. I shall also probably insist on not receiving Mardarescu and Diamandi until they have apologized to the Mission for the letter they sent in regard to the Museums.

In view of the fact that Colonel Vasilescu has always been gentlemanly and accommodating, Colonel Loree took the Colonel and Mrs. Vasilescu to the opera to-night and we had them at informal dinner afterwards.

October 22, 1919.

Last night Colonel Loree and Captain Gore had Colonel and Mrs. Vasilescu to the opera. I was busy in the office until almost eight o'clock, when I joined them at the opera and we had dinner at our quarters about nine. I got Vasilescu into a corner and in due time he waxed confidential, and I learned that our report in regard to the arrest of Prime Minister Friedrich, which implicated the Crown Prince of Roumania, was correct[9]. Vasilescu has been previously referred to in my journal as being an exceptionally fine man, and he is. He has had a tremendous burden to bear on account of the inefficiency and woodenheadedness of Mardarescu. He told me confidentially that the Roumanians were preparing to leave by the end of he month, and that the trouble was that Mardarescu instead of selecting skilled subordinates and holding them responsible for results, required everything to be brought to him for approval and action.

Yesterday I had a call from Rev. Dr. Morehead[10], representing the United Lutheran Church of America and other Protestant denominations, and I gave him much material concerning Roumanian abuse in Transylvania and elsewhere.

At this morning's session we were informed that the Roumanian Colonel, Dimistrescu, was waiting with a message from his government. I immediately brought up the point that I would decline to receive Mardarescu or Diamandi until they had withdrawn their letter of October 4, stating in effect that they proposed to dis-regard our instructions to them of October 1 in regard to the Museum property, and also they must in writing recognize this Mission as being the authorized representative of the Supreme Council before we could transact business with them. General Graziani said that this would practically amount to a rupture, and I told him rupture be damned; that I had been, he had been, and ill of us had been, snubbed time and time again by the Roumanians and I did not propose to allow my government to be subjected to any such additional humiliation. I said, however, that I was perfectly willing to find out what Dimistrescu had to say, but if it were a case of receiving Mardarescu and Diamandi, they would have to come to time before I would have anything to do with them. Dimistrescu was admitted, and he simply made a wooden-faced explanation of recent Roumanian movements to which I had called attention when President of the Day.

There was also received a letter from the Roumanians, explaining that the officer who went up to Friedrich had not the slightest intention of arresting Friedrich, or

9   See diary October 15.

10 Dr. John A. Morehead, of the American National Lutheran Council, in charge of relief work for the Lutheran Church of Europe after the world war. In a conversation with the F.-C. Krüger spoke most highly of the work done by General Bandholtz in Hungary.

anything of the kind. It was such a miserable, rotten explanation that even old Graziani looked nauseated and condemned it in his spicy French.

We also decided to notify the Serbians that, in compliance with our instructions from the Supreme Council, we wanted them to beat it out of the Baranya district, and in particular out of the city of Pécs.

A letter was also received to the effect that the Roumanians were holding forty-three locomotives at Szolnok for shipment into Roumania, and it was decided to notify them to send these locomotives back to Hungary.

October 23, 1919.

Yesterday afternoon at about 5.30 o'clock, Minister Diamandi asked to see me and produced some postage stamps surcharged by the Roumanians on Hungarian stamps for their occupation of Transylvania, and for which I paid him between three and four thousand kronen. I have not the slightest doubt but that the little rascal got them for nothing and was told to give them to me. However, it was far better to have paid him full face value than to have accepted any gifts.

I told him that I was entirely out of patience with he attitude of himself and Mardarescu, first in regard to the Museum communication, and in regard to the evacuation of Hungary. He was still riding his high horse and insisted that they had a right to seize anything at any time and at any place, that came from Transylvania because Transylvania belonged to them; furthermore that the Mission could not give any orders concerning the Roumanian Army, that it was an independent army and that they could not accept orders from anybody; it was never customary in such cases. I informed him that in an Allied combination there was always a Commander in Chief from whom the various allies received orders; that both the British and the American Armies received orders from Marshal Foch; that we as an Inter-Allied Military Mission were in effect the staff officers of the Supreme Council and as such were authorized to give orders in the name of the Supreme Council. He then reverted to his old sophistical argument that this present rumpus between Roumania and Hungary was a private feud and their own little war in which no one else had any right to interfere. Invariably when they make the excuse that we are treating them harshly, they accuse us of treating them worse as Allies than we treat the Hungarians. Whenever they want to pull anything off, they always maintain it is a little separate affair that they are having. I told the little scoundrel that while I enjoyed talking to him-and I did, as it affords me much amusement -that such matters were purely and entirely personal; that while we may

136

get along amicably and pleasantly in such relations, I would fight him to the limit in the execution of my orders, and apparently we could not come together.

Sir George Clerk, having arrived early this morning, General Gorton and I went over to see him by appointment at noon and found that he was coming purely in a political capacity. We gave him some fatherly advice, and I also gave him a copy of the memorandum I had sent to the American Commissioner on the subject of the political parties in Hungary. He also told me that there was no matter of any importance that would come up before next week. So I decided to start for Belgrade tonight, and accordingly wired the American Commission of my intention, adding that there had been no change in the Roumanian attitude.

October 24, 1919.

Last night, accompanied by Colonel Loree, Field Clerk Fenselau, and orderlies Lester and Childstedt, and with Major Body of the Serbian army as liaison officer, I left Budapest on a special train for Belgrade. We arrived at Szeged between two and three o'clock in the morning and, as we could not find the French commander himself, the local French officer in charge refused to give us enough coal to continue to the next station, an hour's journey, where a Serbian locomotive was awaiting us. The result was that we waited at Szeged until the arrival of the Simplon Express which took us on to our Serbian connection, and we eventually arrived in Belgrade at three o'clock in the afternoon. Quarters had been arranged for Colonel Loree and myself at the Hotel Moskwa, and for the rest of the party at the Grand Hotel. The Serbian government placed a limousine at my disposal, and I called that afternoon upon the Chief of Staff. In the evening Colonel Loree and I were entertained informally at dinner by Mr. Dodge, the American Minister.

October 25, 1919.

After spending the night in a room that both smelled and felt like a sepulcher and was located on the top story of the hotel, with no elevator running, we started to make our official calls and paid short visits to the Prime Minister, to the Minister of Foreign Affairs, and to the War Minister, all of whom made the most favorable impressions as men of intelligence and experience.

At twelve-thirty, Minister Dodge gave a formal luncheon on in my honor, to which were invited the main Serbian functionaries and likewise the military attachés of the various legations.

In the afternoon, we took a drive out to the fortress and around through Belgrade, which is not a very prepossessing city. Before the War, it was understood to have had a population of about 90,000, which, when the Serbians re-occupied the city, had dwindled to about 40,000, and which now, owing to abnormal conditions, ad increased to 150,000, with about half as many houses as had originally existed. As a result, there is much congestion and generally high prices.

The Serbian dinar, the standard coin, was exchanging at the rate of 2 ¼ for one French franc, which made it worth in our money a little less than five cents, its former value being the same as the French franc.

In the evening, by appointment, I met Lieutenant-General Bridges of the British Army. We had dinner together at the Hotel Moskwa, and later my party and myself again boarded the train, leaving Belgrade at 11 P.M.

October 26, 1919.

Our return journey was a trifle more successful than our outward-bound trip, owing to the fact that the Serbian locomotive carried us all the way through Szeged, where a Hungarian locomotive met us and brought us the rest of the way to Budapest, where we arrived about one o'clock, just in time for lunch; and, although Budapest is not particularly cheerful under the circumstances, yet it appeared very much like home after our absence in Belgrade.

This evening Colonel Loree, Captain Gore and I were entertained by the Roumanian General, Serbescu, at a most sumptuous banquet in his billet in the palace of the Baron Groedel. The food was well prepared and everything would have been delicious but for the fact that I had Diamandi on my left front and directly opposite to me General Serbescu, who did several marvelous sword-swallowing feats with his knife. On my left was little Mrs. Serbescu, who had a pair of diamond earrings as big as she was; and on my right was a very homely lady who flashed a diamond about the size of locomotive headlight, on her forefinger. Colonel Loree was sure that the Roumanians would try to poison us, it by carefully watching what they ate themselves, and imitating them, we escaped serious consequences.

October 27, 1919.

The Mission met this morning, with General Mombelli presiding.

I related to them my experiences during my trip to Belgrade, informing them that the trip had no political significance, but that I did bring up with the Prime Minister the question of the evacuation by the Serbians the Baranya district, and in particular of the town Pécs.

A letter was received from the Hungarian officials, stating that the shortage of coal was getting acute, and that there was no hope for a solution of the problem until the Roumanians allowed them the transportation. It was, therefore, decided to inform the Roumanians of the present situation and that they would be responsible in case any suffering ensued.

The Museum authorities have sent me word that there were a few boxes in the Museum which really belonged to Transylvania and which they were willing turn over to Roumania. Captain Shafroth had come me with a request for the key to the Museum and for permission to break the seals in order to deliver the boxes in question. I brought this up before the Mission and recommended that, in view of the fact that the Roumanians had taken so many things to which they were not entitled, there need not be any hurry about these few boxes which might properly belong to them. I was sustained by the Mission and the Roumanians were informed that they would have to await the action of the Reparation Commission.

The Roumanians also asked the Mission to designate a delegate to receive the telephone and telegraph instruments which they proposed to return to the Hungarian Minister of War, and it was decided to have our Committee on Army Organization act in that capacity.

A little after ten, Sir George Clerk appeared before the Mission, in accord with our previous telegraphic advices from the Supreme Council, but he really had very little light to shed upon the general situation. We discussed with him the measures to be adopted in case of evacuation by the Roumanians, and it was agreed that we should proceed, to the limit of the means at our disposal, with the rapid organization of the Budapest police, and that the Hungarian Army should not be allowed in the city until the Roumanians had entirely evacuated, in order to avoid any encounters between individuals or small detachments. It was decided to request the Hungarian Minister of War to direct Admiral Horthy and General Soós to report to the Mission at the next meeting, on the twenty-ninth.

A letter was received from the Roumanian Commander in Chief, evidently written with the intention of stirring up friction among the members of the Military Mission. He said that the American Mission had interfered at the jails and had told the Roumanian officials that no prisoners were to be removed except by permission of the American Mission. As it was all a lie, it was decided to file the paper and drop it.

Upon arrival here yesterday, I found a Colonel Raymond Sheldon, who had been a Major of Scouts in the Philippines and whom I have known for a great many years. He recently reported here, had accepted our invitation to join our mess and was very glad to be quartered with us. He had just returned from an extensive trip covering all of the Roumanian prisoner-of-war camps and is now busy, with Doctor Munro and Captain Brunier, in writing up a comprehensive report. In the evening Colonel Sheldon went out to dine with the Italians, and Colonel Loree, Captain Gore and myself dined alone.

October 28, 1919.

As we are apparently out of gasoline and the Roumanians are the only ones who possess any, was forced most reluctantly to go and see little Diamandi. I found him with a bad cold in the head and with a nose on him that looked like a paprika. He said at he would be very glad to give the necessary instructions and that he would telephone General Serbescu to give us what gasoline we needed. In order to drive home the matter, I later went down to General Serbescu's and he said that he would give us immediately 2,000 liters of gasoline and would supply us from day to day as we needed same.

During the day we were threatened with a visitation from a delegation of 10,000 women, but through Colonel Loree, aided and abetted by our Hungarian liaison officers, we managed to stave them off, and later I had word sent to the Hungarian government that I must decline any such delegation as they simply annoyed and embarrassed us, and we could have no transactions whatever with them. Then somebody did a dirty trick and suggested that the delegation go down and visit Sir George Clerk, which I understand they did. I afterwards saw a thousand or more, mostly women, girls, and children, lined up in front of the government building, where Prime Minister Friedrich was addressing them. Down at the foot of the hill we found a company of Roumanians with machine guns drawn up to defend themselves against these women and children.

I have been informed that there has just been issued from Roumanian Headquarters an order prohibiting Roumanian officers from continuing to use rouge and lip sticks. It will certainly be hard on the poor dears.

October 29, 1919.

At the meeting of the Inter-Allied Military Mission today, I presided and there was considerable activity.

We first took up the question of executions in Hungary, in regard to which the Mission was on record as being in favor of General Holban's attitude, which would not tolerate executions until a permanent government had been organized. A memorandum had been received from Colonel Loree explaining that, as the pardoning power by the chief executive did not exist Hungary to the same extent as was usual in other countries, and as the judges were all hold-overs from the older régimes, the decision of the Mission was apparently based upon wrong premises. General Mombelli insisted that the chief executive still did have power, and that he would show the authority. It was decided, therefore, to leave this matter pending until the next meeting of the Mission.

At 10.30 General Schnetzer, the Hungarian Minister of War, accompanied by Admiral Horthy and General Soós, were introduced and I explained to them that they had been summoned so that we might lay before them the situation as we saw it and as it would be affected by a probable early Roumanian evacuation.

I told these gentlemen that Hungary was about to appear before a jury of all the nations; that she was to certain extent discredited on account of having allowed Bolshevism to exist within her borders for over three months; that in case any disorders should result after the Roumanian evacuation, and there should be a recrudescence of Bolshevism, her standing with the Allied Powers would be practically nil; on the other hand, if she conducted herself with the dignity of a civilized nation and permitted no serious disorders to ensue, she would raise herself highly in the estimation the Entente.

I explained to them that there would undoubtedly some young hot-heads of the Hungarian Army who would be crazy to shoot a Roumanian or hang a Jew, and that one or two such could bring discredit upon the whole country. It was also explained to them that on the part of the workmen of Budapest there existed much fear of the so-called "White Army," and that they should show that their army was not made up of a gang of "White Terrorists," but was a well-disciplined and organized National Hungarian Army. The Admiral said that he had his forces absolutely in hand and under control; that they were well disciplined and that he would guarantee that there would be no disturbances.

I explained to him that the general idea was that, when the Roumanians evacuated the city, the Budapest police take over the maintenance of law and order during a short transitory period between the leaving of the Roumanians and the arrival of the Hungarians, and that the time when this should take place would of course be determined by the Inter-Allied liaison officers attached to both forces.

The Admiral complained that he had drawn up a proclamation for publication in the city of Budapest, which the Roumanians had censored in its entirety. He was told to submit any such proclamations to the Mission, which would insist that the Roumanians publish it. Our visitors then left.

At the beginning of the session, I delivered to each member a copy of the report of Colonel Sheldon's committee on inspection of Roumanian prison camps. As it was so voluminous and contained so many disgusting details, it was decided that each member should study his copy until tomorrow, and that in the meantime I should prepare a telegram to the Supreme Council embodying the more salient features of the report. In this telegram I should likewise explain that, although this Mission on October 13 had requested that the Supreme Council either force the Roumanians to evacuate Hungary or relieve the Mission, and despite he fact that on October 19 the Supreme Council had telegraphed to the effect that Sir George Clerk would inform us that the Supreme Council would take all measures to force the Roumanians to comply with requests, there had been as yet no change in the Roumanian attitude, and that each succeeding day the difficulties of the Mission were increasing in geometrical progression. It was also decided to call the attention of the Supreme Council to the fact that the Roumanians had been requested to release immediately all officer prisoners-of-war and interned civilians at Arad, and to arrange with the Hungarian government for the general delivery of prisoners; yet no reply had been received from the Roumanian commander.

October 30, 1919.

This morning I drafted a telegram to the Supreme Council, took it personally in the afternoon to Generals Gorton, Mombelli and Graziani and had them all approve it. General Mombelli was a trifle afraid that we were repeating our ultimatum to the Supreme Council as given in the message of October 3 and, although he talked better French than I did, mine was the stronger flow and he eventually signed in order to close the argument. The telegram sent was as follows:

Armistice of August 2nd between Roumanian and Hungarian forces provided that Hungarian officers should supervise disarming of their own troops and would then be given freedom with retention of arms. Hungarian troops being disarmed, officers were required to report daily but about August 7th despite agreement many officers throughout Hungary were arrested and sent to Arad. Most all so-called prisoners of war were arrested after the armistice and then disarmed, instead of being captured during a gallant advance. During transfer from place of arrest to prisons many of both officers and men were beaten, maltreated and robbed by Roumanian officers and soldiers, and prisoners' female relatives were insulted when visiting prisoners.

Mission's committee sent to investigate prisoner of war camps visited Arad Citadel, Brassó Citadel, Bertalan Hospital, Camp Christian, Camp Rajnow, and Fogaras. Committee consisted of Colonel Raymond Sheldon, U. S. A., Doctor Hector Munro of the International Hospital Relief Association, Captain Georges Brunier of Swiss Army and delegate of International Red Cross, and First Lieut. Francesco Braccio of Italian Medical Corps. All reports of the committee were unanimous, were practically the same as quoted in telegram of October 13th, and in general resembled following extracts from report on interned civilians at Arad, Brassó, and Fogaras:

"At Arad about one hundred men and boys occupy casemates of fortress. No preparation whatsoever had been made for them. No beds or wooden boards to sleep on, floors were of concrete. No heating stoves, weather wet and bitterly cold. Many windows broken, food provided not by Roumanians but by local Hungarian Red Cross under orders from Roumanians. Very few of the men had overcoats, none had blankets, many were without boots and underclothes. Some had no jackets. It would be difficult to describe the abject misery of these men and youths. Many were blue with cold; half starved and worried about their private affairs. Some were quite young, one sixteen years; some upwards of sixty years of age. At Brassó in Citadel we found 121 civilian prisoners, mixed with military and in the same buildings. Latrines are thoroughly unsanitary and inadequate. Among civilian prisoners are six women, one evidently an educated woman who has written poetry. They were housed in a room ten feet by nineteen feet. Five slept on one bench and one in a bed. At Fogaras we found 72 civilian prisoners. They were housed with military, and their condition has already been described. Many of these prisoners had no boots, no underclothing, and one had no trousers. He wore a kilt made of carpet. All were inadequately clad for winter weather. They accused Roumanian soldiers and in some instances officers of stealing their clothes, boots and private property. We found four boys, two of thirteen and two fourteen years old. One old man of seventy- six. Many were suffering from incurable diseases."

Nevertheless we are still allies of a nation guilty of conduct described above, which continues to treat inhabitants of country between Danube and the Theiss as reported in telegram of October 13th, and which has repeatedly ignored or flatly turned down the requests of representatives of the Supreme Council. Roumanians claim many prisoners are Bolshevists, but prisoners deny charges. On October 20th Roumanian commander was asked to liberate immediately officer prisoners of war and civilians at Arad and to arrange with Hungarian government for liberation from other camps, and on October 22nd he was also requested to return from Szolnok to Budapest forty-three idle locomotives that were urgently needed for food distribution. No action taken on any of these requests; not even the courtesy of a reply.

Supreme Council's telegram of October 18th stated that Sir George Clerk would inform Mission that the Council had decided to take all the measures necessary to force the Roumanian government to follow line of conduct it was requested to adopt. There is as yet no noticeable change in Roumanian attitude and situation is becoming intolerable. If Roumanians are allowed to remain until a coalition government is formed, consequences, at the present rate of progress, will be more serious. Difficulties encountered in accomplishing our Mission are increasing rapidly. Under instructions of August 13th even though representing the Supreme Council this Mission can give no orders to Roumanians. In view of Mission's telegram of thirteenth instant stating that either the Roumanians should be forced to evacuate Hungary at once or that this Mission should be relieved it is realized that the Mission will not be held responsible for consequences that may result from Roumanian refusal to evacuate, but it is deemed necessary to present the facts to the Supreme Council.

Upon leaving General Mombelli's quarters, I met General Graziani at the door and we had a little talk about the general situation, and I was delighted to learn that our Latin colleagues were getting as thoroughly disgusted with the Roumanians as are General Gorton and myself.

Later in the afternoon, Captain Gore and I took tea with the family of Baron Groedel. They turned over to me a stamp collection which they wish delivered some time to their home in Vienna.

Upon arriving back at my quarters, I found that the Roumanians had been closing up the Telephone Central and raising Merry Hell in general. Colonel Sheldon of my Mission and Captain Aitken of the British Mission had gone over to investigate the proposition and got all sorts of rough treatment from a bunch of Roumanian rough-necks that were putting the proposition over. Colonel Sheldon went and saw Colonel Vasilescu. The Roumanians disclaimed all knowledge of the occurrence and stated likewise that it had not been done with the knowledge or consent of General Mosoiu. The matter is being investigated.

This evening General Gorton and myself dined with General Mombelli and his family, which consists of his wife and young-lady daughter of about twenty-two years of age, who speaks very good English. One of the guests was an Italian who spoke Spanish; so I was able to get along very well.

October 31, 1919.

The Mission met at 9.30 this morning, with General Gorton presiding.

We first decided to take up the question of executions in Hungary, which had been laid on the table at the last meeting, and it was decided to inform the Hungarian government that our action in concurring with General Holban's decision in regard to the suspension of executions until the organization of a Hungarian government, applied entirely to the portion of Hungary under Roumanian military control, that the Inter-Allied Military Mission did not mix in the internal affairs, and that our previous letters should be so construed.

We then took up the discussion of the report of Colonel Sheldon's Committee on Prisoner-of-War Camps, and it was decided to send to the Roumanian Commander a letter telling him that the report of our Committee indicated that conditions in his prisoner-of-war camps were even worse than reported by Doctor Munro and Captain Brunier; that the conditions were disgraceful; and that, as it reflected upon all the Allies, we must insist that he immediately remedy the same; and he was directed to carry out the following:

> Immediately to liberate by turning over to the Hungarian government, all civilians under eighteen and over sixty years of age, and also all invalid civilian and military persons.
> To send immediately to the hospital all civilians whose condition required surgical attention.
> To take measures so that the quarantine camps should be handled for the purpose of ascertaining the state of health of repatriated prisoners, and not for the purpose of detaining them fifteen days or longer.
> That prisoners of war should receive the pay due them in the future and retroactively from the day on which they were apprehended.
> To see that all camps be furnished suitable arrangements for washing and that the latrines be disinfected and put in condition so that they can be used.
> To arrange so that food should be properly distributed in sufficient quantities.
> To arrest and punish whatever persons, whether military or civil, who had caused the arrest of ladies and gentlemen who were the guests of our Committee in Arad; and finally
> To arrange for the establishment of a courier service between Arad and Budapest, which service should be run in conjunction with the Hungarian Red Cross at Arad, which latter association must be treated according to the rules and customs of war.
> Letters were received complaining that homeless illegitimate children in Transylvania were being deported by the Roumanians in such numbers as to overcrowd the Home in Budapest. Another report was received showing that

the Roumanians were carrying out general religious persecutions[11]. It was decided to inform them that it was difficult to believe how any nation that laid claims to being in a civilized class could handle children along the lines indicated; and in the second case it was decided to report to the Supreme Council as indication of the necessity for obliging the Roumanians to adopt the "Minorities" clause in the treaty.

11 On the condition of religious minorities in Transylvania after the incorporation of that country into Roumania, see *The Religious Minorities in Transylvania*, compiled by Louis C. Cornish, in collaboration with the Anglo-American commission on the Rights of Religious Minorities in Roumania, Boston, 1925. The Commission consisted of representatives of the Presbyterian, Reformed, and Unitarian Churches of England and the United States, and investigated the status of the Reformed, Lutheran, and Unitarian congregations. It summarized its findings in the following words: "The impression gained . . . is that unless a solution can be found for the present problems, racial and linguistic, religious and economic, it will continue to be one of the saddest lands in Europe, and a menacing danger-spot for the peace of the world (p.22)." "The Commission submits that the reply of the Roumanian Government is evasive and inconclusive (p.174)."

November, 1919

November 1, 1919.

Last night Colonel Loree, Colonel Sheldon, Captain Gore and myself were the guests at dinner of Count Edelsheim, who entertained us at the National Club. This is the select club of the Hungarian aristocracy and has been opened only a few days. The other guests were all of them either counts or barons, and included Count Andrássy, former Prime Minister, and Count Károlyi, the President of the Club, but not the notorious Count Károlyi who turned the government over to Béla Kun.

This morning the gasoline situation was so acute that, after having telegraphed General Allen[1] at Coblenz, Secretary of State Polk at Paris, Colonels Smith and Causey in Vienna, and the American Minister in Bucharest each to send me a carload of gasoline, knowing that I could easily dispose of any surplus, I sent Colonel Loree out to round up the Roumanian situation and force them to disgorge a part of the large quantity which I knew that they have on hand here in Budapest. He stuck to the proposition and finally about 5 o'clock this afternoon sent up for a truck to get 2,000 liters. The chauffeur said that there was any quantity of it on the tracks, thereby verifying my well-founded suspicions. The present market price here in Budapest is a trifle over a dollar a gallon, but I have already arranged to buy three or four hundred gallons of the Hungarian government at about thirty-five cents a gallon.

About noon today I had a personal call from my old friend "Archie Duke" accompanied by his son, the young "Archie Dukelet." He is very pleasant to meet socially, and we discussed at some length the general Hungarian situation, and what Hungary ought to do whenever she got rid of the Roumanians. His Royal Highness seemed to think that about the first thing that should be done was to turn loose and invade Roumania. Although he is still technically an enemy and he was talking about one of our Allies, I could not help in my heart sympathizing with him, and I don't know of anything that I would rather do just at present than fight Roumanians.

1   Henry Tureman Allen, Commander of the American Army of Occupation in Germany.

While out on his trip, Colonel Loree telephoned me the sad news that our good friend, Colonel Vasilescu, had been ordered back to Bucharest and would probably leave on Monday. After he leaves, there will be only one advantage in the Roumanian situation, and that is that it will be one of homogeneous rottenness.

November 2, 1919.

Yesterday afternoon about 6 o'clock I got word that Minister Diamandi was waiting in the anteroom, and desired "to approach the east." I sent word that he should be admitted in due form and ceremony. He came in with his little mincing steps and said that between gentlemen (although I could not understand why he used it in the plural), it was always best to speak with frankness, and he wished to enter two complaints about the conduct of American officers.

He started in first and said that an American Red Cross officer had invaded the sacred precincts of Roumanian territory, had gone to the city of Arad and interviewed a lot of Hungarian prisoners there without first having been admitted to the presence of the prefect and, in general, had been guilty of most discourteous conduct, emphasizing the fact that he thought it was a military custom always to advise a commanding officer when his territory was to be invaded. I told his little Excellency that there had been no American Red Cross officer outside of the city of Budapest, and that he was off his nut.

He then read the prefect's complaint, giving the name of the American Red Cross officer as Colonel Raymond Sheldon. I then told him that Colonel Raymond Sheldon was an officer of the United States Regular Army, that he had been sent to Arad as chairman of a committee of four representing the Inter-Allied Military Mission for the purpose of investigating prisoner-of-war conditions there and elsewhere; that forty-eight hours before his departure, General Mardarescu had been advised of it; that Colonel Sheldon had called upon the commanding officer at Arad and every damned Roumanian official he could find, and that he found conditions there that were a disgrace to civilization.

His Excellency then branched out on the topic of American officers having gone to the Telephone Central and of having had trouble there with Roumanian sentinels, stating that he thought that when complaints were to be made of things of that kind, the officers should first go to the Commanding General of Budapest or General Mardarescu and not go and have trouble with sentinels; that the whole thing was an incident that might easily have been avoided. I told him just so, that the two officers concerned were Colonel Sheldon, U. S. Army, and Captain Aitken of the British Army, accompanied by two American field clerks; that the first thing we knew on the day in question was that our telephone service had been stopped; that it was not customary when telephones ceased to operate, to chase up a commanding general of a foreign army of occupation or any other army, but to go direct to the central office to see what the trouble was; that these two officers had gone to the central office and found about eight Roumanian soldiers under the command of a civilian detective, raising Merry Hell; that they were holding up several hundred women and girls from leaving the building; and that when the courtyard was practically vacant of anyone else they had shut the gate, closing in Colonel Sheldon and Captain Aitken; that they had pointed their rifles at them and would not allow them to leave, even for the purpose of reporting the matter to the Roumanian Commander. His Excellency explained that the barred gate, consisting of iron pickets at intervals of about six inches, had been closed apparently to keep the dust out, and he furthermore said that the cause of the whole thing was the fact that a report had been received that some of the Hungarian employees were going to attack some of the Roumanian employees and that it had been decided to stop the Hungarians at the gate and search them for weapons. I told him that it was damned peculiar that both Generals Mardarescu and Mosoiu disclaimed any knowledge of what had taken place, and that it was a funny procedure for soldiers to be placed under the command of a civilian detective and detain hundreds of women and girls, who certainly were not going to attack Roumanian officials; and then to cap the climax I called in Colonel Sheldon, who in unmistakable terms confirmed in still further detail everything that I had said. His Excellency then told Colonel Sheldon that he regretted the incident and that he would further investigate, and although he came into the room with his tail up over the dashboard, he left my presence with it curled up tightly between his legs.

Last night we entertained General and Mrs. Mombelli and their daughter at dinner, and our chef split himself wide open. Everything was deliciously well cooked and prepared, and when it was served was something to tempt the appetite of an Epicure. General Mombelli enjoyed himself so much that later in the evening, when Colonel Sheldon was playing the piano, he accompanied him with a brass gong.

November 3, 1919.

Yesterday morning I started out with young Count Teleki by automobile to visit his uncle's place, which is at a place called Dunatetétlen, between forty and fifty miles down the Danube. This was done because the Roumanians, despite two safeguards given old Count Teleki, had started to make requisitions and were generally acting nasty. Shortly after we started, it began to rain and the roads were very bad. Although there were numerous Roumanian garrisons up and down the river, they are such fine soldiers that the rain kept them all inside, and with one exception we saw no Roumanians on all our outward-bound trip. The exception was a small Roumanian cavalry patrol on the outskirts of the town of Solt, which we came upon rather suddenly. The chauffeur sounded the klaxon and away went the cavalry patrol, Hell split for election, down the road, scattering mud in all directions, and the Roumanians flapping their arms and legs, trying to check their horses. When the horses slowed down a little, we would start up again and sound the klaxon, and away they would go. As here was a deep ditch on each side of the road, we were able to chase them for about a mile before they would turn off into a field. My only regret was that none of them were spilled off their horses on the way. All of them had narrow escapes and were about as rotten a bunch of cavalrymen as I have ever seen.

When we arrived at Count Teleki's home, I found some Roumanian officers there already and, assuming that they were starting to make requisitions, I started in for them good and quick and plenty, and had the Roumanian colonel and two assistants standing at attention, bowing and scraping and trying to explain. I initially learned that they were really there on a decent mission and owing to a complaint that I had sent to General Mardarescu about the conduct of a young Roumanian officer in going to the Count's house while there vas nobody there but his nieces, and insisting on having the prettiest one in a room by himself, in which kind attention he did not succeed. The Roumanian colonel was investigating according to my complaint and cracked is heels together every time I batted an eye in his direction. They finally left, and after an early dinner young Count Teleki and I also left, about 4.30, on our return trip. As it was not raining, we were halted three times by Roumanian sentinels, but we had no difficulty. At this morning's session of the Mission, I related to General Graziani and General Mombelli, -General Gorton being absent- my experiences with Diamandi on Saturday evening, and it was decided to send to the Roumanian Commander a demand for an apology for the conduct of the Roumanian guard at the Telephone Central.

We had a reply from the Czecho-Slovak Republic to our demand for them to evacuate the portions of Hungary which did not belong to them, and they said they would be glad to do so, within five days after three conditions had been fulfilled. One was the assurance that the Hungarians could maintain order in the territory in question; the second that the Hungarians would not attack them; and the third that they should be reimbursed for their expenses in furnishing food to the inhabitants of the occupied section. We replied to the first two, stating that those conditions would be fulfilled, but that the third was ridiculous and preposterous, and we wanted them to get out of there immediately.

A complaint was received also from the Hungarian government to the effect that the Roumanian Commander east of the Theiss was organizing a provisional government of his own with Roumanian representatives, and in general was acting in contravention to all the customs and rules of war in like cases; so it was decided to notify the Roumanian Commander of the same, with instructions to have it stopped.

November 4, 1919.

Shortly after arriving at the office this morning, General Gorton came in with one of his officers and said that the Roumanians were holding back fifty-odd trucks which were absolutely needed by the Food Commission for feeding the city of Budapest, that they had Roumanian drivers on the trucks, sentinels over the garage, and claimed that the trucks were war booty and would not be given up. I insisted that General Gorton accompany me to Roumanian Headquarters to tell the Roumanian Commander that we would have to have those trucks. He finally consented to go, and accompanied by Colonel Sheldon, U.S.A., and Captain Doumalle of the British Service, we chased over to the Hotel Gellért and were promptly ushered into General Mardarescu's presence. After sitting down for a few minutes and indulging in the ordinary persiflage usual on such occasions, I nudged General Gorton and he brought up the question of the trucks. General Mardarescu then stated that these trucks were considered booty of war, and that they had a right to them. I interrupted and told him that that was a mooted question and that I did not agree to this. Colonel Sheldon interpreted to Mardarescu that I considered that he was a liar, at which he begged to assure me that it was not the truth; that they did consider them booty of war. It was finally explained to him that he had not been called a liar, but with the mental reservation that the epithet would always be appropriate. After considerable palaver and after General Gorton had offered to sign a receipt for the trucks, he agreed to turn them over on condition that when we were through with them they should be turned over to the Roumanian authorities. As, of course, when we were through with them, they would be in charge of the Reparation Committee, who could theoretically turn them over and immediately take them back, we consented to this.

I then asked General Mardarescu how he could explain that with the beautifully disciplined Roumanian Army- and I got no further because he interrupted to explain that they really had a finely disciplined army. After he had rattled on for some time, I asked him if he would keep still long enough for me to state what I desired to state. I then asked how it could be that in such a well-disciplined army, the officers and soldiers absolutely disregarded the commanding general's safeguard, or property-protection certificate, and made requisitions in spite of it. He then indulged in a Hell of a lot of circumlocution, and finally stated that he would immediately investigate the concrete case of Count Teleki's estate, which I gave to him, and punish the guilty offenders.

Before we left, I think he invited General Gorton and myself to luncheon on Thursday as a sort of farewell party. If it is really a farewell, I may be inclined to attend.

From Roumanian Headquarters, General Gorton and I went to see Sir George Clerk to discuss the general situation as regards the organization of the Hungarian government. Sir George seemed to be having trouble with Minister Friedrich, who is apparently blocking the proposition. He was, however, optimistic and finally told us that Diamandi had been there yesterday and told him definitely that the Roumanians would start to evacuate Budapest on the ninth, and would finish by the eleventh. In view of the fact that Mardarescu and Diamandi both, at a session of the Mission, informed us that they would immediately advise us of any prospective evacuation plan as soon as they knew themselves, it is rather strange that Sir George Clerk should have been informed twenty-four hours in advance of the Military Mission, especially in view of the fact that Sir George had nothing whatever to do with the evacuation.

November 5, 1919.

Last night I attended a large dinner party given by Sir George Clerk. Among other guests present were Admiral Troubridge, Generals Graziani, Mombelli and Gorton, Admiral Horthy, Minister of Foreign Affairs Somssich, Countess Somssich, the two Baronesses Podmaniczky, and Mrs. Mombelli and her daughter. It was a very good meal, but not quite up to the standard of our own chef.

Shortly after arising from the table, Sir George Clerk asked General Gorton and myself into his cabinet and informed us that the Italian consulate had received a telegram from Paris which stated in effect that the Supreme Council was studying three points of the Hungarian question. The first was the resignation of Friedrich, on account of his inability to organize a coalition government; the second was the immediate evacuation of Hungary by the Roumanians; and the third was a proposition to send as an army of occupation into Hungary two divisions under Inter-Allied officers, one division of Czecho-Slovaks and one division of Jugo-Slavs. Sir George was himself much opposed to this last, and read us the draft of a telegram stating that in his opinion it would be injudicious to take any such action.

At this morning's session, General Mombelli presided and we first brought up the question of Diamandi having notified Sir George Clerk that the Roumanian evacuation would begin on the ninth of November, and the President of the Day was directed to send a letter to General Mardarescu stating that both Minister Diamandi and he, at an open meeting of the Inter-Allied Military Mission, had assured us that they would give us immediately all possible advance notice as to the date of evacuation, and all details connected with the movement of troops; that Sir George Clerk had informed us that Minister Diamandi had given him such notice on the third instant, but that up to this date no word had yet been received by the Military Mission in regard to a proposed evacuation. An explanation was demanded. We next brought up the question of the telegram Sir George Clerk had seen in regard to the occupation of Hungary by a Czecho-Slovak division and a Jugo-Slav division. While the discussion was going on, I drafted a telegram to the Supreme Council, which was approved by the Mission and sent. The telegram read as follows:

This Mission is aware that a telegram has been received in Budapest from Paris covering three points. First the Friedrich Cabinet, second the immediate Roumanian evacuation, and third the occupation of Hungary by two divisions under Inter-Allied officers, one division of Czech~Slovaks and one division of Jugo-Slavs. Against this third proposition the Inter-Allied Military Mission unanimously and urgently protests. Such procedure, it is believed, would stir Hungary into revolution and would destroy all prospects for an early solution of the Hungarian question. It is furthermore urged that the Roumanians, the Jugo-Slavs, and Czecho-Slovaks be all required to retire at once behind their respective lines of demarcation.

During the session, a letter was received from Roumanian Headquarters, which was turned over to me on account of Colonel Sheldon's interest in the matter. I therefore wrote, and sent to General Mardarescu, the following self-explanatory letter:

"1: During the forenoon of November 4, 1919, accompanied by General Gorton of the British Army and Colonel Sheldon of the American Army, I visited the Headquarters of the Roumanian Army of Transylvania, and during the conference with General Mardarescu brought up the question of an incident which had occurred at the Budapest Telephone Office between an American Officer and a British Officer and some Roumanian soldiers. I explained that the telephone service having been interrupted, the two officers mentioned were sent to the Telephone Central to investigate as to the difficulty and that they naturally would not first go to the Roumanian commanding general for such a trivial matter until after an investigation; that once arrived at the telephone office and inside the fence they had the gate closed and locked on them, and were held prisoners for at least four minutes during which time they were threatened by Roumanian soldiers with fixed bayonets and pointed rifles and that as soon as they could leave the enclosure they promptly went to Roumanian Headquarters and made the complaint.

"2: Nevertheless letter Number 436 of November 4, 1919, from the Headquarters of the Army of Transylvania states as follows:

"(a) The Allied officers in interfering directly in this matter endeavored to impose their will upon Roumanian soldiers which they had no authority whatever to do. If the Allied officers had applied direct to the Roumanian Headquarters it is certain that these gentlemen would have had no complaint whatever to register," all of which is in direct contradiction of my statement to General Mardarescu made in the presence of General Gorton and Colonel Sheldon on the 4th instant, and which I resent as an official reflection upon my veracity, and I am therefore regretfully obliged to inform the Roumanian commander that under the circumstances and until satisfaction is given for the entire incident it will, of course, be impossible for either myself or my officers to meet him and his officers at any social occasion such as the luncheon to which we were invited for the 6th instant."

At the same time, a letter was received from General Mardarescu stating that, as a result of their investigation, they had found that the statements made by the British Major Foster about not having broken seals at Gödöllô Palace, had not been confirmed, which they regretted. In other words, they politely said that Major Foster was a liar. General Gorton therefore sent General Mardarescu a letter similar to, but more gentle than, the above.

At noon today, accompanied by Colonel Loree, I paid a call upon my old friend "Archie Duke" in his own palace. The building had been originally a magnificent edifice and was still so as regards the structure. The Bolshevists, however, had cleaned it out pretty thoroughly and it was apparently not in its former beautiful condition. "Archie Duke" and his son, the "Dukelet," met us in all the panoply of war, and dolled up with all the concentrated splendor of several Fourth of July celebrations. "Archie" himself was such a mass of scintillating gold and decorations that it was difficult to pick him out from amongst the mass. He, however, really is a charming fellow, and all Hungarians are loud in praise of his actual personal bravery during the War. The Archduchess was afterwards introduced and joined in the conversation, which was mainly confined to the reorganization of the Hungarian government and the evacuation of the Roumanians. I finally wound up by inviting both the Archduke and his son to dinner for tomorrow night, which invitation they accepted.

November 6, 1919.

Last night Colonel Loree, Colonel Sheldon, Captain Gore and myself were entertained at dinner by Mr. R. M. Haan, the proprietor of the Hotel St. Regis of New York City, who has daughters in Budapest married to Hungarians. The dinner, despite the food scarcity, was really a sumptuous banquet, but it was rather long drawn out, and we were glad to return home.

This morning I found Colonel Dimistrescu awaiting me in my anteroom with a letter from General Mardarescu, in effect apologizing for his letter which contained an official reflection upon my veracity. It was explained that the letter to which I objected had been signed and sent before General Mardarescu had seen me, and before he had even received Colonel Sheldon's report, and that he regretted the incident, and would be glad to investigate the affair at the Telephone Central whenever a representative from the Inter-Allied Military Mission had been designated. As that still leaves the second portion of my ultimatum in regard to satisfaction for the manner in which the American officer was treated in *statu quo*, I shall of course pay no attention to my ally beyond acknowledging his letter and accepting so much of his apology as applies to the case.

Our whole household is in considerable excitement over the proposed dinner to the Archduke and the "Dukelet" tonight. They are turning out so much new furniture and stuff that I regret that we did not invite His Highness at an earlier date.

I think I forgot to mention in my memorandum at the time that on October 31 we had our first snowstorm and it has been cold and nasty for several weeks.

Diamandi told General Gorton yesterday that the Roumanians would be ready to evacuate on the ninth, would begin to do so on the eleventh and be finished by the thirteenth, and that he was astonished that the Military Mission had not yet received official notice to this effect.

During the day I received a telegram from the American Commission, requesting that a copy of it be furnished Sir George Clerk, and which translated was about as follows:

The President of the Peace Conference on the 3d of November in the name of the Supreme Council sent the following telegram to the French Minister at Bucharest:

"The Supreme Council has decided to instruct the Allied Ministers at Bucharest without delay to notify the Roumanian Government jointly that it has received a bad impression from the arrival of General Coanda, sent by the new Roumanian Ministry as Special Envoy to Paris, without bringing the Roumanian response to the last communication from the Powers, under the peculiar pretext that the Italian Representative had not reported at the same time as the Ministers from France, England, and the United States. The Supreme Council desires to state that it wishes with the least possible delay a clear and positive reply from the Roumanian government covering the points in discussion. The situation in Hungary requires immediate decision in order to re-establish the normal conditions necessary for the security of Central Europe, and the Allied and Associated Powers cannot permit a prolongation of the dilatory Roumanian negotiations on the three questions submitted on the 12th of last October. I beg you to deliver this communication in the name of the Conference to your colleagues collectively, who will not need to await special instructions from their governments on account of the urgency of the case.

[Signed] S. Pichon"[2]

The foregoing is a most encouraging sign and looks as though the Supreme Council was finally getting tired of Roumanian tactics.

At 6.15 I received a letter from General Mardarescu, explicitly regretting the detention of our officers at the Telephone Central, so he has finally made complete apology for the entire occurrence, and we will now lunch with him tomorrow.

November 7, 1919.

Last night we had our big dinner for the Archduke and the "Dukelet," in addition to whom there were Count Andrássy, Count Somssich, Count Edelsheim, and Baron Than. "Archie" blew in all decked up like a Christmas tree, and we gave him a good square feed, and the party seemed pleased, judging by the fact that they stayed until about midnight.

At this morning's session I presided, and General Mombelli informed us that Mardarescu told him on the fifth instant that the Roumanian evacuation would begin by the departure of Minister Diamandi on Tuesday. He will be followed on Wednesday by the General Headquarters, on Thursday by our cute little friend Mosoiu, and on the night of Thursday and Friday the Roumanian troops will leave Budapest.

We also received word that the Czecho-Slovaks had come to the conclusion that they wanted to be good and would evacuate Salgótarján at noon on the eleventh instant. It was therefore decided to notify the Hungarian government of this action and to telegraph the Supreme Council accordingly.

2   Pichon, Stephen Jean Marie. Journalist, politician, diplomat, and Minister of Foreign Affairs of France from 1906-11, March, 1913- Aug., 1914, and Nov., 1917-July, 1920. An ardent nationalist and follower of Clemenceau.

General Graziani suggested, and very wisely, that we send word to the Roumanian Headquarters that it was desired, in view of its international importance, that the radio station at Budapest, prior to the departure of the Roumanians, be turned over to the Hungarian government, and that we send an Allied officer to take charge of the same.

It also afforded me much pleasure to read to the Mission the correspondence that I had had with General Mardarescu relative to the incident at the Telephone Station. Both Graziani and Mombelli kept their pencils busy making notes while I was reading it.

A red-hot letter was received from Mardarescu complaining bitterly of the conduct of our Committee in investigating prison camps. He reported that everything was beautiful and serene, and that our Committee had grossly maligned the humane and civilized Roumanians. It was noted, however, that the beautiful conditions to which he referred were all included between dates subsequent to our investigation of the camps.

Pursuant to promise, all my officers and myself chased over to the Roumanian Headquarters at the Hotel Gellért at one o'clock and went through the torture of an official luncheon with General Mardarescu and his bunch of forty thieves. It was certainly trying to have palatable food placed before you and have to sit facing Mardarescu and at the same time to be sandwiched in between Mosoiu and Serbescu. Fortunately Diamandi with his gargoyle face was not there; so matters were not as bad as they might have been.

During the day, I received a code telegram from Mr. Polk, which indicated that the French are up to something. They are apparently against Horthy as Commander of the Hungarian Forces and against Friedrich. For some reason or other, the French and the Italians are not working together. It will now be up to us to see just exactly what the cause of the separation is.

At eleven o'clock Prime Minister Friedrich, accompanied by Count Somssich, called and asked to see me and we spent about an hour and a half discussing the general political situation. Friedrich stated that the whole country depended upon him; that his party comprised between 80 and 90 per cent of the entire Hungarian population; that they had absolute confidence in him; and he insisted that he remain at the head of the government. He said that personally he was perfectly willing to resign, but in case he did so chaos would result. I told him I wished to talk to him in a purely personal manner: that he knew or should know that America had nothing whatever to gain over here in the way of indemnity or

157

territorial acquisitions, but that we were interested in a square deal for everybody, in having peace ratified between Hungary and the United States, and in having a well-organized government in control of the destinies of the country, and that I proposed to speak to him frankly and in the manner that one gentleman of intelligence should address another. I stated:

"I do not propose to defend the feeling in the Supreme Council or in any of the Allied countries and I shall grant you that they are all wrong, but you must bear in mind that the two great democracies, America and England, will look askance upon the reorganization of a government which would appear to be dominated by the Hapsburgs, and that France and Italy are likewise in opposition. Now, undoubtedly, if given sufficient time, a year or two, you could by propaganda and by a demonstration of your own worth convince the American and British people that you are right, but in the meantime where in Hell would Hungary go to? I consider that you are confronted by a condition and not a theory, and that every patriotic Hungarian must be prepared to sacrifice something at least along the lines of personal ambition. It is up to you Hungarians now to cooperate with Sir George Clerk and organize as quickly as possible a government that will be acceptable to the Entente, so that you can be recognized and have elections, and reorganize your country. Once that is done, it will not matter what party is in power.

Friedrich stated he thought it was the policy of the Supreme Council to allow the Hungarian people to do what they wanted, and that they should have their own way. I asked if, during the months of the Roumanian occupation, he had had very much of his own way; if the Hungarians had had their own way in letting the Roumanians run away with their railroad stock, clean out their machine shops, and loot all their farms. He said that would not have happened if the Entente had put an end to Béla Kun. I asked him why go into ancient history, why bring up the question as to why Napoleon Bonaparte invaded Egypt; and that we could likewise ask, why had the Hungarian King fled, why had the Hungarians allowed Károlyi to come into power, why had they allowed Béla Kun to succeed Károlyi, and that all this was begging the issue; that there was no use crying over spilt milk and that the condition was exactly as I had placed it before him, that the Entente would not recognize a government in which he, as the representative of the Hapsburg dynasty, was at the head; that as long as he was Prime Minister, even though an election were held and resulted triumphantly for him, nothing would convince the Entente but that such election result was due to the fact that he was in power. I advised him to give up his job as Prime Minister and to accept some other cabinet portfolio. He said even if he did, he would still run the cabinet. I told him that was another proposition; that if he amounted to a damn I thought he would; but what they must all do, and do quickly, was to turn out some government which the Entente would recognize, and thus enable us to clear up the whole situation. When he left me, he said he would go over and see Sir George Clerk and talk the situation over with him.

Later in the evening I saw Sir George Clerk and let him read the code telegram I had received from Mr. Polk, and asked him also about his interview with Friedrich. He said that Friedrich was still somewhat stubborn, but he thought that my talk with him had rather weakened his props, and he was optimistic as to a satisfactory outcome.

From there I went over, had a late dinner, and for once was able to stay at home with my official family.

November 8, 1919.

When we first arrived in Budapest, I engaged a large building for the quarters of my detachment and, as it was too large, I suggested to General Gorton of the British Army that we put our two detachments together, and he gladly accepted the suggestion. Later on Admiral Troubridge asked, through our Captain Gregory, if I would object to having some officers pertaining to the Commandement du Danube, located in the same building. I likewise acquiesced to this. Two or three times, our British naval brothers-in-arms have been a little bit condescending about allowing us in the building, and matters came to a climax on the sixth, when a British naval officer told Captain Gore he would like to have us move our detachment out of the building. On the seventh, a British officer directed our detachment to vacate, and on the same date Admiral Troubridge's Chief of Staff, Colonel Stead, sent a note to Colonel Loree asking him if he could not without too great inconvenience move the American detachment from the building, as it was needed by the British. I immediately drafted a slightly sarcastic note to Admiral Troubridge, but decided to see him personally, which I did this morning. The Admiral had already heard of the matter, said of course the building was ours by right of first occupancy, and that to suggest we leave the building was equivalent to the way in which the Roumanians had been firing the Hungarians out of their houses; that he regretted the entire incident and had told his men if they needed more room to get it elsewhere. He told me he did not blame me for sitting as tight as a drum, and that he hoped we would have more men instead of less. So this incident was ended.

We decided to give a party tonight, and accordingly invited the son-in-law and daughter of Count Edelsheim, the family of Count Szirmay, a number of young Hungarians, and also General Mombelli and his family, to come in after dinner and see what we could do in the way of an extemporized dance. We engaged a fine Hungarian Gipsy band, which could not show up, however, intil half past ten. It was the original intention to begin at 9.30 and stop at 12, but it appears that Hungarian custom is opposed to any such early termination. The result was that festivities were continued until about 3.30. Anyway the party was a success and everybody seemed to enjoy himself.

November 9, 1919.

Today, being Sunday, bade fair to be very quiet, until my Falstaffian friend, General Mosoiu, rolled in about noon to give me in large and bull-like tones a report on a trial of a Hungarian judge for alleged maltreatment of Roumanian prisoners two or three years ago. To impress me with the popularity he had attained among the Hungarians, he told me that they had given him a big banquet when he left the town of Czegléd, and had him photographed by the moving pictures.

November 10, 1919.

General Gorton presided at the meeting of the Mission this date, and we had a big session with a Roumanian representative who came to explain the details of the proposed evacuation. They have agreed to begin on the thirteenth with their withdrawal, when they will retire to the outskirts of Buda, going over to the Pest side of the river. At eight o'clock the Hungarians will come into Buda, and Inter-Allied troops will guard the various bridges until 10 o'clock. Before 10 o'clock, the Roumanians will entirely quit the city of Pest, at which hour the Hungarians can enter and occupy. From that time on, the evacuation will proceed by daily stages until the line of the Theiss has been reached, where the Roumanians will establish with five bridgeheads, including the important centers of Szolnok and Csongrád. We called Colonel Dimistrescu's attention to the fact that the Supreme Council had notified the Mission that all occupying forces, whether Roumanians, Jugo-Slavs, or Czecho-Slovaks, were to be required to retire at once to the lines of demarcation prescribed by the Peace Conference, and asked him to have us furnished with the least possible delay with a schedule for the Roumanian retirement from the Theiss River to their line of demarcation. He replied that as yet they had received no instructions from Bucharest relative to retirement beyond the Theiss. We next asked him what the Roumanians proposed to do in regard to the temporary bridges across the river, and he stated that, as he understood it, if they retired from the river all such bridges would be removed. He was told that it was our desire that they remain, not only on account of their necessity for the organization of eastern Hungary, but also in Roumanian interests, to perfect liaison.

I then brought up the question of prisoners-of-war and said I had two questions which I wished to ask. The first was whether the Roumanians had as yet furnished the Hungarians with a list of prisoners-of-war; and the second, why in the past few days the prisoners at Czegléd had been reduced from 10,000 to 5,000. Colonel Dimistrescu stated that they were preparing the lists of prisoners, but had not yet finished them. I told him that our Committee wanted a list to verify the transfers and that, in regard to the depleted camps between the)Danube and the Theiss, I wanted to know in addition if they were removing all the more important prisoners and were leaving only physical derelicts and Bolshevists to be turned over to the Hungarians. He said that he was sure nothing was happening, except that of course they were retaining Transylvanian prisoners. I told him that I knew they had just recently received at Brassó a number of Hungarian prisoners from Czegléd, and that I did not like the appearance of the situation.

I afterwards helped General Gorton draft a telegram to the Supreme Council, calling attention to the fact that the Roumanians were preparing to evacuate only to the Theiss, and that they were apparently transferring to the east all their more important prisoners-of-war; and recommending that they be obliged to continue with their retirement to the line of demarcation, and to liberate immediately all prisoners-of-war, giving the latter the option of remaining as Hungarian citizens, or becoming Roumanian citizens, and not obliging them to become the latter on account of possessing property in Transylvania.

Prime Minister Friedrich called to see me again about 5 o'clock this afternoon and I am not yet decided as to what his object was unless to suggest that he thought that Sir George Clerk was overly intimate with the Social Democrats[3]. He started in by saying that he was in touch with the situation in Austria, which he thought was on the verge of a revolution, and the restoration of the monarchy under the kingship of Otto, the son of the former Emperor Karl, with Archduke Eugen as Regent. He stated furthermore that King Karl had never resigned as sovereign of Hungary and that he was still considered by the people to be such; that he had it from reliable authority that Karl was contemplating a return, and was afraid that in case he should return the people would shout "Vive le Roi!" He wanted to understood that he was against the restoration of the Hapsburgs under such conditions, even to the extent of going to Transdanubia to oppose Karl.

He then launched on another subject and stated that all the bourgeois parties had come to him and expressed a desire to collaborate with him and his party, that all prospects along these lines were bright, but that the Social Democrats were

3   Compare note on Sir George Clerk, October 20.

blocking the proposition. He said that he had offered to meet Garami, the leader of the Social Democrats, but that Garami had refused; that he had had an engagement to meet two of the other Social Democrats at 6 o'clock this date, but that they had sent word that they preferred to write him a letter instead of coming. He said the Social Democrats insist on several portfolios, in particular those of the Interior and of Commerce, which they could not have; but that he was willing to concede them two portfolios, those of Labor and People's Welfare, and a third cabinet position without portfolio. I repeated to him what I had said at our previous interview, that it was up to the Hungarians to organize some cabinet that could be recognized by the Entente, and that the Entente certainly would not stand for the return of Karl or for the immediate restoration of any Hapsburgs.

November 11, 1919.

Yesterday afternoon while down town, I called upon Count Szirmay's family, and while there the Countess Teleki, daughter of the owner of our house, came in and remarked upon the delightful time they had had at our party. Knowing that she had been very strongly impressed by one of our officers, I asked her if she did not think that Colonel Sheldon was a delightful gentleman. She said: "Yes indeed, he is, and I do so like that young boy, Captain Gore, with his pink baby face." Evidently Colonel Loree and myself made no impression.

Just as we were finishing dinner last night, an urgent letter came in from Count Somssich, brought by a gentleman and a lady, who had just received word that three members of their family, including a three-year-old child, had either been killed or badly wounded by the Jugo-Slavs. Human life seems to have lost all its sacredness in this section of Europe. All I could do for these two poor people was to give them a letter to my friend, the Serbian Minister, asking him to do everything within his power to help them get to their family.

After Prime Minister Friedrich left me yesterday afternoon, I went over to see Sir George Clerk and gave him in detail my whole conversation with Friedrich, in order that he might not be hampered in his work. This morning Lieutenant-Colonel Causey came in from Vienna and told me that the situation in Vienna, as regards food and fuel, was far worse than in Budapest and was really critical. He was also interested in the Hungarian political situation, as he knows the Social Democratic leader, Garami, very well. He promised to see him and try to bring him to reason and to form some understanding with Friedrich.

Despite their oft-repeated and solemn promises, the Roumanians continue to steal property right and left. It is simply impossible to conceive such national depravity as those miserable "Latins" of Southeast Europe are displaying.

November 12, 1919.

This morning's session of the Mission was held at General Graziani's headquarters, owing to the fact that we have no fire in the Palace. In his connection, it might be added that although this is the twelfth of November, and it has been damnably old, I have been able to have a fire in my room only one day.

When I arrived at the French Mission, General Graziani met me, rubbing his hands and shivering, and stated that, although yesterday they had had plenty of heat, their supply of firewood had given out since then and unfortunately our session would have to be held in a room as cold as any in the Palace.

Right off the bat we had a beautiful little evidence of the "fine Italian hand." At the previous meeting, we had sent a communication to the Roumanian Head-quarters directing them to turn over to the Inter-Allied Military Mission the big Hungarian wireless station during the Roumanian evacuation, and between ourselves we had arranged that the only wireless expert with the Mission, an Italian officer, should be placed in charge of it until the Hungarians occupied the city. General Mombelli, before we had hardly got started on the session this morning, stated that he was now prepared to take over the wireless station and would establish an office at his own headquarters where he would be very glad to have the members of the Mission send any wireless messages which they wished to have forwarded to Paris or elsewhere; that fortunately he had an expert and was well prepared to run the wireless station. I told him that all this sounded sweet and alluring, but asked by what authority we proposed to take over the wireless station; that we were not an occupying army; that the Berlin station and the Vienna station had not been taken over; that if we took over the wireless station, we should also take over all the Hungarian telegraph and telephone stations, which we could not do; that my understanding was that we take the station over only during the evacuation by the Roumanians, and that it then be restored unconditionally to the Hungarians. General Graziani heartily accorded with my views, and then and there ended the Italian dream of monopoly of aerial communication in Hungary.

General Mombelli then stated how he had been informed that the Hungarians proposed to give a big manifestation, including the presentation of a bronze bust and the freedom of the city, and a number of other things, to the Italian Colonel

Romanelli, on account of his services during the Bolshevist régime[4]; how he had frowned upon this, and that now they were proposing to give a manifestation at some theater, which, according to his views, might result in a counter manifestation by the Roumanians, and was, therefore, not advisable. This brought out more clearly than usual the fact that for some reason or other there is friction between Mombelli and Romanelli, the latter being on more of a diplomatic than a military mission. However, everything considered, it would be most inappropriate at this time, despite our hostile feelings towards our allies, the Roumanians, and our friendly feelings towards' our enemies, the Hungarians, either to participate ourselves or o allow any of our subordinates to participate in pubic demonstrations, and we decided that nothing of the and should be allowed.

We directed the President of the Day to send a communication to the Hungarian government, to the effect that we desired to have submitted to us a list of all he prisoners-of-war liberated by the Roumanians, against whom the Hungarians proposed to institute proceedings either criminal or for treason. This was done because undoubtedly there will be many attempts on the part of the Hungarians to even up personal and political matters whenever they can get their hands on certain of their compatriots, now held as prisoners by the Roumanians.

I brought up again the Roumanian complaint against our Committee that investigated their prison camps, and proposed that we write the Roumanians a letter acknowledging receipt of their communication; informing them that it was noted that all the good conditions which they described as existing in their prison camps covered dates subsequent to the time of our investigation; that we were glad there had been any improvements; and that many of their statements, among which was one to the effect that our Committee had been accompanied by a Hungarian interpreter, were based upon false premises or were entirely groundless. The object of this letter was to show on our records that we had received the Roumanian letter and replied thereto, as otherwise they would make the statement that they had given us a reply that was simply incontestable. It was then decided to send a copy of the Roumanian reply to the Supreme Council and enclose therewith a copy of Colonel Sheldon's critique on the same, which is drawn up on the plan of the deadly parallel.

We also sent a telegram to the Supreme Council recommending that the Roumanians be required to return a specified amount of rolling stock, including motor trucks.

Yesterday afternoon, accompanied by Colonel Sheldon, I went over to see that miserable little scalawag, Diamandi, to intercede for a Hungarian judge named Miskos, who had formerly been in charge of Roumanian prisoners-of-war in Hungary, and whom the Roumanians were now swamping under a deluge of preposterous charges. The miserable little rascal, knowing it he had me on the hip, said of course he could not tolerate any interference with the sovereign rights of Roumanian government to try its prisoners, but if were asking it as a favor of course it would be gladly granted, and he would take the matter up with General Panaitescu. Colonel Sheldon and I therefore accompanied him downstairs with some other new arrivals, and cooled our heels in the corridor for ten or fifteen minutes while Diamandi and Panaitescu held a star-chamber session. They then came out and stated that General Mosoiu would be over very soon to see me about it and Panaitescu immediately plunged into a characteristically Roumanianesque circumlocutory dissertation on court-martial in general and on the Miskos case in particular. It took the combined efforts of Colonel Sheldon and myself for some minutes to succeed ally in choking him off and telling him we did not give a damn about that; that it would be discussed with Mosoiu when necessary, and we wished to know why in Hell the Roumanians, in violation of their solemn promises, were seizing all the tobacco stored in Budapest. He then stated that he had given orders to have it stopped and to take only what was actually necessary for their troops, and he would see that all requisitions were stopped. This being about the four-thousandth time that some Roumanian high official has made this statement, it had a corresponding effect and, so as to avoid giving them the satisfaction of keeping me waiting for Mosoiu, I left the building.

During the Bolshevik régime, the Italians maintained suspiciously friendly relations with the Bolshevik government. They furnished Béla Kun arms and ammunition in exchange for breeding horses, jewelry, etc. when Béla Kun escaped to Austria, the Italian Military Mission gave him an escort, thus guaranteeing him and his company safe conduct. The head of the Italian Military Mission was then Colonel Romanelli. He often used his influence with the Hungarian Soviet government to make it act more humanely in the treatment of its adversaries at home, and he frequently secured the pardon of condemned political prisoners. See Cécile Tormay, *An Outlaw's Diary,* New York, 1924, pp.175 and 185. The relationship of Italy to Hungary was guided by her interests in the Fiume question. She apparently liked to see her other allies in trouble, so that their attention would be diverted from the Dalmatian coast.

Later on, Mosoiu came over to my office and fortunately I was out, and Colonel Loree told him if he wanted to see me he would have to come the next day.

About noon today he came in, puffing and blowing, rolled up to me, spit in my eye, told me how much he admired and loved Americans in general and myself in particular, assured me that he was a thorough and honorable soldier, that he had won the love and admiration of the town where he had been stationed before, that it was a public calamity that he had not been earlier placed in command of Budapest, and assured me that Judge Miskos and his companions would receive only the best and kindest of treatment, and then whispered to me, in a voice that made the Palace tremble, that he was sure that Judge Miskos would be liberated in a few days. I then spit in his eye, wished him "au revoir," and the session ended.

November 13, 1919.

Shortly after arriving at my office this morning, Colonel Dimistrescu came in to say "Good-bye" and, while I was giving him my opinion about various kinds of conduct on the part of the Roumanians, Colonel Loree burst through the door to tell me that one of the Roumanian companies in town was engaged at that minute in breaking into and pillaging houses. This started my visitor off on a new tack, and he promised to get busy immediately with his headquarters and stop the looting. While he was talking the matter over in Colonel Yates' office, I received word at the Roumanians were violating a safeguard and were robbing a farm; so I went out where the Roumanian was talking to the others, and told him in rather forcible language that I was now put to the necessity of telegraphing Paris that the Roumanians, on the verge the evacuation, were beginning to pillage and loot like a band of robbers.

Yesterday Colonel Sheldon went out to one of the prison camps, in connection with the turning over to the Hungarians by the Roumanians of prisoners-of-war, and found that practically no arrangements had been made for this work. Today they are to take over some sick prisoners whom the Roumanians have been keeping in a Hungarian hospital, attended by Hungarian doctors and at Hungarian expense.

Yesterday morning there appeared in the papers a notice from Roumanian Headquarters that they proposed distribute large quantities of food to the inhabitants of Budapest. Then in characteristic Roumanian style, they broke into the food depôts belonging to Hungarian government and distributed these supplies right and left, thereby completely upsetting the ration system of Budapest, but during the process being photographed as international philanthropists. It is understood that that little rascal, Diamandi, was present himself at one place where they turned out some company kitchens, then robbed a nearby restaurant of food supplies and called together a lot of children in order to be photographed while feeding the poor. As no wood was handy, they got some newspapers, crammed them into the stove and, while they were burning, had a rapid photograph taken in order to complete the picture.

November 14, 1919.

Late yesterday afternoon, Colonel Sheldon had called up Colonel Dimistrescu to tell him that it was reported that the Roumanians were threatening to bombard the town of Kecskemét because the body of a Roumanian soldier had been found near that place, and to tell him that such action was contrary to international law and to the customs of civilized warfare. In view of the fact that Dimistrescu asked Colonel Sheldon three times whether the protest was being made in the name of the Inter-Allied Military Mission or in the name of the American Mission, about 9.30 I went over with Colonel Sheldon to the Hungaria Hotel, routed Colonel Dimistrescu out to inform him that whenever any member of the Inter-Allied Military Mission sent a message to Roumanian Headquarters it was necessarily in the name of the Mission, and then asked him what he meant by asking if the protest emanated from the American Mission, and what he would have done had he been told that it was only the American Mission. He squirmed around and lied like a true Roumanian and said that his question had really meant nothing, but in their records they kept track of the various Missions separately and it was solely for that purpose that he had made the inquiry.

This morning before daylight, the Roumanians pulled it and the Hungarians came in, at least to the west portion of the town, the City of Buda, where detachments lined up at the bridges to wait until the signal after 10 o'clock for crossing the Danube and occupying likewise the city of Pest. The whole evacuation of Budapest by the Roumanians, and its reoccupation by the Hungarians, bids fair to pass off without noteworthy accident.

At the session of the Mission this morning, at which General Mombelli presided and which on account of the cold in the Palace was held in the Italian Mission, we brought up the question of Roumanian liaison, and General Graziani stated that Colonel Dimistrescu had told him that he thought for a few days at least it would inadvisable for any Roumanian officer to remain behind in Budapest, all of which speaks well for the courage of the Roumanians.

I suggested we notify the Hungarian government that, in view of several inquiries received by individual embers of the Mission, this Mission exercised no control over private property in any of the museums and the Hungarian government was free to restore any such its own judgment.

November 15, 1919.

Today was a disagreeable, nasty day, with some snow and slush under foot.

The Hungarians continued to come into the city and are in actual occupation.

Yesterday afternoon I went over to the Hungarian National Museum and returned to them the key which I had taken possession of on October 4, and I removed the seals from the doors. They gave me a receipt for the key and asked permission to retain, as a historic document, the seal from one of the three doors upon which they were placed. I gave them one, retained one for myself and gave the other to Colonel Loree.

As we were barred from attending the big celebrations given by the Hungarians in honor of the Roumanian evacuation, we accordingly invited a number of people, including General Gorton, General Mombelli and his family, our host Count Edelsheim, and the families of Count Szirmay and Teleki, and had a little dance.

November 16, 1919.

This is the great day for the entry of Admiral Horthy's army, and the bells began to ring early to indicate the arrival of the troops. Unfortunately, none of us could witness this for fear of international complications, so we worked as usual. They were to have a big public mass in front of the Parliament Building. Tonight they are to have some kind of big celebration at the opera, to which, of course, none of us can go, for the same reason that kept us away from the parade.

Mr. Dubois, representing the United States Department of State, called this morning to explain that he was on a mission to endeavor to compile a report on the political situation of Central Europe, and asked for my assistance in getting together data and in preparing his report in general. This of course I was very glad to furnish him, as he will undoubtedly be able to check up many of the reports that come to me.

November 17, 1919.

Yesterday was a big day in Budapest and fortunately everything passed off with dignity and decorum. There was a cold rain in the morning, which rather dampened the ardor of those participating the public mass, but it cleared up in the afternoon and at night, I understand, the opera House was packed. Although no members of the Inter-Allied Military Mission were in attendance, the British Admiral Troubridge and the French Admiral on duty in Budapest both, accompanied by their staffs, occupied conspicuous boxes, thereby making the rest of us conspicuous by our absence.

I presided at this morning's session of the Mission, and view of the fact that Sir George Clerk is wiring the Supreme Council scare-head telegrams, we decided to send a report to the effect that conditions in the city of Budapest and vicinity, since Hungarian reoccupation have, everything considered, been excellent; that Admiral Horthy's troops have shown themselves to be well disciplined and under control. I also sent a personal report of attendance at the opera of the British and French admirals.

Sir George Clerk is still much concerned about his work, and properly so. He does not seem to be able to handle these people at all and keeps on paying overmuch attention to the complaints of Garami and the other Socialist leaders[5]. As a result of all this, Friedrich is proceeding serenely on his way and paying very little attention to anybody else. Some of the Hungarians have made the statement that, as long as the Entente cannot force the Italians out of Fiume[6] and could not even oblige a little nation like Roumania to obey its orders, there is no reason why Hungary should be unduly concerned about such a feeble combination.

Just before General Mardarescu left Budapest, General Gorton and I went to see him and he promised faithfully to leave behind fifty-three motor trucks for the distribution of food. When our men went to get the trucks, instead of fifty-three, they found only thirty-six, not one of which was serviceable and most of which were lacking in wheels, motors, or something equally important; and then when Mardarescu left, he even took these along. We have, therefore, wired the Supreme Council recommending that the Roumanians be required to return the fifty-three trucks which they took.

5   Compare note on Sir George Clerk, on October 20.

6   Gabriele d'Annunzio had seized Fiume on Sept. 13 and Zara on Nov. 4, in defiance of the decision of the Allies.

November 18, 1919.

This has been the coldest day that we have had. It froze hard all day and at night a heavy snowstorm began.

I was down in the city, both in the forenoon and in the afternoon, to see how matters were progressing, and everything is remarkably calm.

Sir George Clerk, in evident fear that he is not going be able to accomplish his mission, sent some scare-head telegrams to Paris, which apparently gave the impression that Admiral Horthy and Friedrich were arresting all of their political opponents. As a matter fact, the arrests that were made were practically insignificant, and none were made that were not perfectly justifiable. Under the circumstances, I was obliged to telegraph the American Commission accordingly, in addition to which Colonel Loree left Budapest last night for Paris in order personally to explain the situation, they are apparently bewildered by the conflicting telegrams from Sir George Clerk and the Inter-Allied Military Mission.

This evening we had for dinner Major Moffat of the American Red Cross, Captain Weiss, formerly on duty with Mr. Hoover and who is now about to return to the United States, and Captain Richardson, who is in charge of the American organization for feeding children. At present he is feeding daily in Hungary 33,000 children, over half of whom are in Budapest, and he expects soon to increase the number to 100,000.

November 19, 1919.[7]

7   On this day Bandholtz wrote a letter to the British foreign minister, severely criticizing a confidential memorandum written to Earl Curzon by British Charge d'affaires Rattigan from Bukarest. The two documents are included at the end of this diary.

It snowed good and hard last night and early this morning, with about four inches of snow on the ground, and it snowed practically all day. As a result many sleighs were in evidence.

At the session of the Mission this morning, General Gorton presided, and showed a telegram, which by courtesy of Sir George Clerk had been handed to him, giving the decision of the Supreme Council in regard to the various Hungarian boundaries. Among other things, it stated that the Supreme Council was still considering the question of the exploitation of the coal mines at Pécs by the Serbians. As a result of this, we directed the President of the Day to telegraph to the Supreme Council, informing them how we had received this copy of their telegram, deprecating that they had not seen fit to advise us directly in regard to a matter so essentially military, and requesting that they sustain our action in requiring the Serbians to evacuate immediately all of the district of Baranya[8]. One letter, received sometime ago from the Serbians in regard to the evacuation, contained the statement that in view of the fact that the Entente had not forced the Roumanians to evacuate, they could see no reason why they should pay any attention to such requests.

As our good friend, Sir George Clerk, had been apparently badly rattled over prospective arrests during the first days of the Hungarian reoccupation, and had apparently thought that the blame lay a good deal with the police, which was under the supervision of Colonel Yates of the American Army, I submitted to the Mission some statements in regard to actual conditions during the evacuation, and the Mission decided unanimously to congratulate Colonel Yates on the excellent manner in which everything pertaining to the police situation had been handled.

As a telegram of the day before yesterday from Mr. Polk indicated that Sir George Clerk's scare in regard to the outcome resulting from Hungarian reoccupation had permeated to the Supreme Council, I went over this morning and had a personal interview with Sir George, showing him Mr. Polk's telegram, telling him our wires had undoubtedly got crossed, and that if any such idea obtained in the Supreme Council as the retention of the Roumanians in Hungary, I considered that results would be most disastrous. Sir George promised me to telegraph immediately to the Supreme Council, stating that everything was lovely and that prospects were most encouraging.

8   The main city of this district is Pécs, or Fünfkirchen.

At the session on the seventeenth, there had been presented by the French Mission a proposition for the turning over to the Roumanians of three batteries of our guns each, of 10.4 centimeter howitzers, in exchange with the Roumanians for an equal number of 8 centimeter guns. The whole proposition looked a little bit fishy, especially in view of the fact that sometime before, when General Gorton was President of he Day, a communication was sent to the Roumanians stating explicitly that this deal was off. It appears that he whole proposition was a little private transaction between Lieutenant-Colonel Berthon, French, and Colonel Dimistrescu, Roumanian. At the session this morning, we received a protest from Admiral Horthy in regard to such a transfer, and it was decided that it would not take place. Later on, a telephone message was received from the Roumanians insisting that such a transfer should take place not later than the twenty-first. They will be politely invited to side-step to Hell.

At noon Admiral Horthy called upon me and we spent about an hour in conversation. He is a fine-appearing, intelligent-looking officer, and I believe is sincere in his desire and intention to do everything for the best. He deprecated Friedrich's obstinacy and I think is afraid that he may have to remove him sooner or later by force, although at present it looks as though some sort of an agreement could be arrived at. The Admiral promised me that it would be his constant and earnest endeavor to prevent any excesses on the part of his countrymen or the pulling off of any stunts that would affect the situation.

November 20, 1919.

It continued to snow all day, and sleighs were in evidence throughout the city.

Owing to the coal shortage, all the street cars have stopped running and the electric current has been reduced by 50 per cent.

In the evening at 6 o'clock, accompanied by Colonel Sheldon, I called upon Admiral Horthy and went into considerable detail concerning the situation. I also informed him of the rumor that we had heard that the Supreme Council had sent a final ultimatum to Roumania, giving her eight days for reply, and demanding that she reply affirmatively without quibbling, equivocation or prevarication, to the various points presented to her, and requiring that she immediately evacuate all of Hungary and sign the Peace Treaty, including its Minority clauses.

From all word received, it is apparent that the Roumanians are seriously contemplating progressing directly east of the Theiss River, instead of stopping there as they had originally determined.

The Admiral informed me that he would probably remain with his headquarters as at present at the Hotel Gellért, in the same place where General Mardarescu had had his headquarters, that he would then move for short time up to the War Office, and would eventually establish headquarters outside the limits of the city of Budapest.

During the day, I arranged to send Lieutenant-Colonel Moore to southeastern Hungary, to that portion of Baranya where the Pécs coal mines are, to investigate to conditions. When he approached the Serbian Minister in regard to the matter, that poor little toy balloon nearly burst and did all sorts of vehement protesting, stating that he could not visé any passports or anything of the kind. As the territory Colonel Moore is to visit is, according to the terms of the Armistice, to be permanent Hungarian territory, I gave Colonel Moore a letter of instruction informing whom it might concern that he was proceeding on this duty by order of the Inter-Allied Military Mission, which in giving its orders was acting in strict conformity with its authority from the Supreme Council. We will now await developments.

We had no guests tonight and spent a quiet evening in our quarters.

November 21, 1919.

During the evening the snow turned into rain and fog, and today it is indescribably disagreeable. There is slush everywhere and, owing to the stoppage of the street cars, the streets are full of struggling pedestrians.

The meeting of the Mission was held at General Graziani's quarters, in the house which is owned by the Countess Széchényi, the sister of my friend, General Cornelius Vanderbilt. They had hoped that the American Mission would occupy the building, and we really had first choice at it. I decided, however, that I did not want to have Nelly Vanderbilt chasing me up afterwards and asking me what I had done with any property that might be missing from his sister's home.

At the session, General Gorton and I in turn explained what we had gathered from Colonel Moore's verbal report on conditions at Szolnok, to the effect mainly that he had gathered from Colonel Dimistrescu, not by a direct statement, but from his general conduct and bearing, that the Roumanians were apparently going to continue their evacuation up to the line of demarcation; but adding that these signs might mean nothing, seeing that they came from Roumania.

173

I then explained Colonel Moore's experience of last night with the Serbian Minister, and stated what I had done in this case. It was approved by the Mission. It was further decided to telegraph the Supreme Council requesting that the Serbians be required to evacuate immediately all portions of Hungary they were holding and retire behind their line of demarcation, and it was added in particular that it was recommended that they be required to withdraw from the town of Pécs. It had been intended to include this in the telegram of the day before yesterday, but through error it had been omitted.

Colonel Yates stated this morning that he thought the Hungarians were making far more arrests than they were reporting, and I instructed him to investigate and see whether or not they were emulating the illustrious example of the lying Roumanians.

November 22, 1919.

Last night we entertained the Envoy Extraordinary and Minister Plenipotentiary from The Kingdom of the Serbs, Croats and Slovenes to the Inter-Allied Military Mission, meaning thereby our old friend, Dr. Lazar Baitch, his colleague Major Body, and Mrs. Body. We also had Colonel Yates and Major Moffat of the American Red Cross. The Hungarian champagne warmed up the cockles of Lazar Baitch's heart to such an extent that he was soon waltzing with Colonel Yates while Colonel Sheldon played the piano, and later on wound up with a skirt dance.

At noon today there was a big meeting at one of the schools, to which I was invited as the senior American representative, and where we listened to several most eloquent addresses in Hungarian. The eloquence was to be judged only by the gesticulations, as Hungarian is a language which no one can read or understand without swallowing a paper of fish hooks. Before we wound up, a little girl came up and made some remarks in what purported to be English. Anyway she handed me a big bouquet of chrysanthemums, and I kissed her on the right cheek, to the accompaniment of vociferous applause.

I have acquired a new Hungarian valet, who speaks only German and Hungarian, and forces me to go back to my childhood of forty-five or fifty years ago, when German was almost as easy as my native tongue. He insists on making me do a great many things that I do not want to do. Among others, he tries to force me to take a warm bath in the morning when I am determined to take a cold bath. However, when his back is turned I let the hot water out and turn the cold water in, so I am able to circumvent to a certain extent his devilish intentions.

174

We just received word today from our beloved allies, the Roumanians, that they have decided to remove the pontoon bridge at Szolnok, all this despite their solemn promises that they would leave it. The Roumanians are really the most reliable people in the world when it comes to depending upon their breaking any promises they make.

November 23, 1919.

Last night Colonel Sheldon, Captain Gore and I were guests at dinner at the house of Baron von Groedel, and while there we met young Baron Weiss, whose family is the wealthiest in Hungary, and whom the Roumanians robbed of eight hundred million kronen worth of property.

Yesterday morning a staff officer from the French Admiral called at my quarters to say that three weeks ago he [the Admiral] had called upon me and left his card. He was wondering if I had received it as I had never returned the call. So later in the afternoon, accompanied by Captain Gore, I went to the Admiral's quarters, found him in, and told him that within twenty-four hours his call had been returned and my card left at his quarters, but I wished that there should be no misunderstanding and therefore I had come personally this time to make sure that there could be no mistake. Not to be outdone, he called upon me again my office early this morning, so that we are now quits.

The newspapers announce that the Hungarians at last have formed a new cabinet with Huszár[9] as Prime Minister and Friedrich in charge of the War portfolio. is to be hoped that Sir George Clerk's labors are now approaching their end and that he can proceed to his proper Station as Minister to Czecho-Slovakia.

November 24, 1919.

Last night we entertained Admiral Horthy, General Soós, Count Edelsheim, General Gorton, and Colonel Yates at dinner, and our chef absolutely surpassed himself.

At this morning's session at the Italian Mission, where course General Mombelli presided, General Graziani gave us a report of Colonel Berthon's trip to Szolnok,

9   Karl Huszár, a Christian Socialist.

175

by which arrangements were made for internationalizing the railroad bridges across the Theiss River; and we were informed that the Roumanians had already removed the pontoon bridge at Szolnok.

General Graziani also read from the Hungarian papers a retraction which had been made by the Hungarian Colonel Lehár, of the ridiculous statements attributed to him in a previous issue of the *Pester Lloyd*, in which he was quoted as having said that Hungary had the only disciplined army in all Central Europe.

Lieutenant-Colonel Moore, of my Mission, was later brought in, having just returned from a trip to the Pécs coal mines where the Serbians are in occupation. He stated that the Serbs were running rampant through the whole section, that even many kilometers beyond Pécs, which is itself about thirty kilometers inside the Hungarian lines, the Serbians had established complete civil government, and were intimating in no uncertain terms that they proposed to stay permanently. The troops that they had in garrison were in a rotten condition of discipline, and conditions on the whole were most unfavorable. He reported that of the one hundred and fifty carloads, of ten tons each, that were turned out daily by the Pécs coal mines, about one hundred and twenty carloads were taken over by the Serbian government and the rest only was used for local consumption. The Serbs had even gone so far as to demand verbally, as a tax, 20 per cent of all the private deposits in the banks.

After the meeting, I went with Captain Gore and Major Moffat to see the American Red Cross at work and was very much gratified. In one place they were systematically issuing to the poor large quantities of clothing in appropriate individual lots, and in another place they were furnishing food and clothing to infants. is work of this kind that immensely raises the prestige of the American name.

November 25, 1919.

Yesterday afternoon was a very busy afternoon, owing to the fact that our courier was leaving for Vienna, which, taken in connection with the morning session of the Mission, jammed things all together in the last half of the day. Unfortunately this courier business does not mean much because, although leaving here Monday evening and arriving in Vienna Tuesday morning, our mail will lie over there until Monday before going on to Paris.

This morning I received several telegrams from Colonel Loree, among others, word to the effect that he had seen General Bliss and Mr. White of the American

Commission and explained to them that it would hardly be advisable to continue this Mission in case the American Commission to Negotiate Peace were permanently dissolved[10]. This was absolutely along the lines my instructions to Loree before his departure, and likewise strictly in accord with my own personal ideas. When I mentioned the matter, however, to one or two Hungarians, the first one being Count Somssich, the minister of Foreign Affairs, he simply collapsed and said the mere fact that an American Mission was here gave them confidence in the future, and assured them of a square deal. He assured me it would be nothing short of a calamity in case we left here before the elections in January and the establishment of a permanent government. I interrogated him and several others and told them plainly that I had no delusions of grandeur, was not a megalomaniac, and wanted to know whether they were trying to tell me things which would be most grateful to hear, or whether they were really sincere in their belief that the American Mission should continue for a while longer, and that in any event I should remain on account of my knowledge of the situation, absorbed from nearly four months' stay. Their protestations that it was necessary that the Mission, as now organized, remain, were undoubtedly sincere, so I felt obliged to telegraph Colonel Loree that the Hungarians felt that their main guarantee for a square deal lay in a continuation until after election of the American Mission, but I added that, personally, the sooner I could go home the better I would be pleased. It will now be a question of waiting two or three days to learn what the final decision is.

The Roman Catholic Cardinal, who is called the Prince Primas of Hungary, called upon me this morning, accompanied by a bishop as interpreter, to thank me, not only for what I had done for Hungary, but in particular for having saved most of his treasures which were in the Museum that the Roumanians were going to rob. Like all high functionaries of the Catholic Church, he was a jolly old fellow, and I enjoyed his visit very much.

November 26, 1919.

At this morning's session of the Mission, at which I presided, General Mombelli was very sore because Sir George Clerk had not sent notice to the Mission of the fact that he had recognized the new Hungarian government under Huszár. As a

---

10 On Nov.19 the United States Senate had definitely rejected the Treaty of Versailles.

matter of fact, Sir George did notify us, but through rather devious channels. He sent a letter to the Italian counselor giving a list of the ministry and telling him he had recognized the new cabinet, then sent General Gorton a copy of the same and asked Gorton to let the rest of us have copies. In view of the fact that the Italian counselor had not a damn thing to do with the government or anything else, neither Mombelli nor Graziani could understand why Sir George had adopted such a peculiar method. I don't think he meant anything by it, but just didn't know any better.

It was decided to send another telegram to the Supreme Council, calling attention for the third or fourth time to the fact that the Serbs had planted themselves in the Baranya district apparently for life, and also to he fact that the Supreme Council had never yet given us any decision as to whether or not the Serbians were to remain or to beat it. We therefore asked specifically for a statement that the Serbians were immediately to evacuate territory which did not belong to them, or that the territory was to be given to them.

The day before yesterday I was the recipient of a long tale of woe from Baron Than, representing the Archduke Joseph, to the effect that the Czecho-Slovaks were seizing the private property of his estate in Czecho-Slovakia, including his wife's personal letters, and were proposing to sell the whole thing at auction. I immediately telegraphed our Minister at Prague that it was inconceivable that any civilized nation could be guilty of such rotten conduct, informing him that I had likewise notified the American Commission in Paris. At the same time, I sent a copy of the telegram to General Mombelli, who was President of the Day, and he put in a vigorous protest with Minister Hodza, the Czecho-Slovak representative in Budapest. The whole situation throughout southeastern Europe seems to be a "go as you please" game.

As a report had been received that the Roumanians, despite the fact that an Armistice was in existence had shelled the defenseless town of Tokaj, killing several of the inhabitants, it was decided to call upon the Roumanians for an explanation of their peculiar yet characteristic conduct, and also to invite their attention to the fact that they were still raiding private estates.

A commendatory letter was drafted and given to Major Edward Borrow, of the British Army, for his excellent services, particularly in connection with keeping track of the rolling stock that the Roumanians had seized.

Yesterday afternoon I went down town and had some dental work done by a Hungarian dentist named Dick, who had been a student of Dr. Brophy in Chicago. Colonel Sheldon and I both went to see him again this afternoon.

Owing to the coal shortage and the early nightfall, all stores now close at either three or four o'clock, and the city is decidedly gloomy by mid-afternoon.

November 27, 1919.[11]

General Gorton told me this morning that, having heard of the possibility that my Mission might close up shop and leave in a few days, had wired the British Commission in Paris protesting and requesting that we remain here until after the Hungarian elections.

Some way or other, the Hungarians today found out at it was our Thanksgiving Day and I received large bouquets of flowers with cards from the Archduke, from Cardinal Csernoch, the Prince Primas of Hungary, from the Prime Minister, from various other cabinet ministers, from Admiral Horthy, from General Soós, from the Mayor and Council of Budapest, and any others. The Cardinal came over about noon with big flock of counts and barons, countesses and baronesses, and we had quite a celebration. The Prime Minister also came in, not only to felicitate us on our national holiday, but to express his thanks for the justice and sincerity with which the American Mission had operated from the beginning, and for the interest that had displayed in unfortunate Hungary. I told him that neither my country nor myself had anything to gain whatever, that we desired nothing but fair play, at America has always sympathized with and endeavored to aid unfortunate nations and people, and that if I had succeeded in impressing them with that idea, I had really accomplished my mission; that the various expressions of thanks and appreciation from all Hungarian officials I accepted, not as coming personally to me, but as coming to my country.

About 6 o'clock a code message came from Colonel Loree to the effect that the American Commission would meet tomorrow and decide whether or not the

11 On this day the Treaty of Neuilly was signed with Bulgaria. The Roumanians and the Jugo-Slavs were not permitted to sign it until they had signed the Treaty of St. Germain, with its Minorities provision.

American Military Mission should continue, whether I should remain with a small body as an observer, or whether we should entirely quit Hungary.

In view of the fact that it was Thanksgiving Day, I gave a dinner at my quarters to all the American officers in Budapest, those attending being Colonel Sheldon, Lieutenant-Colonel Moore, Captain Shafroth, Captain Gore, Captain Weiss, Major Moffat of the American Red Cross, Captain Richardson of the American Children's Welfare Association, and my Hungarian Aide, Lieutenant Count Teleki. Before the dinner, most of them attended the Grand Opera which was turning out a musical enigma called the "Magic Flute." Captain Gore and I did not arrive until within about three-quarters of an hour of the conclusion of the performance, because we were obliged to remain at home to decode Colonel Loree's telegram. However, we saw too much of the performance even at that late hour. All that I could gather was that a gray-headed young man with robust body and spindle-shank legs had to go through seven kinds of Hell in order to win a little squirt of a prima donna with a face like the head of a tabasco bottle. Some of the dancers in connection with opera might have been worth going through one or two Hells for, but only a lunatic would have gone through seven for the prima donna.

Our chef, in a strenuous effort to turn out a real American Thanksgiving dinner, turned out the rottenest meal since we have had him. He asserted in raucous tones, interpolated with the usual number of Hungarian consonants, that he knew how to make a pumpkin pie and he did. It was pumpkin all right, and it was pie, but it was the same kind of a crust that we had on our chicken potpie, and the pumpkin was chucked into in cubes about an inch square. Another time we will limit him to his well-known repertoire.

November 28, 1919.

As General Gorton left last night for Vienna to meet Mrs. Gorton, who is expected to are there in a day or so, General Graziani presided and met at the French Mission. General Graziani read a translation from one of the Hungarian papers of what was supposed to be a report on an address by Friedrich the Christian-National Party, of which he is the head, and which contained one particularly strong sentiment as follows:

"I state frankly that we cannot and must not have confidence in the Entente."

It was decided to write Herr Friedrich a letter, calling attention to this, and requiring an explanation and retraction in the paper.

Telephone reports came in yesterday that, whenever a Hungarian appeared at the bridge at Szolnok he was promptly shot at by the Roumanian sentinels on the other side, despite the agreement the Roumanians made that the bridges at Szolnok and elsewhere would be opened to traffic for the Hungarians. This is the usual Roumanian style of keeping a promise.

We also received word that the Serbians were retiring from Pécs and pulling off all sorts of rotten stunts. Therefore it was decided to send a committee of four officers, one from each Mission, immediately to Pécs to investigate and handle the situation.

While I was attending the session of the Mission, Colonel Kelly of the U.S. Engineers, called, and Colonel Sheldon very properly invited Kelly and Mrs. Kelly to informal luncheon.

November 29, 1919.

Last night we had Colonel and Mrs. Kelly to dinner, and they left this morning by boat for Belgrade.

I recently received a clipping from a Roumanian paper, which in big headlines had the following:

"A reply from General Mardarescu."

"The following was sent to Vienna from Budapest."

"The conduct of the Roumanians with regard to the Hungarians and the Allies is best characterized by the reply of General Mardarescu as given to the protest of the Inter-Allied Military Mission against requisitions:"

"Gentlemen, you have four telephones but I have 80,000 bayonets."

Of course the old scoundrel never said such a thing or we would have choked him on the spot, but the worst part of it is that if he had said it, it would have been the truth, which is still further proof that he never did it.

Last evening I received a very touching telegram from Mr. Halstead, of the American Mission in Vienna, which he stated:

"Regret exceeding carelessness of a clerk this Mission caused pouch for your Mission to be returned to Paris and your pouch for Paris remain here. Greatly chagrined. Pouch be returned from Paris by courier leaving there Monday and sent down by Thursday train first available.

Halstead.

His chagrin was nothing compared to our disgust. I also received a telegram from Mr. Polk in which he asked me to telegraph him fully as to whether or not was still necessary to keep up the Inter-Allied Military Mission, adding that he desired to withdraw all Inter-Allied Military Missions as far as possible, in order not to become too deeply involved in European politics, and to avoid any criticism from Washington. He suggested that I should remain as High Commissioner until the arrival of the American civil representative. I replied that in my opinion the Inter-Allied Military Mission could well be dispensed with, as it had carried out its instructions as far as possible. I might have added that it had never received any backing from the Supreme Council all the time it was here, although my people always backed me to the limit. I also suggested that I reduce my force to about one-half of what it has been in the past.

By the same messenger, I received a cable from the United States which was the best that I have received since being over here. It was from my young friend Littwitz, who sent only three words:

"Wife improving splendidly."

It is a pleasure to be of service to anyone as appreciative as Littwitz has been of the few things I did for him.

November 30, 1919.

This morning, accompanied by Colonel Sheldon, Mr. Zerkowitz and my Hungarian Aide, Lieutenant Count Teleki, I called upon His Excellency, Prime Minister Huszár, and we were received with all the pomp and circumstance with which Hungarian officials delight to surround themselves. A magnificent major-domo all dolled up like one of the old time drum majors, met us at the entrance and led us by a whole line of obsequious flunkies, each of which was shining with oriental splendor. By a circuitous route, so as to take in all the swell rooms, they led us to the reception room, where the Prime Minister met us at the entrance.

It then became evident that I need not have brought Mr. Zerkowitz along as interpreter because there was a young man named Bárczy who came forward, and who had the most beautiful flow of English I have ever heard, at least as far as the flow is concerned. His Excellency would spout and spit Hungarian for about one minute, then M. Bárczy would open the floodgates of his eloquence and spit ornate and flowery English for fifteen minutes. It was all to the effect that the Hungarians appreciated all that the Entente had done for them and, of course, in particular America. They wanted us to stay by them until after the elections, of course again in particular America, and most particularly myself. I responded with like hyperbole, and after half an our the meeting terminated and His Excellency escorted us all the way out to the head of the stairs. He greatly admired my heavy riding crop, and wanted to know if it was the same one with which I had driven company of Roumanians out of the Palace courtyard, and which had been my sole weapon when I stood guard over the government office when the Roumanians were threatening to come up and arrest the whole cabinet. Upon my replying in the affirmative, he asked that I turn it over to their National Museum, so I suppose that will be the end of my fine old riding crop, which I shall miss damnably.

Colonel Sheldon has been bitten by the philatelic microbe and his case, for the present at least, seems to be more hopeless than my own. If he is introduced to a high official, the first thing he says is:

"Has Your Excellency any stamps in his pants?"

and the inquiry has become so stereotyped that I am afraid he will address it to the countesses and baronesses who seem to be flocking into his office, but of whom he allows none to penetrate into my sanctum unless they are older than the devil or as ugly as Hell, in this respect emulating the example of one Colonel Taber Loree.

December, 1919

December 1, 1919.

Last night Colonel Sheldon and I dined with our dentist, Doctor Dick, and had a horrible time. It was one of those occasions during which the host and hostess are so annoyingly attentive, and so insistent upon one's making a garbage can out of one's self, that much of the joy of the occasion is lost. After the dinner we adjourned to a sitting room, where some she-musicians piled on agony, and one of them in particular fiddled out a lot of dirges.

This morning the Mission met at General Mombelli's quarters, with him presiding, as General Gorton had not yet returned from Vienna. I read to them Colonel Yates' report to me, to the effect that General Mardarescu maintains that he has no instructions about retiring beyond the Tisza[1]; that he thinks he should remain there until a treaty of peace is signed with Hungary, in order to keep an obstacle between himself and the Hungarians; that he sees no necessity for a liaison officer, as he understood that the Inter-Allied Military Mission was to arrange only for the evacuation from Budapest to the Tisza. Mardarescu's statements are always so palpably lies that there is never any use discussing them. However, he clearly outlined the plans of the Roumanians.

I then informed my colleagues that last night Colonel Moore had called me up by telephone from Pécs and had told me that the Serbs declined to recognize any commission from the Inter-Allied Military Mission, stating that they had received no orders from their government and could not discuss evacuation or anything of the kind; and that I had, therefore, ordered Colonel Moore to return.

I then informed my two Latin colleagues that I had got damn sick and tired myself of having two miserable little misfit nations like Roumania and Serbia insult the United States of America through its unworthy representatives; that I was equally sick and tired of sending urgent telegrams to the Supreme Council with the strongest possible recommendations, without even receiving the courtesy of a reply; and then I suggested that we consider the advisability of informing the Supreme Council that in our opinion our usefulness had practically ended, and the relief of the Mission was advisable. They all solemnly

1 Or Theiss, in German.

185

concurred in my remarks, but thought the question of taking up the matter with the Supreme Council should receive a little longer consideration. I learned afterwards that both the French and Italian officers are receiving as allowances several times what their pay would be in case they were relieved and returned to France and Italy, all of which accounts for their reluctance to give up a remunerative job.

General Graziani confirmed the reports that I had received in regard to the Czecho-Slovaks, and seemed to be of the opinion that things were in a ferment over there and that something would pop before long.

We received characteristic letters from Mardarescu, stating that he would now allow the bridges to be repaired at Tokaj, Szolnok, and Csongrád; that he proposed to return, on the sixth, 1,840 Hungarian soldier prisoners-of-war and 886 officers, and that he would like to have arrangements made so that goods en route through Hungary to Roumania would not be delayed.

After the meeting of the Mission, accompanied by Colonel Sheldon and Captain Gore, and likewise by Major Foster, representing the British in General Gorton's absence, we went to the reception given by Dr. Baitch, the Serbian Minister. Here we went through some kind of ceremony on the anniversary of the creation of the Kingdom of Serbs, Croates and Slovenes in succession to the Kingdom of Serbia. Eventually, toward noon, we escaped from the Serbian Mission, and then after lunch loaned all of our cars to the English Mission because one of their captains, named Graham, is going this afternoon to marry the Hungarian Baroness Podmaniczky.

December 2, 1919.

This morning I sent a car down to meet Colonel Causey, who was returning from Vienna with General Gorton. Colonel Causey is still left by our government as adviser to the Austrian government on railroad and other similar matters, and he reports conditions in Vienna to be most deplorable. He doubts if there will be an outbreak of Bolshevism, despite the fact that there is dire distress from shortage of both fuel and provisions. We had Colonel Causey to luncheon and invited him to dinner also, but he had a previous engagement with General Gorton.

In the forenoon I went to the city and attended an art exhibit and arranged for the purchase of a couple of paintings, which I hope to be able eventually to install in Constantine, Michigan[2].

In the afternoon General Gorton called upon me and I gave him a résumé of what had happened during his absence of a few days in Vienna to meet Mrs. Gorton. He retaliated by inviting me to dinner tomorrow night and I accepted on condition that I be allowed to tell Mrs. Gorton all that I knew of his horrible derelictions prior to her arrival. He tried to buy me off but the price was not high enough.

December 3, 1919.

General Gorton having returned from Vienna, the Mission met in his office with him in the chair, and it was one of the most unimportant sessions that we have had, with practically no business before us.

The Hungarians sent in a request that certain persons, whom they desired to place on their list of peace delegates, were in Roumanian occupied territory and they were very anxious to have arrangements made so that these persons could come to Budapest and proceed with the Hungarian delegation. All the Mission could do was to repeat their request to the Supreme Council.

General Graziani tried to calm me down and told me to be patient, that we had done a great deal here after all, and that there was no occasion to get worried, but that we should bide our time and all would be well. I told him that sounded bully, but that I couldn't see why four generals should be hanging around Budapest and practically doing nothing; that I was of course willing to wait for instructions, which I was now doing.

Last night there was a report current that Minister Friedrich had been implicated as accessory to the murder of Count Tisza. This morning the report is denied.

A Mrs. French, from California, who is over here on some sort of a suffrage proposition, was in to tell me about a meeting that took place in Budapest and, if all her statements are true, there is still a wild-eyed bunch of fanatics who will have to be skinned before much progress is made in Hungary. She said that a Catholic priest, at a public meeting on the thirtieth of November, said:

The Bible tells us we must forgive our enemies. I say we can personally forgive our enemies as Christians, but not as Hungarians. The Hungarian people must never forget

2   General Bandholtz's hometown in the United States.

and the Jews must be punished. They say it is shameful to have pogroms, but we say it is just as shameful to have communism in the twentieth century, and we had it.

The second speaker was a professor by the name of Zarkany, who after giving some left-handed compliments to the Entente, stated:

The Jewish question is a national one for the Hungarian people to settle and we will settle it[3].

3   Before the world war and the rule of Bolshevism, there existed no anti-Semitic movement in Hungary to speak of. Hungary contained in its population a relatively large percentage of Jews, but they felt as strongly Hungarian as the old German Jews felt German. In contrast to their racial confreres in Roumania and Russia, Hungarian Jews did not suffer from persecution or exceptional legal treatment.

   But a disproportionate number of Jews participated in establishing Bolshevism in Hungary and they were its most cruel exponents. Ninety-five percent of the communist leaders were Jewish, and, of the twenty-six Commissars, eighteen were Jews, though there were only one and a half million Jews among the twenty million inhabitants of Hungary. Furthermore, a very large number of the Jewish Bolshevik leaders had immigrated into Hungary only recently and could really not be called Hungarians in any true sense. The conservative and national Jewish-Hungarian element despised these foreigners as much as did their Christian compatriots. Unfortunately, however, the despicable behavior of many of the Jewish Communists caused the Hungarian people, after the overthrow of the Bolshevik rule, to turn against all Jews.

   It is deplorable, but quite natural, that the reaction against the Red Terror was accompanied by excesses and persecution of the Jews though the account of it is generally greatly exaggerated. The attitude of the better element is expressed in the following words of Count Paul Teleki: "I would like to say that it is a mistake to think that the anti-Jewish movement, which really existed and which still exists in Hungary, is one against the Jewish religion or Jews in general. If I had to characterize it as a historian it would be rather with the words 'anti-Galician movement.' " *The Evolution of Hungary and its Place in European History*, New York, 1925, p.141. A few examples of the anti-Semitic feeling and actions in Hungary are given in this Diary.

December 4, 1919.

Things are getting quieter and quieter. Now that the Roumanians are out of Budapest and have practically cut all communications, there is comparatively little doing. A French officer, however, came over today to say that General Graziani could communicate by telegraph direct to the Roumanians in very few minutes, so it would appear that, although the latter do not care to establish liaison with the Inter-Allied Military Mission, they are doing so with the French mission, which, when everything is considered, not to be wondered at.

Count Somssich came in to see me and I arranged with him to send a telegram to the Supreme Council from the Hungarian government, acknowledging receipt of the invitation to send peace delegates to Paris and explaining how impossible it was to make satisfactory arrangements while the Roumanians were still occupying one-third of Hungary.

As previously stated, I had permanently assigned to me the Royal Box in the Opera House, but in view of the fact that there is now a recognized government in Hungary, I sent the following letter today:

To His Excellency, the Hungarian Prime Minister.

The undersigned is deeply grateful for the courtesy and the honor conferred upon him by the assignment of the large central box at the Opera House. As long as there was no government in Hungary that had been recognized by the Allied and Associated Powers, there was no apparent impropriety in the use of this box as assigned. Now, however, that the Government of which Your Excellency is the honored Minister President has been duly recognized, and as it is understood the box in question is the one usually reserved for the Head of the State, the undersigned, with sincere thanks and grateful appreciation of the past honor conferred upon him, desires to relinquish the box in question, and with assurances of the highest respect and esteem begs to remain,

Most respectfully.

If this currency keeps on tumbling, it will not be worth the paper it is printed on. The krone, which in ante-bellum days was worth 21¼ cents, is today worth just 8 mills or 4/5 of a cent, and today I converted a few dollars at the rate of 125 kronen to the dollar.

December 5, 1919.

This morning's session was held at my quarters and I presided, and we had a hot old time. General Gorton stated that last night he had received communication, as President of the Day, from the diplomatic representative of the Kingdom of the

Serbs, Croates and Slovenes, complaining that Hungarian regular troops to the number of one thousand had crossed he Serbian line, attacking the Serbian forces and capturing prisoners in the vicinity of Redics; asking that he Hungarians be required to release the prisoners immediately, and that a committee be sent from this Mission at once to investigate the facts in the case. We asked the Hungarian Prime Minister to send an authorized officer to explain this matter to us, and accordingly General Soós reported at 10.15, bringing with him maps and all data in connection with the incident, which occurred on November 29.

It appears that there are no Hungarian regular troops in the vicinity mentioned, and only one company of seventy gendarmes. These gendarmes were going through military exercises near the Serbian line, and the Serbian soldiers got scared and came out and surrendered to them, thinking the Hungarians were preparing for an attack. The people of the town, at this, came out and, on account of the repeated Serbian atrocities, begged the gendarmes to go to the neighboring town as there were no Serbians there. However, upon arriving in this town, the Serbians at long range opened fire with infantry and artillery, at which the Hungarians, although two of them were wounded, withdrew without replying. The Hungarian commander investigated the matter and sent a messenger with a flag of truce to the Jugo-Slav commander, explaining that the whole incident was due to a misunderstanding and was a mistake.

It was accordingly decided to send a letter to the diplomatic representative of the Jugo-Slavs, giving him a synopsis of General Soós' report, calling his attention to the fact that all of the incident had occurred on purely Hungarian territory from which the Serbs had been repeatedly requested to withdraw by this Mission, and adding that in view of the fact that a committee, sent by this Mission to Pécs, had been refused recognition as representative of the Supreme Council by any of the Serbian officials or authorities, it would not be practicable to send any other such committee until assurances had been received from the Serbian government that any committee from this Mission would be recognized as authoritative and would have its labors facilitated in every way possible.

A telegram was also sent to the Supreme Council to the same effect, and adding that General Soós had stated that unless the Entente required the Roumanians and Serbs to withdraw immediately beyond their line of demarcation, it was manifestly only just and proper that the Hungarians be allowed to defend themselves against the pillaging, murders and other atrocities committed by occupying forces.

All the way through, this has been a hectic day. I was not only President of the Day of the Mission, but our mail came in with a whole raft of official and other letters to be signed.

This afternoon the Prince Ferdinand Montenuovo called upon me to make complaint about the Serbians robbing his property, and several counts and a few barons were floating around, in addition to much lesser fry.

Tonight we are invited to dinner with Baron Weiss.

December 6, 1919.

Last night Colonel Sheldon, Captain Gore and I dined with the family of Baron Weiss, and had a very delicious dinner. The Baron is about the wealthiest man in Hungary, owns immense factories and has other large interests. The Roumanians looted some of his various plants property to the value of eight million dollars, but he still seems to have enough for turning out a square meal.

After the usual routine in the morning, and when things were beginning to look as though we would have quiet day, a code message was received from Mr. Polk, informing me that the Supreme Council had decided to relieve the Inter-Allied Military Mission, but that I would be left by my government as the United States representative in Hungary until the arrival of Mr. Grant Smith, who had been sent by the Department of State and who was due to reach here in three or four weeks. The telegram wound up with the statement that the American Commission thoroughly approved my entire administration of affairs while on my present duty.

Later in the afternoon, a couple of fine-looking young Jewish boys were brought in, who had been beaten up by Hungarian soldiers at the railroad station, so I sent for General Soós, who promptly came over, and told him that I was damned sick and tired of any such conduct; that although I could understand how the Hungarians would naturally feel sore over the fact that most of the Bolshevist leaders had been Jews, nevertheless, neither America nor England could understand any such barbaric conduct; that one of England's greatest Prime Ministers had been a Jew, and the present Chairman of the Military Committee in the American House of Representatives is a Jew[4]; that if reports got out that Hungarians were lapsing into the same form of barbarism as the Russians, it would seriously affect their whole future; that I could now give him a concrete case and information as to who the responsible Hungarian captain was who had been guilty of such brutal conduct, and I wanted him punished. I also informed the General that other reports had come to me from the outlying districts, and I gave him the minutes of a meeting which had taken place in Budapest, where pogroms were openly advocated. He promised me that he would take immediate and drastic action to cut short this growing evil.

One of my office force brought me in a translation of an article in one of the Budapest papers, which is as follows:

Statements of General Bandholtz to the Representative of he *Pesti Napló*[5] on the future of Hungary.

In the apartment of Queen Zita, the walls of which are covered with silk and adorned with beautiful pictures and Gobelins worth a fortune, I had an opportunity of conversing with Harry Hill Bandholtz, General of the United States Army. This General of world fame has been entrusted with a very difficult military and diplomatic task, that of representing the United States in Budapest during Hungary's most trying time. How energetically, successfully, and at the same time how tactfully, he fulfills this mission, could best be told by the members f our government. They could tell how uplifting was the message of General Bandholtz sent through Premier Huszár, which in as follows:

"It is now that we are beginning to appreciate you," said the American General to the Premier. "I have just read your history and am becoming acquainted with the Hungarian nation. A nation that appreciates itself, must needs obtain the general appreciation of the world. We see that your nation is a martyr and the sympathy of America is now with you."

These noble words of the General have induced me to call on him concerning our misery and our future. General Bandholtz was busily engaged when my arrival was announced, but he immediately stopped work and received me with an extremely obliging kindness. The General, to whom I was presented by Ministerial Councilor Emil Zerkowitz, was sitting at desk, putting in order a batch of papers, telegrams, reports, letters, and petitions. When I entered, he arose, came quickly towards me, shook hands in a friendly manner and offered me a seat.

General Bandholtz is a man of middle size, his head is getting bald, his moustache is white, his look friendly and candid. His age may be about fifty. If I wanted to characterize him in a brief manner, I should say he is kind and human. In his work, is guided by a thorough impartiality, for he considers himself not only the representative of America, but also one of the delegates of the Allied Powers. He does not look upon the future of Hungary from the viewpoint of a rigid soldier, but with the feeling and understanding soul of a man. He is indeed watching the state of affairs in Hungary with the cleverness of a diplomat; he has learned to understand the history of this thousand-years-old nation, so full of sad and glorious events, and his friendly feelings are not merely grounded on the sympathy of the kind man, but on the American tradition that always takes the side of the friendless and the weak.

4   The late Julius Kahn, of California.

5   The *Journal of Budapest*, a Liberal morning daily.

The uniform of General Bandholtz was ornamented by three rows of decorations, on the collar of his coat we see nothing but the two letter "U. S." The General is a veteran soldier. He was one of the first leaders of the Philippine war, where he also rendered extremely valuable service to his country as governor. American punctuality and readiness for work are characteristic of him. His working capacity is unparalleled. In his office, that occupies fifteen rooms in the Royal Palace, punctuality is the motto, but with his subordinates he is a commander only while matters strictly official are being handled. The next minute he talks to everybody who works with him in the most amiable manner. He has smiling brown eyes and a serene temper. After work, he likes to mix with the distinguished society in Budapest; you can frequently see his limousine in the Váci utca where he does some shopping. He is an enthusiastic stamp collector and a great art patron. He likes Budapest very much and everybody can see that he is very happy amongst us.

I had a formidable array of questions ready for the General, but with the skill of a practiced diplomatist, he picked out those questions that he could properly answer. My attack on some of the most important questions was repelled by General Bandholtz with a cruel persistency.

"I beg your pardon, General, but this question is of great military and political importance for us; you would oblige me extremely by giving further information. Hungary is about to hold elections and in the territory which the Roumanians occupy and where they are requisitioning mercilessly, there lives a pure-blooded Hungarian population. We must know about the Roumanian withdrawal."

He replied: "I must remind you that the Entente has given orders for Roumania to retreat as far as the line of demarcation. Naturally the Entente will not tolerate that the Roumanian Army remain for any length of time on this side of the line of demarcation, in contravention of orders."

I mentioned to the General the latest action of Food Commissioner Hoover, the essence of which is that America is ready to despatch foodstuff to Hungary, especially to Budapest, providing sufficient official guarantees are forthcoming from the state, and that America is ready to facilitate this transaction as regards the rate of exchange, adding that the dollars intended to be sent home by the Hungarians living in America would considerably facilitate this arrangement.

General Bandholtz showed great sympathy in this matter, and said: "Upon request of Charles Huszár, Premier, I recently forwarded a telegram to the Hungarian Relief Committee in New York. In this telegram, the Premier expressed his thanks to the Committee for the support given by the relief funds collected by the Hungarians, and begged the Hungarian brethren living in America not to forget those that are suffering want in Hungary. I forwarded the telegram with the greatest pleasure, and I am always ready to help to alleviate suffering and to give my support to humanitarian institutions."

At this moment my glance fell on the General's desk, and I was touched to see a scroll sent by a Hungarian peasant woman to the kind-hearted General of the United States Army. The lines were scribbled on a large white sheet and I committed the impropriety of reading a few lines.

The letter began: "Blessed be Jesus Christ!" followed by the address: "Right Honorable Mr. General!" Then a long epistle. The letter was signed: "With the deepest respect and hope, dated: Hahót, 27th Nov. 1919. Mrs. Stephen Horváth."

What a world cataclysm must have taken place to make it possible for Mrs. Stephen Horvath, from a small thatched cottage at Hahót, to have anything to do with the Royal Palace and with General Harry Hill Bandholtz!   (Signed) Miklós Vécsei.

December 7, 1919.

Last night Colonel Sheldon, Lieutenant-Colonel Moore, Captain Gore and myself attended a large reception given by the Prime Minister, and the friendliness of the Archduke and the Archduchess, of the Prime Minister, of Admiral Horthy, and others, towards the American delegation was most marked and conspicuous.

It appears that the former Prime Minister, Friedrich, is completely at outs with the present Prime Minister. Friedrich openly advocates a postponement of peace negotiations, because he says that the Entente can do nothing with Czecho-Slovakia, Roumania, and Jugo-Slavia, and can, therefore, do nothing with Hungary; that the three small nations first mentioned, are now on the verge of an upheaval and will probably split into separate parts, so that all that Hungary should do is to bide her time and take advantage of the upheaval.

Huszár, on the other hand, although also of the opinion that the upheaval referred to will take place, advocates conservatism without reaction; a prompt conclusion of a peace treaty with the Entente, which will then back Hungary in her just ambitions and desires, enabling her to gain more from any upheaval among her neighbors than she would by antagonizing the Entente.

This morning I received a long telephone message from Colonel Causey in Vienna, complaining that the Czecho-Slovaks would not allow timber or dynamite to be sent to the Tata-Bánya mines, where it was badly needed, as otherwise the mines could not operate. He repeated that the Czecho-Slovaks had absolutely no use for the timber or the explosives, and needed the money badly, but were acting like a herd of swine, which conduct has characterized them in practically all their relations with their neighbors.

While at the Prime Minister's reception last night, I took my colleague, General Mombelli, "apart" and gave him a hint that the days of the Inter-Allied Military Mission were numbered, and he nearly collapsed. I have not yet broken the sad tidings to my other colleague, General Graziani, but shall probably do so tomorrow at our session, which I hope will be the last one. It will be much more convenient for me to work as a free lance here and to coöperate with General Gorton. It will not only give us more time, but it will also give us greater freedom of action.

December 8, 1919.

At the meeting today, I submitted a letter written by Lieutenant-Colonel Moore explaining the necessity for obtaining clothing without delay for the Hungarian police, and it was decided to notify the Hungarian government that this Mission would approve of the purchase of such clothing wherever it could be found.

As there is a steady flow of complaints about the Serb's seizures and general misconduct in the vicinity of Pécs, it was decided to send for the Serbian diplomatic representative, Doctor Baitch, to be present at the next meeting of the Mission, which will be held at the French Headquarters. General Graziani was rather reluctant to have this occur when he was chairman, but he was forced to yield to a majority vote and finally consented to send for Baitch.

There were also received several complaints of abuses on the part of the Hungarian "White Army" and others towards Jews, and it was decided to refer all of these to the Prime Minister of Hungary, with the statement that it was understood that he would immediately take suitable action.

On November 25 the Supreme Council sent another last ultimatum to the Roumanians[6]. In general, Roumania was invited to take without discussion, reservation, or conditions, the following resolutions:

First. To evacuate entirely Hungarian territory, without drawing within the definite frontiers fixed by the Conference.

Second. To accept the constitution of the Inter-Allied Commission provided for to decide, control and base judgment upon the requisitions made in Hungary since the beginning of the Roumanian occupation.

Third. To sign the Austrian Treaty and the Minorities Treaty under the conditions indicated by the note of the Supreme Council of October 12, 1919.

The Roumanian government was first given eight days in which to send an answer, but as there was some delay in transmission of the message, the time was

6   This was in fact the last and definite ultimatum, the fourth. It was accepted by the Roumanian government, which, on Dec.10, signed the treaties with Austria and Bulgaria, containing the Minority Clauses so obnoxious to them. The signatures were affixed to these treaties just after the American delegates had left Paris.

extended, and on the last day it is understood they signed the treaties, but so far no information has been received that would indicate any intention on their part to abandon the line which they are holding on the Theiss so I telegraphed the American Commission to that effect this date.

In conclusion the ultimatum of the Supreme Council stated:

Should this reply not be satisfactory to the Supreme Council of the Allies the latter has decided to notify Roumania that she has separated herself from them. They shall invite her to recall immediately her delegates to the Peace Conference, and they will also withdraw their diplomatic missions at Bucharest. As the questions concerning the settlement of boundaries are still to be made, Roumania will thus by her own action deprive herself of all title to the support of the Powers as well as to the recognition of her rights by the Conference. It would be with the profoundest regret that the Supreme Council of the Allies should see itself forced to sever relations with Roumania, but it is confident that it has been patient to the very last degree.

The communication also contained the following paragraph:

In short the Roumanian Government has continued for the last three and one half months to negotiate with the Conference from Power to Power, taking into consideration no other rights or interests than her own and refusing to accept the charges of solidarity although she wishes to enjoy the benefit of them.

And then continued:

The Conference wishes to make a last appeal to the wisdom of the Roumanian Government and of the Roumanian people before taking the grave resolution of severing all relations with Roumania. Their right to dictate rests essentially on the fact that Roumania owes the priceless service of having reconstituted her national unity, in doubling her territory and population, to the victory of the Allies. Without the enormous sacrifices consented to by them at the present time Roumania would be decimated, ruined and in bondage without any possible hope. Roumania entered the struggle for her freedom at the end of the second year of the war, making her own conditions; it is true she made great sacrifices and suffered heavy losses, but she finally consented to treat separately with the enemy and to submit to his law; her liberty and her victory, as well as her future she owes to the Allies'. How can such a situation be lost sight of and so soon forgotten by the Roumanian statesmen?

7   The truth is that the Allies had not kept their promises when the Roumanians entered the war on their side, and had left the Roumanians in a bad military situation. They could hardly do anything else but conclude peace. It cannot he denied that the Roumanians had a right to harbor a bitter feeling against their allies in this respect.

196

December 9, 1919.

It is a pretty cold day when I am not photographed by a new royal photographer. As near as I can ascertain, all the photographers in Budapest spent most of their time photographing royalty, and they are now concentrating on the poor defenseless members of the Inter-Allied Military Mission.

The newspapers have also begun their interviews and I have so far waded through five. As it is understood that there are seventy-six such newspapers in Budapest, the beginning has hardly begun.

The following is an extract of an article which appeared in the *Pester Lloyd* [8] of December 5, 1919.

General Bandholtz on Hungary

Budapest, 4th December.

The statements made by Brigadier General Bandholtz, the worthy leader of the American Military Mission, to Prime Minister Huszár at the celebration of Thanksgiving Day and later during the visit paid to him by the Premier, have made a deep impression on the whole country. These statements are further proof of the fact that the fate of Hungary is duly appreciated by the United States and that the American Mission in Budapest, of all others, has studied and grasped thoroughly our position and thus greatly contributed to putting right the erroneus opinions existing with regard to our country. Nearly four months have now elapsed since General Bandholtz has started his work in Budapest. His arrival coincides with the darkest days in Hungary's history; the country and the capital bad hardly recovered from the terrors of Bolshevism, when armed hordes of foreign troops of occupation invaded Hungary. In consideration of the modesty of General Bandholtz, we dare not yet adequately appreciate what he has done for us during this period. The time will come when we shall be able to give a more detailed account of his work, of that of the American Military Mission under his charge, and also of the Claim Office within its sphere of action. Then the public will be able rightly to appreciate this work.

Our reporter has today called on General Bandholtz in the apartment of the former Queen at the Royal Castle, or National Palace, as it is at present called, where the General's offices are. The General had just returned from a meeting of the Inter-Allied Military Mission when our reporter was intro duced to him by Ministerial Councilor Zerkowitz.

Although the General was engaged and very busy, he has had the goodness to reply to the following questions:

8   A well-known Liberal newspaper written in the German language.

197

. . . . . .

The well-known leader of the American Army in the Philippine War continued to converse without restraint with our representative concerning the position of Budapest, making some enthusiastic remarks about the beauties of the capital, expressing warm feelings for the population, and speaking with confidence about the future of the country. We have found in General H. H. Bandholtz a true friend of Hungary and an impartial and just leader of the American Mission.

December 10, 1919.

Yesterday afternoon at 4.30, accompanied by Colonel Sheldon, I went over and took tea with my old friend "Joe," always alluded to here with much kowtowing and genuflexioning as the Archduke Joseph. Although I had called on "Joe" some time ago with Colonel Loree, the Palace had not then been in shape, on account of the fact that the Bolshevists had removed most of the furniture. This is all back now, and it really is a magnificent building. When we arrived at the antechamber, I didn't know whether the gorgeous personages awaiting us were generals or flunkies, but I thought I would wait to see whether they offered to shake my hand before making the first step myself. As they offered to help me off with my coat, I compromised by letting them keep it. We then entered a beautiful room and ran into a small flock of little "archduchesslets" and the young "Archdukelet." "Joe" then advanced smilingly to meet us and we were escorted into a room pretty well filled with the *créme de la créme* of Hungarian nobility, and including General and Mrs. Gorton. It was noted that no members of the French or Italian Missions were present.

I got planted next to Countess Somssich, the wife of the Minister of Foreign Affairs, and was buzzing her good and plenty when "Joe" came over and insisted that I give the Archduchess the benefit of some of my conversation, so I approached the royal presence in the usual humble American spirit and turned my buzzing apparatus loose on "Augusta." It took her a little while to get on to the American pronunciation, as she spoke only English, but after a while I was able to produce several giggles and we had a genuine good time until the meeting broke up, when most of the party went down to the opera, which was of such political significance that we could not attend; While Colonel Sheldon and I went down to see a Jewish printing office that had been wrecked by a mob.

The Mission met this date at the French Headquarters, with General Graziani presiding.

There was first brought up the question of whether or not members should accept an invitation from the Archduchess Augusta to a cinematograph performance to be given in the Archducal Palace for the benefit of widows and orphans of the Hungarian National Army. In view of the fact that this invitation was of a semi-personal nature, it was decided that each member could follow his own inclination.

It was noted that General Graziani had received many messages from the Roumanians, which showed conclusively that the French and Roumanians are in very close touch, as no one else was receiving any such messages.

Reports keep coming in that the Serbs in Pécs are acting along the same lines as the Roumanians have done heretofore and are still doing east of the Theiss. While we were discussing this proposition, Baitch, the Serbian Minister, came fox-trotting in, and General Graziani, as President of the Day, explained to him that we could not send any committee, as he requested, to investigate the reported incident at Redics, on account of the fact that the Serbians had not recognized the committee that we had previously sent to Pécs. Graziani then went on to tell about the complaints we had had of Serbian seizures, etc., in Hungarian territory still held by them, and wanted to know when the Serbs were going to evacuate and carry out the instructions given them. Little Baitch gave us a characteristic diplomatic smile and said that he had noted in the Paris papers and elsewhere that the Serbs were charged with appropriating property; that he had called the attention of the Belgrade government to this matter, and that they had replied, telling him to deny this absolutely as being without foundation. As it was about time that I had an inning, I stated that I should like to address a few remarks to the diplomatic envoy of the Kingdom of the Serbs, Croates and Slovenes, and as little Baitch and I are boon companions and as he understands English fairly well, I looked him in the eye and said:

My dear Doctor, why in Hell do you insist on imitating the Roumanians in everything? We know that your people are requisitioning and seizing property around Pécs; you know that they are doing it; and the proofs are right here before you. Now, why imitate and blindly follow Roumanian tactics, and try to lie out of it under all these circumstances?

He smilingly admitted that the Serbs were following a bad precedent, and that he would look into the matter.

The Mission then adjourned.

Upon arriving back at the Palace, I had a talk with General Gorton and, while there, a Canadian officer who is attached to the British Food Commission, reported that the Serbs were making a big hullabaloo about the Redics incident, that they had had a special session of the Parliament, and that they had decided in view of this that no food would be allowed to cross the Hungarian boundary line until reparation had been made for same.

After considerable difficulty, the Captain got in touch with a high ranking officer in Belgrade and got him to consent to lifting the embargo on exportation of food into Hungary if the Hungarians should voluntarily comply with the following conditions:

1. Apologize for the incident;

2. Set free unconditionally any Serbian prisoners who had been taken;

3. Pay the families of any Serbs who had been injured, according to amount fixed by an Inter-Allied Committee;

4. Give assurance that there would be no repetition of the incident.

As General Soós had already practically complied with these conditions through the Inter-Allied Military Mission, General Gorton and I sent word to the Hungarian Premier suggesting that he act likewise directly through the Serbian diplomatic envoy.

Before leaving the session of the Mission, in view of the food crisis now existing in Budapest, I insisted that the Mission telegraph the Roumanians to the effect that the present situation in Budapest was primarily due to the damned-fool requisition methods of the Roumanians in the beginning, and was intensified by the fact that they, despite their repeated promises, had sent no food supplies into Budapest.

General Graziani apparently did not like to send the message, and dislikes exceedingly to give any bad-tasting medicine to either the Roumanians or the Serbs.

Today I received from the Hungarian Prime Minister a reply to my letter returning the Royal Box, and his reply read as follows:

Hungarian Prime Minister

Budapest, the 9th of December 1919

To his Excellency

General H. H. Bandholtz

Chief of the American Mission to Negotiate Peace

Budapest

Sir,

in reply to your kind note of the 4th of December in the matter of the Opera box I beg most respectfully to ask you to keep the box in question in the future as well.

It caused me as well as to the other members of the Government real pleasure to give you by offering you the box, another sign of the respect and esteem we are feeling towards your Excellency as to a real and sincere friend of the Hungarians and a protector of our just interests.

Believe me Sir

very respectfully yours

[Signed] Huszár

Prime Minister

Today we received a telephonic message from Colonel Loree, who is now as far back as Vienna on his return. Owing to the congestion in passenger transportation, it will probably be three or four days before he can make the short run from Vienna to Budapest.

In reply to Prime Minister Huszár's letter I sent the following:

Budapest, Hungary

10th December 1919

To His Excellency

M. Charles Huszár,

Prime Minister of Hungary

My dear M. Huszár:

Your characteristic letter of the ninth instant insisting that I retain the large central box at the Opera has affected me more than I can express. I shall consider this act as being intended to indicate the most kindly feeling towards my country and I cannot do otherwise than gratefully accept your repeated offer.

Most sincerely,

H. H. Bandholtz

December 11, 1919.

Last night the Count and Countess de Troismonts gave what they called a "nine-thirty o'clock tea," which was in reality a sort of at-home *thé dansant*. The crowd was decidedly mixed; practically all of the French officers and Italian officers were there, and a scattering of Hungarians, with Captain Gore and myself from the American Mission, as Colonel Loree had not yet returned and Colonel Sheldon was somewhat under the weather. It was noted that no British officers were present. The little "Archdukelet" was there, having the time of his life, and danced considerable attendance on one of my adopted daughters.

The room was so full of wood smoke from the stoves and tobacco smoke from cigarettes, that fortunately one's eyes were considerably dimmed, and a young lady who was dancing in what looked like a very décolleté nightdress, did not attract as much attention as might otherwise have been the case.

This afternoon is the cinematograph affair that the Archduchess is giving, and I have sent my regrets, as one cannot be chasing around with royalty all the time and likewise attend to one's business.

This morning, in view of the fact that the food situation in Budapest is rapidly approaching a crisis, I went down and saw my boon companion, little Lazar Baitch, the Serbian Minister.

Bringing up the subject of the Redics incident, mentioned before, I told Baitch that I was astonished that the Serbs were falling into the horrible error of blindly imitating the Roumanians in their rotten traits. I repeated the talk I had given him yesterday at the session of the Mission and told him that the Roumanians had lost the chance of a lifetime in not handling their occupation of Hungary properly, and that I did not want the Jugo-Slavs to make a similar mistake.

I then whispered in his ear that there was now in Budapest the representative of one of the great New York dailies, and asked him how he would like to have scattered broadcast through the United States in large headlines, something to the following effect:

Serbians worse than Roumanians. Using a trivial frontier incident as pretext, they proceed to starve 2,000,000 people,

all to be followed by the harrowing details which only newspaper correspondents know how to bring out. I told him it was all right to demand an apology from the

Hungarians, and a promise of punishment to the guilty, and of adequate arrangements for the prevention of a repetition of similar incidents, but that they ought now to break their necks to let into Hungary immediately the five thousand carloads of provisions which they were holding up and which, worst of all, the Hungarians had already paid for. He promised me that he would telegraph his government immediately. I then suggested to him that in view of the fact that both Roumania and Italy were both already hostile to Serbia, I thought it almost suicidal for her to force Hungary into a similar position, whereas by retaining Hungary as a friend she could separate the Italians and the Roumanians. He agreed likewise with this.

I then went over to Admiral Horthy's Headquarters, finding him out; but did find General Soós, to whom I gave friendly advice in the way of immediately apologizing to the Serbs for the Redics incident, in order to admit food. After General Soós I went to see Count Somssich, the Minister of Foreign Affairs, and had a similar talk with him. He promised to take up and push the matter immediately.

In the afternoon Mr. Arno Dorch-Fleurot, the *New York World* representative referred to in my conversation with Baitch, came in to say good-by, as he was on his way through Belgrade to try to get into Southern Russia.

About noon I received a code telegram in Mr. Polk's name, stating that Grant-Smith was due to arrive in about two or three weeks and would have a party of seven with him. I was asked to arrange for quarters, food and fuel for the party, to leave two automobiles for them and to transfer chauffeurs, and it was added that no reason was known why they should not continue with the offices and quarters that I was now occupying. It is most apparent that Mr. Polk himself never saw the telegram, and I replied as follows:

Budapest, Hungary

11th December 1919

American Embassy

Paris

Number E 5 Polk from Bandholtz. Replying to your 132 of December 9th. Quarters now occupied by me are part of Count Edelsheim's house which he does not care to rent after my departure. Offices are in part of Royal Palace which our occupancy saved from Roumanian looters but which would not be appropriate for permanent representative. I shall take immediate steps to make tentative arrangements for suitable quarters. There are now here three Cadillac automobiles, two limousines and one touring car, and all are understood to be State Department property. Unless contrary instructions are received they will be left here. They were all received in bad condition and two at a time usually undergoing repairs. To do my work it was necessary constantly to hire two to three other cars. An effort now being made completely to overhaul Cadillacs. My American chauffeurs are all soldiers who do not desire to remain. I have also hired Hungarians when necessary and will try to have two or three trained on Cadillacs. It is suggested that one or more American chauffeurs of mechanical training accompany any new party, that a complete set of spare parts, extra tubes, tires, etc., be brought, and that another carload of gasoline be sent to arrive here by January 20th. Contract for fuel will be made, but a general food supply for at least three months should be brought along. Local prices are exorbitant.

Bandholtz

Budapest, Hungary

11th December 1919

American Embassy

Paris

Priority Number E4. Polk from Bandholtz. Your number 132 answered in detail by my number E5. As Commission is supposed to sail on thirteenth I shall consider myself automatically relieved as member of Inter-Allied Military Mission on that date unless contrary instructions are in meantime received. Please inform me as to my official designation.

Bandholtz

December 12, 1919.

The Mission met this morning at the Italian Headquarters, with General Mombelli presiding. Considering my telegram of yesterday, this undoubtedly was my last sitting with the Mission as a member. I could not, however, as yet, notify my colleagues of this fact, and took the same apparent lively interest in the proceedings that I have taken heretofore.

I called their attention to the fact that the Roumanians had received an ultimatum in regard to the immediate evacuation of Hungary, signing all treaties, etc.; that they had signed the treaties, so I understood, but were still hanging on to eastern Hungary. Generals Mombelli and Graziani both said they had heard nothing of such an ultimatum, and that they had never seen it. I told them I had seen it, had a copy of it, and would be glad to furnish them one the next day. It was decided, therefore, to telegraph the Supreme Council along the lines indicated. It is frequently commented upon that the Supreme Council has practically forgotten our existence. As near as I can make out from telegrams from my own Mission, we really do not exist, at least officially, but the Supreme Council has neglected to notify us that we have petered out. As the others are having so much fun about it, I decided to let them plug on and enjoy themselves, but on Sunday, the fourteenth, unless I receive contrary instructions in the meantime, I will inform them that I can no longer sit as a member.

When I got back to my office after the session, General Soós, came in to tell me that his government had complied with my suggestion and had sent its regrets through the Serbian Minister for the Redics incident. I complimented him on the wisdom of the policy they had pursued, and hope that there will be no more difficulty about getting in the five thousand carloads of food from Jugo-Slavia.

Colonel Loree arrived about 10 o'clock this morning from Vienna, which did not surprise me, as I knew that he would be on the train if it was humanly possible for anybody to get on.

Colonel and Mrs. Kelly arrived in Budapest this morning, on their return trip from Belgrade and Bucharest. Colonel Kelly states that he found both places to be just about as I had described them; that the Roumanians were decidedly inhospitable and did not care to see Americans; that Roumania was full of loot, sidetracks were filled with cars which they had not yet had time to unload, and in general the whole country showed that the Roumanians were utterly lacking in system and organization as well as in decency. We had Colonel and Mrs. Kelly to dinner, but they left early as they had had a very hard trip.

December 13, 1919.

This morning, Colonel Loree, Captain Gore and myself tried to do a little Christmas shopping, but there was mighty little to be bought.

Lieutenant-Colonel Hume, of the Army Medical Corps, who is our senior Red Cross representative in Serbia, came up to see me, being en route from Paris to Belgrade by automobile with his wife, who just recently arrived from the United States. We therefore had them to luncheon. It was fortunate that he arrived, because Colonel Sheldon is somewhat under the weather and it is a comfort to feel that we have an American medical officer to look him over. Colonel Hume states that at any time we need anything of the kind he will send, if necessary, both a doctor and a nurse from Belgrade, as he considers it is more important to look after Americans than anybody else.

As on this date, per my telegram to Mr. Polk of yesterday, I shall automatically cease to be a member of the Inter-Allied Military Mission, I drew up several letters, signed them and will deliver them tomorrow. These letters were as follows. To Generals Graziani, Mombelli, and Gorton, I sent each the following letter:

My dear General:

It is with a feeling of real regret that I am obliged this date, as per my official communication to the Inter-Allied Military Mission, to sever for myself the close and harmonious official relations that have from the beginning existed between me and my colleagues of the Inter-Allied Military Mission.

My association for four months with three generals of international fame has been for me a great honor, a privilege and an education.

Your patience under the steady fire of my Americanisms has been admirable, but has also been appreciated. I shall ever retain most pleasant and affectionate recollections of each and all of you.

Very sincerely,

H. H. BANDHOLTZ

Brig. Gen., U.S. A.

13th December 1919

From:Brigadier General H. H. Bandholtz, U.S. A.

To:Inter-Allied Military Mission

Subject: Change of Status

1: In compliance with telegraphic instructions from the American Commission to Negotiate Peace, the undersigned this date ceases to be a member of the Inter- Allied Military Mission.

H. H. BANDHOLTZ

Budapest, Hungary

13th December 1919

From: American Military Representative in Hungary

To: Hungarian Prime Minister

Subject: Information as to change of status

1: I have the honor to inform Your Excellency that on this date, pursuant to instructions from the American Commission to Negotiate Peace, I shall cease to be a member of the Inter-Allied Military Mission, but shall remain temporarily in Hungary as American Military Representative [should have read "Commissioner"].

H.H. BANDHOLTZ

Brig. Gen., U.S. Army

Just as things were going along swimmingly in the automobile line, we ground out another axle bearing in one of the limousines, so that both of them are now in the shop and we are plugging around in open cars.

At present everybody seems to be out of gasoline except ourselves and our popularity is as great as it is undesirable. It will be a pleasure to accommodate Colonel Hume and people who have been nice to us, and it will be likewise a pleasure to be unaccommodating to a few others.

December 14, 1919.

Last night Colonel Loree, Captain Gore and myself attended the opera, having with us the Szirmay family and Colonel and Mrs. Hume, who were mentioned yesterday as being en route to Belgrade. The opera was "Rigoletto" and it was the best that I have yet seen. My taste along the lines of grand opera, however, is so depraved that whatever I like is probably inferior. Still our musical expert, Captain Gore, admitted that it was very well presented.

This morning I dropped in to see General Gorton and, as he will be the President of the Day of the Mission for tomorrow, I handed him my letter notifying the Mission that I was ceasing to function as a member thereof. He stated that he had talked the matter over the night before with General Mombelli, and Graziani thought that my notice to the Hungarian government of my ceasing to be a member of the Mission should be sent through the Mission. I told General Gorton that, with all due respect to General Mombelli's astuteness, he was off his nut; that I did not recognize the Mission and never had recognized it as being my superior; that I had been relieved by my own commission and I recognized no other channels.

Colonel Sheldon is laid up in bed with an attack of tonsillitis, which, however, has not yet reached a serious stage, and we hope to have him cured up in a day or so.

December 15, 1919.

It is very annoying to be quite as much in demand as the American Mission now seems to be in Budapest. The fact that I bought a painting at the exhibit has been pretty well advertised, and I never imagined that there were so many paintings in the world as are now being offered me. The newspaper articles have also given us a widely circulated advertisement and there is a steady stream of invitations to attend all sorts of openings, meetings, celebrations, etc.

Then for the evening I was invited by the officers of the British Mission to be their guest at an opera and dinner party. Not having one of those technical ears that listen for beautiful notes in the bell-like tones of sopranos and the bull-like tones of basso profundos, I arranged to arrive at the opera about half an hour before its conclusion. They intended to give "The Flying Dutchman," but I saw in the paper that it was to be "Lohengrin." My timing was accurate, as the opera begins at six and ordinarily ends at nine, so I arrived at about 8.20, but it appears that "Lohengrin" is a musical endurance test and the damned thing lasted until after 10 o'clock.

We then went with the British officers to their "B" Mess, where we had a delicious dinner to the tune of "cigány"[9] music. After dinner they prepared to do what the British called "take the floor," which means to dance. This latter began about midnight and my party beat it at one o'clock.

It seemed good to be able to come to my own Headquarters this morning and tackle my own work without being obliged to waste the whole forenoon with an emasculated Military Mission that could issue instructions and ultimata and get snubbed for its pains.

Yesterday afternoon the young Archduke called up a friend of mine and said that he was in a Hell of a fix, or words to that effect; that he and his sister had been invited to General Bandholtz's birthday party on December 18, but that Papa Archduke and Mama Arch duchess had not been included; that papa and mama were crazy to come, but were a little bit afraid of General Bandholtz and did not know how he could be approached, and would my friend be so kind as to try to arrange the matter?

9   Gypsy music.

Accordingly, accompanied by Colonel Loree, I went over to see his Royal Highness at half past twelve, told him that I had seen his son enjoying himself at Count Troismont's dance, and had therefore asked the young Archduke and his sister to come over to my birthday party; that I was not sure whether their Highnesses would themselves care to attend such a function, and I had, therefore, come personally to ask him, with one lady in waiting, to butt in on the scene in case they cared to come. "Archie" was tickled to death and showed it, and said he sure would be there with the whole Archducal family.

During the course of the conversation he spoke about my length of stay, and I told him I was very anxious to get home, that although I had only a son and a daughter-in-law in America, with seven daughters in Budapest -at which he interrupted me, with admiration marking his entire pose and expression, saying: "What already!" I then explained to him that they were all adopted and were from families of friends of his, at which his admiration passed away to a certain extent, and I was no longer the wonder he thought I was.

Count Apponyi, who is to be chairman of the Peace Delegation to Paris[10], came to see me and ask if I could help him get to his estate, in territory now occupied by the Czecho-Slovaks, for the holidays and then return. The Czecho-Slovaks had announced that they would either not let him come, or if he did, that they would not let him return here. I told him that I would send a telegram to Prague which I

10 Count Albert Apponyi. From 1906 to 1910 he was Minister of Education in the Wekerle cabinet. He succeeded Francis Kossuth as president of the party of Hungarian independence and was an advocate of the introduction of universal suffrage in Hungary. During the War, he was a loyal supporter of the government. After the outbreak of the revolution in 1918, he retired to private life. In 1919 he was elected a non-partizan representative of the National Assembly. He developed more and more as a man above the parties, and enjoys today [Written by Krüger in 1932.] great prestige as the Grand Old Man of his country.

Apponyi's anecdotal description of his experiences, excerpted from his *Memoirs* published in 1933 is included in the Appendix.

The other leading members of the Hungarian Peace Delegation were Count Paul Teleki and Count Stephen Bethlen.

thought would fix the matter, but I suggested that he come with me to the Mission, which was in session. I called General Gorton out of the meeting, explained the situation to him, and left them together. The Count later returned to me and said that the Mission would back him, and with my backing also he now felt safe to go home for the holidays.

Count Andrássy came in, likewise, to see about get ting passes to Czecho-Slovakia and return, so I gave him the same kind that I gave to Count Edelsheim two or three months ago, in the shape of a letter, stating that he had been of service to the Mission, and we trusted that he be extended every courtesy in his contemplated journey to and from Czecho-Slovakia, the passes being written in English, German, French, Hungarian, and Czech.

Colonel Sheldon came down to dinner tonight with his usual appetite and now seems well on the road to recovery.

December 16, 1919.

General Gorton came in this morning and said that he had been mistaken about Mombelli thinking that my notice to the Hungarian government in regard to separation from the Mission should have been sent through the Mission, but that he referred to the telegrams which had been received by me from the Supreme Council for the Hungarian government and which I had delivered directly.

I told General Gorton that this was the characteristic Italian way of doing things; that instead of coming to me and making his complaint he went to someone else, and I was going right down to see General Mombelli and tell him that when he had any growls coming that I wished he would growl at me and not do it vicariously; that the telegrams which I had delivered to the Hungarian government did not come to me from the Supreme Council, but came to me from the American Committee, with instructions to deliver to the Hungarian government; and that I did not give a whoop in Hell how many Italians, French, and others felt hurt, and that I proposed to carry out my instructions.

I then chased down to the Italian Mission to say the same thing to General Mombelli, but found him away on a hunting expedition, so it will be reserved for another occasion. At the time I did not know that he was away hunting, but thought he was simply out of his office; so I went to the French Mission to see General Graziani, and was told by his aide de camp that the Italian General was with General Graziani. He asked me if I would wait. I said that I would not, but that I would be very glad to have him send my name in to General Graziani and see what the result would be, this mainly with the idea of seeing both Graziani and Mombelli together.

I was immediately ushered in and found out that it was not Mombelli, but another Italian General, who had been sent here on the Reparations Commission. He promptly beat it on my arrival, so I had a little chat with Graziani. It appears that at their meeting yesterday they were somewhat concerned as to how they might use the American telegraph line and as to whether or not it would be necessary to write me a request for general use or for each time. I told General Graziani for Heaven's sake to come off his perch, that I was here to do business and not to spend all my time in reading and dictating letters, that the line was at the disposal of the Mission exactly the same as it had been when I was a member thereof, that my relations with my former colleagues would continue on the same amicable footing, and that I would coöperate to the fullest extent.

I then told the General that I was going to have a birthday in Budapest on the eighteenth and would like to have him and his Chief of Staff attend. He said he would be charmed, and I beat it.

In view of the fact that my separation from the Mission seemed to cause some uneasiness in the city, and to prevent any misunderstanding, I then drew up for publication, and sent each of my former colleagues, a copy of the following notice:

CHANGE IN THE INTER-ALLIED MILITARY MISSION

It has been known for some time that the American Commission to Negotiate Peace would leave Europe early in December, the original date for their departure being scheduled for December 5. The Commission, however, did not sail from France until December 13, 1919.

As a natural result of the Commission's departure, General Bandholtz, the American representative on the Inter-Allied Military Mission, was automatically relieved as a member thereof. It is understood, however, on the best of authority that this change in the Inter-Allied Military Mission has no material significance. The remaining members will continue as heretofore, and General Bandholtz will remain temporarily in Budapest as American Military Representative and, although no longer a member of the Inter-Allied Military Mission, his relations with his former colleagues will be those of the representative of one of the Allied and Associated Powers with the representatives of other such Powers, and he will cooperate with the Mission in every way practicable.

Later in the day I received a letter from General Gorton, of which the following is a copy:

16th December 1919.

My dear General Bandholtz

The letter which you have sent to the Interallied Military Mission announcing the termination of your membership therein, contains sad news for us all, but for none more than for your British colleague.

I take this opportunity of expressing my admiration for your energy and ability which have inspired our meetings, as much as your flowers of speech and elegancies of metaphor have enlivened them.

I should like also to say how proud I am that the relations between your Mission and mine have been of so pleasant a character. We could not have been more in unison had we been comrades of long association instead of newly-found cousins.

Accept, my dear General, my best thanks for the ready assistance and kind fellowship for which I and my officers are indebted to you and yours, and believe me to remain,

Yours very sincerely,

R. S: G. Gorton

I knew damned well what he alluded to by "my flowers of speech and elegancies of metaphor," and rather think he enjoyed my frequent breaks into the stilted and ordinary conversation of a Mission of distinguished generals.

When I arrived at home I found waiting for me a letter from General Graziani, of which the following is a free translation[11]:

Budapest, 15th December, 1919

My dear General:

Like you, I shall ever retain pleasant memories of those four months of collaboration, which has always been marked so plainly by harmony, cordiality and frankness. It was perfectly natural that each one of us should, in our discussions, be influenced by his temperament, but we were always soldiers, talking to other soldiers, and we were, therefore, always on the ground of perfect understanding.

I regret greatly your withdrawal, but fortunately it is only relative since, although you leave the Mission, you do not leave Budapest.

Believe me, my [dear] General, with most cordial and sincere sentiments.

[Signed] General Graziani.

In view of the fact that General Mombelli had gone hunting and I could not see him today, and that there would be a meeting of the Mission tomorrow, I decided to send a formal communication concerning the criticism which had been made in regard to my transmitting telegrams directly to the Hungarian government. The following letter was therefore dictated and sent to the President of the Day.

Budapest, Hungary

16th December 1919

From: American Military Representative

To: President of the Day-Inter-Allied Military Mission

Subject: Criticism of Procedure.

1: There has come to my attention the fact that I have been criticized for transmitting to the Hungarian government telegrams that it was thought should have been forwarded through the Inter-Allied Military Mission.

2: As this happened repeatedly while I was a member of the Mission I cannot understand why the criticism was not then made.

11   5 Budapest, le 15 - XII - 19

Mon cher Général

comme vous, je garderai un souvenir ineffacable de ces quatre mois d'une collaboration qui a toujours été marquée au coin de la bonne harmonie, de la cordialité et de la franchise.

Il était très naturel que chacun de nous apportat, dans nos discussions, son tempérament; mais nous étions des soldats parlant it d'autres soldats et nous devions, dès lors, trouver toujours un terrain d'entente.

Je regrette beaucoup votre éloignement mais il nest, heureusement, que relatif puisque, si vous quittez la commission, vous n'abandonnez pas Budapest.

Veuillez croire, mon cher Général, à mes sentiments très cordialement dévoués,

[signed] G'l. Graziani,

3: While regretting that my action may have created doubts in the minds of any of my former colleagues, I must add that I did and do consider it to have been perfectly proper under all the circumstances.

4: The telegrams which I transmitted to the Hungarian government were all of the same general form of arrangement and composition, which in effect was as follows:

"General Bandholtz

Budapest

You will please deliver the following message to the Hungarian Minister President:

[here would follow the message, usually from Clemenceau]

[Signed] Polk Admission."

5: My letter of transmissal was invariably limited to the customary stereotyped form, embodying the message.

6: Each entire transaction was one in which the American telegraph line had been utilized, and in which I received and obeyed orders from my immediate superiors, and it was one in which the Inter-Allied Military Mission had no direct concern or control.

7: I fear that the exaggerated headlines and distorted versions that appeared in the local press in regard to such telegrams, and for which I was in no-ways responsible, gave an entirely erroneous impression which could have been quickly cleared away by a few words at the time.

8: I repeat that I regret exceedingly that any doubts whatever should have arisen in the minds of my former colleagues, whose good will and opinion I so highly prize, and I trust that the foregoing explanation will be satisfactory. If I have not made myself perfectly clear, I shall be pleased to go into further detail either verbally or in writing.

With assurances of the highest esteem and respect, I am,

Very sincerely:

H. H. Bandholtz

Brig. Gen., U.S. A.

December 17, 1919.

Last night Colonel Loree, Captain Gore, and myself were again the guests of Count Edelsheim at the Nemzeti Casino, the finest club of Budapest. The Count explained that in view of the fact that I was daily meeting diplomats, politicians and military officers, he would try and give me as brother guests civilians only. I cannot recall the names of other Hungarian guests, but they were all very charming gentlemen, and we had an excellent dinner and a pleasant evening.

Yesterday four communists, who had smuggled themselves in some way or other from Austria to Hungary, endeavored to blow up the Gellért Hotel, where Admiral Horthy has his Headquarters. Fortunately they were discovered and apprehended before they did any damage. In this connection it might be mentioned that today we received several seats for the hanging of twelve Bolshevists, which is to take place in a day or so.

Now that I no longer have the sessions of the Mission to attend, and there is no Supreme Council or American Commission to Negotiate Peace to whom I can send frequent reports, my work has fallen off materially, but we still have a great number of visitors who seem to think that the American Mission can accomplish results when all others fail.

December 18, 1919.

My birthday today seems to have been pretty well advertised on account of the little celebration we are giving at our mess.

Admiral Horthy sent over his aide with his best compliments, and the Mayor of the City sent me the following letter:

Budapest, the 18th of Dec.1919.

Dear General,

I have the honour in the name of the City-Council to deliver our best wishes at the occasion of your birthday. May the Lord grant you a long, happy and sorrow less life.

Permit us to hope, dear General, that you will preserve for our unfortunate Country and City the greatly appreciated sympathy and attachment which you have always so kindly shown to us.

Yours truly,

[Signed] D. Bódy

Mayor of the City of Budapest.

The Prime Minister came in person to offer his congratulations and to pay the respect of the Hungarian government.

The largest paper here, the *Pester Lloyd*, burst into melody of which the following is a translation:

Harry Hill Bandholtz:

Tomorrow, the eighteenth of December, is the birthday of Brig. Gen. Harry Hill Bandholtz, U. S. A., the leader of the American Military Mission to Hungary, who won fame in the Philippine war. It is not essential for us to know where he was born and what age he will be tomorrow, as we respect in this son of the great Union only the noble, energetic, kind-hearted, and strong man, who combines the virtues of the old soldier with the qualities of a most capable diplomat.

Yes, we love and honor General Bandholtz, who visited Budapest as the first representative of the United States, thus awakening within us those sympathies which we have ever harbored since the beginning of the War, for the nation of George Washington, Abraham Lincoln and Thomas Jefferson. He has since done everything to increase this enthusiasm and sympathy. We owe this noble man a great debt of gratitude for his work of mediation, which he is doing for us in all quietude, but none the less energetically in our much-tried country. We avail ourselves of this opportunity to express to him the warmest wishes of every Hungarian and trust that he may live to see many a happy return of this day, in good health and good spirits.

One gentleman sent me a beautiful gold cup; my British colleague sent me a fine silver dish; and in fact all of the birthday presents of my past brief existence combined would hardly come up to what has been showered upon me today.

While the Prime Minister was here, he also discussed the political situation, explained that he was having a great deal of difficulty in keeping the extreme Right factions and the extreme Left factions from clashing constantly, and that as a result the anti-Semitic group had separated from the Christian-Socialist party.

He stated that one of the papers yesterday came out in an editorial strongly advocating pogroms and persecution of the Jews, and that he was having the editor punished.

He seems to be of the opinion that the Socialist members of the Cabinet will resign at an early date because they have been unable to push through many of their communistic schemes. He says he himself has been threatened many times, but is paying very little attention to it; that he recently went to investigate the abuses reported from Kecskemét and that he put a stop to them; that he was going to leave again at an early date for Csongrád, which is the Socialist center, and he hoped to be there nominated for Parliament and to beat the Socialists out of business.

He then went into details about how the Roumanians are completely gutting the country east of the Theiss in absolute defiance of the Entente, and in total noncompliance with the ultimatum of November 5. I included the substance of his remarks in a telegram to the American Embassy in Paris, adding that fourteen Bolshevists were hanged this morning in Budapest, and that instead of all four of the party who came from Vienna to blow up the Gellért Hotel having been captured, only one of them had been captured, but that the plot had nevertheless been frustrated.

In the evening we had some of my adopted family to dinner and then wound up with a dance. The Archduke, the Archduchess, their two children, General Gorton, and wife, General Mombelli, his wife, daughter and aide, and General Graziani with aide, were also present. By special request of Her Royal Highness, the Archduchess Augusta, they danced a Hungarian dance called the "Csárdás." In this, you face your partner squarely, the lady puts both arms upon your shoulders and looks soulfully into your eyes, you place both hands on her hips and ditto the soulful stunt. You then wiggle back and forth to the right and left with a couple of side jumps, occasionally intermingled with a hundred- yard dash speed on a ring-around-the-rosy with your partner. After watching the celebration for some time, I got the step and when the elder Countess Teleki ambled up, dazzling my eyes with her tiara of two hundred and ten big diamonds and her ten-carat diamond earrings, we took a catch-as-catch-can hold and then showed the Archduke and assembled multitude how the Csárdás should be danced. "Joe" applauded vigorously and General Gorton nearly cracked his monocle by his rapid change of facial contortions. The Archduchess had intimated in the beginning that she wanted to be treated in a strictly American manner and she surely got it.

We tried to close up the party about half past two, but my young Hungarian aide, Lieutenant Count Teleki, under the inspiration of several libations of Kümmel, etc., and some of the others, having got started, could not shift their gears, and it was only at 5.30 that we were able to stop the formation by use of the emergency brake. All participants voted the affair a grand success.

December 19, 1919.

In view of last night's celebration, this forenoon was practically used up. However, I rose at 10 and the others got up at 11.30.

The newspaper people came in to offer belated congratulations, and several others who had not known of my approaching birthday did likewise.

I sent a telegram to the American Embassy to the effect that Sir George Clerk, when here, had in the name of the Supreme Council promised the Hungarians immediate Roumanian evacuation, in case they would organize a coalition government as he desired; adding that the Hungarians assert now that they have complied in the spirit and in the letter with all of their instructions, but that the

Supreme Council has not complied with its promise to force the Roumanians to evacuate the country immediately, and that the latter were still on the banks of the Theiss and had already done incalculable harm.

During the day the following letter was received from the Hungarian Prime Minister:

Hungarian Prime Minister.

6703   ME.

To his Excellency General

H. H. Bandholtz

American Military Representative in Hungary

Budapest.

I am thanking you for your note of the 18th Dec. a. c. informing me that you ceased to be a member of the Interallied Military Mission.

I take this opportunity of expressing in my own name as in that of the whole government my most sincere thanks for the friendly and appreciative attitude your Excellency has taken towards Hungary in these sad days of her trials. I can assure your Excellency that the country will remember with gratitude your noble and valuable activity.

t causes me great pleasure that your Excellency will still remain in Budapest as the American Military Representative in Hungary and I beg to express my hope that your Excellency will stay in our midst for an extended period.

Believe me Sir

Most faithfully yours,

[signed] Huszár

Prime Minister.

The following letter was also received today[12]:

Inter-Allied Military Mission Budapest, 17th December 1919

Italian Delegate

To General Bandholtz, Chief of the American Military Mission Budapest.

My dear General Bandholtz,

It is with the greatest regret that I have learned you have ceased to form part of our Inter-Allied Military Mission.

Your collaboration has been very efficient and your activity as well as your firmness have always been highly appreciated.

Please remember me with the same amicable and grateful recollection I shall always have for you and permit me to express to you as well as to all the officers of your Mission my most sincere sentiments of friendship.

Very cordially yours,

The General of Division Mombelli.

12 Commissione Militare Interalleata

Delegazione Italiana   Budapest, 17 Decembre 1919

Il Generale.

A Mr. Le General Bandholtz Chef de la Mission Militaire Américaine Budapest

Mon cher Général Bandholtz,

C'est avec le plus grand regret que j'ai appris que vous avez cessé de faire part de notre Mission Militaire Interalliée.

Votre collaboration a été très efficace et votre activite, ainsi que votre fermeté ont été toujours hautement appreciées.

Veuillez vous rappeler de moi avec le même souvenir amical et reconnaissant que je garderai toujours de vous et permettez moi d'exprimer à vous ainsi qu'it tous les Officiers de votre Mission mes sentiments de sympathie la plus sincère.

Très cordialement à vous.

Le General de Division,

[Signed] Mombelli

December 20, 1919.

Yesterday I received word from Count Apponyi that the Czecho-Slovaks had sent him intimation that in case he ever showed up again in their territory he would be immediately arrested.

All this billing and cooing at the Peace Conference has apparently resulted — instead of leaving a whole dovecote of peaceful little squabs— in leaving a ravenous flock of turkey buzzards. Each one of these miserable little countries down here is utterly and absolutely devoid of all sense of international decency, and spends most of its time in devising schemes for robbing and irritating its neighbors. If the three great powers had been able to keep armies and could have sent them immediately to any place where trouble was brewing, it would have been entirely different, but the Supreme Council's prestige went aglimmering when a steady stream of ultimata had no effect whatever upon that miserable little nation of Roumania. The Hungarians, although down and out on account of Bolshevism, are a much more virile nation than any of the others, and it would not astonish me at any day to see them turn and lick Hell out of the Czechs, aided and abetted by the Poles, who would probably attack the Czechs on the Northeast, and then turn back on the Roumanians.

The Serb, although as unprincipled a looter as any of the others, is a mighty good fighter, and in all probability the Hungarians and the Serbs will some time or other get together and be a hard combination for the other weaklings to go against.

Today Colonel Sheldon and I got inveigled into a tea, and although I attended I did not do any tea lapping. It was a sort of farewell tea given by my protégés, who tomorrow start for the country to be gone over the holidays. It appears that anybody in Budapest who has any social standing whatever must go out to the country and have a family reunion in some miserable cold hole in order to hold his own in the upper crust of society.

A cablegram was received from Secretary of State Lansing, asking me to leave here at Budapest the two State Department automobiles for the use of my State Department successor, Mr. U. Grant-Smith, who is scheduled to arrive about January 22. This is the nearest to any definite date that we have had in regard to Mr. Grant-Smith's arrival. He is surely welcome to the two old arks that were left here by General Jadwin. Both of them have gone through every possible stunt in the way of breakdowns that an automobile can go through with.

December 21, 1919.

This is supposed to be the shortest day of the year and I am thankful for it. After having been freer from colds than ever, I am now coming down with a miserable one which makes days seem longer whether so in reality or not.

We have pretty good information that, although it was expected that the Hungarians would be limited to an army of between twenty and thirty thousand, they already have about eighty thousand, which is rather confirmatory of my belief that they are getting in shape to take a fall out of the Czechs and then the Roumanians.

Yesterday the Roumanian Commander of the Army of Occupation in Hungary sent word to the Inter-Allied Military Mission that he did not care to receive any more messages from the Mission, as he considered that their relations had ended when he crossed the Theiss, and that in the future he desired to have such communications sent to Bucharest, all of which was in direct contravention and disregard of the explicit instructions from the Supreme Council. Fortunately I am no longer a member of the Inter-Allied Military Mission, and this latest Roumanian insult passes me by.

I have also just received a telegram from the American Embassy in Paris to the effect that my automatic relief of myself from the Inter-Allied Military Mission, on December 13, was approved. As a matter of fact, they could not do anything else but approve it.

In acknowledgment of the beautiful silver dish that General Gorton presented me with on my birthday, I sent him the following note:

Budapest, Hungary

21st December 1919

My dear Gorton:

In proper acknowledgment of that "pippin" of a birthday present, as scintillatingly substantial as your attractive self, I have endeavored anon and again to indite a touching epistle that would induce the weeps and melt your tinkling monocle, and which, in return for the oft-repeated and outrageous verbal assaults committed against my archducal dignity, would be as coals of fire upon your stiff and bushy pompadour.

And now, in despair at doing the subject justice, I will simply say, many many thanks and God bless you and yours.

Your devoted friend, General R. St. G. Gorton

H. H. Bandholtz

December 22, 1919.

Thanks to a liberal supply of adrenalin, with which I have been spraying my mouth and throat at frequent intervals, my cold seems to be decidedly better, and was put to a severe test because I went up for my first sitting at the studio of the celebrated artist, Gyula Stetka, who is going to paint my portrait.

In the news summaries from Vienna, the *Arbeiter Zeitung*[13] of the seventeenth of December, gave the Americans honorable mention, and among other things said:

An American Commission which visited Kecskemét found sixty-two corpses lying unburied and hanging on the trees of a neighboring forest. This paper is in position to prove by an official document that this wholesale murder was committed by order of the functionaries of the Hungarian state, with the knowledge of the highest authorities and of the Ministry of Justice, and that it was hushed up, though the number of victims is said to be about five thousand.

The Allied Powers are about to conclude peace with this government of murderers and thus to receive them into the community of civilized humanity. The Roumanians kept these men in check, but hardly had they left when the slaughtering began. English, French, and Americans did not permit them to protect the lives of these miserable people. The American Colonel Yates undertakes the supreme control over the *Brachialgewalt*, that is, the new forces. Now, under the Stars and Stripes of the United States, who could hold back these monsters, the murderous work will go on.

The above translation was sent me by Mr. Halstead, the American Commissioner in Austria, and immediately upon receipt I telegraphed as follows:

Budapest, Hungary

Mr. Halstead,22nd December 1919

Vienna.

B 225 Reference your Press Summary Number 81 your regrets about action of Vienna press apply particularly to article from *Arbeiter Zeitung* of December 17 quoted in your Press Summary Number 85. Every statement in this article as received and regarding Americans is false. No American Commission visited Kecskemét. Colonel Yates returned to his permanent duties in Roumania over three weeks ago. The American member of the Inter-Allied Military Mission was relieved from same on December 13. Report that Colonel Yates undertakes supreme control over the new forces and that murderous work is going on

---

13 Organ of the Social Democratic party. It has a wide circulation.

under the Stars and Stripes of the United States is inexpressibly false and libelous and it is requested that prompt and efficacious action be taken adequately to punish the perpetrators, to force the *Arbeiter Zeitung* to retract its false statements, and to prevent a repetition of such a scurrilous publication. B. 225.   Bandholtz.

December 23, 1919.

In order to complete the portrait painting sooner, I went to M. Stetka's studio at half past ten and stayed until about noon, when the light played out. The old duffer says that he is putting his soul into the portrait and I am curious to see what sort of a composite will result from my physiognomy and his soul.

The people in this section of the world remind me so frequently of my old friends, the Filipinos. They do not and cannot look at things the same as we do. I was approached by a proposition to arrange for the entry into Hungary of six carloads of sugar from Czecho-Slovakia, the proposition being that if I could arrange and guarantee the return to Czecho-Slovakia of six empty cars for the cars bringing the sugar, there would be no difficulties. This I did; then to my surprise found out that a contract was being made between the sugar people and the American Mission by which the American Mission engaged to use six carloads of sugar at a value of about twenty thousand dollars for its own use. This meant that I was to be a party to the contract and then turn the sugar over to somebody else to dispose of. Quite naturally I stepped on the proposition good and plenty. If they want to bring the sugar in to relieve suffering, which I understood was the case, I am for it. But getting mixed up in any kind of a private deal is a little bit too much.

Another thing, before my favorite adopted daughter, Juliska, had left for the country, I noticed that she frequently referred to individuals as being "damned fools" and damned things pretty generally. I must caution Colonel Loree, Colonel Sheldon, and Captain Gore to be more particular in their conversation. Young men are so prone to be thoughtless in the selection of their adjectives.

Last night Colonel Loree and I went to the opera to see what we thought was going to be a ballet. Instead of that, it was a combination of babes being lost in the woods, angels coming down the ladder, witches riding broomsticks, and children burning up witches, explosions, animated toys, etc. In addition to Colonel Loree, there were hundreds of other children in the Opera House.

December 24, 1919.

Again I reported at ten-thirty at the studio for my daily sitting, and found the rotund little artist chasing back and forth across the room with an overcoat on and a muffler around his neck and no fire. He explained that there would be no fuel until Saturday, and the best he could do would be for me to come again next Sunday and resume the sittings.

I met Captain Gore just in front of the studio, so we went down town to look at Christmas presents and found that during the past few days practically everything had doubled in price.

A short time after arriving back at the office, I received a call from Count Apponyi, who has been previously referred to as the chairman of the Hungarian Peace Commission which is to be sent to Paris. It appears that Count Apponyi, owing to the recent change in boundaries, had his estate shifted out of Hungary into Czecho-Slovakia, where he was residing when he received an urgent appeal from the Hungarian government to come to Budapest with a view to helping out in the organization of the new Cabinet and ultimately to becoming chairman of the Peace Commission. He was assured protection by the Inter-Allied Military Mission and the message was delivered by a Czech officer who courteously escorted him across the border.

The Count would now like to return to his home for the holidays, but the Czechs refuse to allow him to return, and stated that if he once arrives there he will be arrested. On the other hand, the Countess Apponyi, who was left behind in Czecho-Slovakia, is not allowed to leave the country. The Czechs give as their reason that a person who is commissioned to represent the interests of Hungary at the Peace Conference against those of the Czecho-Slovak Republic, cannot be allowed to sojourn in the territory of the latter. This is such a peculiar attitude that it is impossible to analyse the thought that produced it. All I can do, of course, is to report the matter to Paris where, I know, nothing will be done.

The whole trouble is that Czecho-Slovakia is entirely dominated by the French. The French papers have lately come out in strong opposition to Count Apponyi being a member of the Peace Commission, and they are, therefore, using their puppets, the Czechs, to make it uncomfortable for the Count.

When the American Army was in France and we heard so much of the Czecho-Slovaks, we formed a very high opinion of them, but I am afraid that this opinion was based entirely on propaganda, because, in all the asinine and ridiculous stunts lately pulled off in this corner of Europe, the Czechs have been ahead of all other small nations.

There is no question, however, but that they are going to get theirs good and plenty and before long. The Slovaks are determined to separate from them, and would make a move now, were the Hungarians ready to help them out. When they do move, the Hungarians and the Poles will combine with them and it will all be up with the Czechs. At the same time, we know that there is a delegation of Croats trying to get in touch with the Hungarians with a view to separation from Serbia and reunion with Hungary; and to complicate the situation still further, the Serbs are flirting with the Hungarians with the object of an offensive and defensive alliance against the Roumanians. It looks as though, if the Hungarians were shrewd and played first one and then the other, that they would rapidly be able to get back all that they lost by the War.

It is rather remarkable that we are at war with Hungary, because our troops never faced each other and we had no hostility whatever against this little country and, had they not been a part of the Austro-Hungarian Empire, we would still be at peace with them the same as with Turkey and Bulgaria.

My sugar-contractor friend came in this afternoon, so I called Colonel Loree in to be a witness to our conversation. I told the gentleman in question, a Mr. Guthard Imre, that the proposition as advanced to me was simply to guarantee to the Czechs that the Hungarians would return six good empty cars in exchange for an equal number that would bring in the sugar; that when it came to being a party to a contract in which the American Mission guaranteed to use the sugar exclusively for its own purposes, I must decline to have any participation. He said that it was intended to use the sugar entirely for distribution by the Hungarian government among the families of employees of the railways, posts and telegraphs. I told him this was a most praiseworthy object and that I would be perfectly willing to undertake to assure the sugar company of the Czecho-Slovaks that the sugar would be disposed of for that purpose, but that there was nothing doing on any contract in which the American Mission was a party of the first or the second part. He left, assuring me that he would see the agent of the sugar company and try to have the matter adjusted.

December 25, 1919.

This morning I spent over at the office, from ten o'clock until noon, to get off a memorandum on traffic control which had been requested by Colonel Youngberg of the Engineers.

Late in the afternoon Captain Aitken, of the British Mission, came over to invite all of us to come to the British "B" Mess about ten o'clock and celebrate with them. As I knew I could not, with the damned cold, do myself or the subject justice, I sent Colonel Loree and Captain Gore to represent us. They found the representation apparently quite pleasant, because it was well towards morning when they returned. I understand that one of the favorite beverages of the evening was a "Black and White" whisky high ball in which flat champagne was substituted for water. After a few libations they indulged in playing charades, blindman's buff and other childlike games.

December 26, 1919.

Mr. Zerkowitz, the Hungarian gentleman who from the beginning attached himself to this Mission and has rendered us such valuable service, induced my old portrait painter, Stetka, to transfer his operations from his atelier to my office. So he rolled in this morning with canvas, easels, tubes of paint, brushes, etc., and got ensconced in the corner where I had always kept my desk, promptly ranking me out of this location, but thereby assuring the completion of the portrait before we finally leave Hungary. The various amateurs who have dropped in and seen the old man's work all have criticisms to make; some say the nose isn't right; some that the face is too broad; others that it is too narrow, etc. It is probably all of these and results from his trying to make a composite of his soul and my face. However, as he has the reputation of being one of the best painters in Europe, I think it will eventually turn out all right.

December 27, 1919.

Last night when I went over to the Post after five o'clock, there were evidences everywhere that the Hungarians were laying off for the holiday week, the same as the Filipinos, and they certainly do resemble the Filipinos when it comes to laying off for holidays. All the way from Buda to the Elizabeth Bridge, which is usually a very busy thoroughfare, I met only three vehicles.

This morning my old friend, the painter, showed up on time and I had three hours of very tedious sitting.

This afternoon I sent for Mr. Unger, who is representing the Czecho-Slovak sugar concern and told him that, while I was interested in any humanitarian movement, I could not and would not make any contract in the name of the American Mission by which sugar would be bought solely for the Mission's purposes; that I was willing to arrange for the return of the empty cars and to supervise and do my best to see that the sugar upon arrival in Hungary was turned over as represented to me, for the use of the families of employees of the railways, posts, telegraphs and telephones, instead of being allowed to fall into the hands of profiteers. He said that this was perfectly agreeable to him and that he would endeavor to ship the sugar along these lines.

December 28, 1919.

For sometime past, the city of Budapest has been placarded with posters protesting against the dismemberment of Hungary, and as a result a society has been formed called the "Association for the Preservation of the Old Hungarian Boundaries"— or words to that effect. This morning a delegation of several hundred people came up to the Royal Palace in front of the Ministry of Foreign Affairs, and called for Count Apponyi, who will be Chief of the Hungarian Peace Commission to Paris, and implored him to use his utmost endeavor to preserve Hungary in her original entirety. In a speech which he made from the balcony, he pledged himself to do his utmost. In view of the fact that Hungary is already practically dismembered I am afraid his utmost cannot amount to very much.

In the afternoon, I had a meeting with Mr. B. A. Unger, representing George Morgensen of 50 Broad Street, New York City, which firm has loaned to the Czecho-Slovak state one hundred million dollars in raw materials and taken as security the Czecho-Slovak sugar crop. There were with him Mr. Imre Guthard, who is negotiating for the six carloads of sugar before referred to, Mr. Zerkowitz as interpreter, and Colonel Loree. To clarify the situation, I handed Mr. Unger a letter, of which the following is a copy:

Budapest, 27th December, 1919.

Mr. B. A. Unger

Prague, Czecho-Slovakia

My dear Mr. Unger:

Relative to the six carloads of sugar which are to be shipped into Hungary, the understanding is that there is no contract in which the American Mission enters at all. In the interest of humanity and with a view to relieving suffering, I will, however, do my utmost to facilitate the transaction.

There is enclosed herewith a copy of a communication from the Hungarian Railroad Commissioner agreeing to turn over at Szob Station six empty cars immediately upon the arrival of the six cars loaded with sugar.

In addition to this, I shall be glad to arrange for the delivery of this sugar to the proper person, for distribution, as I have been given to understand, among the officials and employees of the Hungarian railways, posts and telegraphs.

With this understanding, you may ship the sugar addressed to the Mission and arrangements will be made for turning over as above outlined.

H. H. Bandholtz

Brig. Gen., U.S. A.

I then informed Mr. Guthard that he must bring to me a communication from the Food Minister designating him as the person to receive the sugar for distribution among the employees of the railway service and posts, telegraphs and telephones. This he agreed to do, and the matter was ended.

During the day, Colonel Loree brought in a communication asking for twenty-five carloads of sugar for distribution among the various other governmental employees, and I told Mr. Unger that I would be very glad to help in any such matter, under the same conditions as indicated in his letter.

A few days prior to this, one of my stamp friends, who is a journalist, informed me that the journalists of Budapest and their families, representing some eight hundred people, had contracted in Jugo-Slavia for fifteen carloads of supplies which the Serbs were holding up, and he implored me to use my influence with the Serbs to induce them to allow the food to enter Hungary. This occurred some time before Christmas. So I took the gentleman in to Colonel Loree, told him to give the data to Colonel Loree, and I would send him immediately over to see the Serbian Minister. My stamp friend then said that he could give it himself, but that the director of the association would have to furnish it, and in view of the fact that the Holidays were approaching, he did not think much of anything could be done until after New Year's. Colonel Loree informed him that we were not starving and, if they were not sufficiently interested to bring it up before New Year's, it made no difference to us. Everything in this neck of the woods must make way for holidays.

December 29, 1919.

Shortly after arriving at the office, General Mombelli called informally, just to talk things over. He said things were very quiet at Mission meetings now and that they missed very much my occasional thumping of the table and saying, "I'll be damned if I'll do it." He also said that he understood that a British diplomatic representative was due to arrive to take charge of the diplomatic situation, thereby relieving General Gorton from the same. The Italian representative is already here, the

American representative is expected, but we have had no word yet in regard to a Frenchman.

I received a short letter from my adopted family, stating that they hoped that the "damned cold" was better. It is astonishing how rapidly young Hungarians take up English.

December 30, 1919.

Today in order to make sure of getting rid of the damned cold, I also stayed in and am feeling decidedly better.

December 31, 1919.

According to the doctor's advice, — am still hanging on to my room for today in the hope that when New Year's breaks tomorrow I shall be able to get out and raise Hell with the boys.

Yesterday I received a cablegram from Mr. Polk stating that Mr. Grant-Smith had already sailed from the United States and suggesting that I communicate with him in Paris. This opens up the field a little and it looks as though we can begin to see the end of our Budapest tour of duty. I imagine, however, that Mr. Grant-Smith will stay in Paris for a week or two before coming down here, and I shall have to stay a week or two after he gets here. So we probably will depart early in February.

January, 1920

January 1, 1920.

Today is another day like yesterday, with fog banked up so thick that one cannot see across the street. I was not feeling fit to receive callers, but there certainly was a raft of them, and I have a pack of cards several inches high.

A telegram was received from our Embassy in Paris, stating that Grant-Smith had sailed from the United States on the seventeenth and that they would advise me when he arrived in Paris. As he has had more than ample time, had he gone direct to a French port, it is presumed that he stopped in England en route, and my original schedule about getting away from here about February 1 will undoubtedly be carried out.

Mr. de Pekár, the former Hungarian Minister of Liaison, insisted on seeing me today and gave me one of the medals of the National Museum with a dedication on it to myself from the grateful Museum. This honor was conferred upon me on account of my having saved the Museum from being looted by the Roumanians.

The whole situation is beginning to get on the nerves of all of us, and we shall all be mighty glad to get headed towards home. I hope this time I will not be held up at the eleventh hour and stuck off on some other skunk-skinning detail.

January 2, 1920.

This morning I rose at six o'clock, feeling much refreshed after a cold bath, had breakfast at seven, and Colonel Sheldon and I took a special train at eight for Dunatetétlen, where we arrived at 11.10.

After arriving at the house and lunching, I assembled my whole adopted family to the number of about fourteen, including servants, etc., got them to the railroad station and started exactly on time, at four o'clock. After leaving our protégés at their house in Budapest, Colonel Sheldon and I immediately came up to our quarters, where we had dinner and all retired fairly early.

Word was received that Colonel Yates and Colonel Poillon had arrived, the former on his way to the United States and the latter from Bucharest in order to see me and talk over the Roumanian situation. I shall, therefore, see them tomorrow and hope to be able to start Colonel Poillon off right as regards those liver-complexioned Roumanians.

January 3, 1920.

Most of the morning was spent at the office catching up with back work, and in an effort to start in well with the New Year.

This afternoon I spent in winding up private affairs.

January 4, 1920.

This morning, being Sunday, I went to my office at 9.30 and had been there but a short time when General Bridges, of the British Service, came in with the new British High Commissioner to Hungary. Apparently the latter had been instructed to get in close touch with me and has made several appointments for interviews before my departure.

Colonel Poillon later came in and we had quite a conference, during which he informed me that the Queen of Roumania had told him that I was a Jew, that Colonel Loree was a Jew, that my aides were all Jews, and that everybody about the office was a Jew; that we were buying up a vast quantity of articles, which was a very bad policy; and, in general, good Queen Marie gave us Hell and repeat[1]. I gave Colonel Poillon considerable information on the general situation and in particular about the Roumanians, and had him to lunch, after which we continued our conversation for two or three hours.

In the evening Colonel Loree and I were invited as guests to a dinner, given by General Bridges and Mr. Hohler, the British High Commissioner[2], to General Franchet d'Espérey, at the Hotel Ritz. The other guests present were Generals

1 Compare this to Diary on September 8, and footnote.

2 Thomas Beaumont Hohler was appointed High Commissioner of Great Britain in Hungary on January 5, 1920. During his stay in Hungary, he became very sympathetic towards the problems of the Hungarians. Charles à Court Repington says in his diary, *After the War* (Boston, 1922): "I saw Hohler after lunch. He is fully of opinion that great injustice has been done to the Magyars under the Treaty" (p.165).

Graziani and Mombelli, each with a staff officer. The dinner was rather elaborate, and either it was decidedly heavy or sitting opposite one Frenchman, with another one on my left, gave me the first attack of acute indigestion I have had in months.

While at coffee, the British High Commissioner asked me to talk over the situation with him, which I did in as much detail as possible under the circumstances, and he has arranged to come and see me daily in order to get wise to what has occurred in the past.

January 5, 1920.

Today I received confidential reports from Admiral Horthy, covering the Bolshevist activities in this section of Europe. It appears that the Communists have a well-perfected organization in Vienna, which has become the center of their activities, and their plan is in February or March to have general uprisings in Hungary, Czecho-Slovakia, Austria and Italy. They feel confident that they will be most successful in the last-named country[3].

Their plans were obtained from the confessions of a party of four or five who were sent over to Budapest from Vienna for the express purpose of blowing up Admiral Horthy's Headquarters, the Royal Palace where General Gorton and myself are located, the Government Building, the Coronation Cathedral and the Opera House. Fortunately this little bunch was spotted and arrested before they did any damage and, as a result of their confessions, it is believed that much danger may be averted. I am having copies of all their confessions made and forwarded for the information of our State and War Departments.

This afternoon I received a letter from Lieutenant-Colonel Moffat, the American Red Cross representative in Budapest, enclosing a cablegram from the United States in which I am asked to make recommendations in regard to the continuation of Red Cross activities in Budapest. In compliance with this I sent the following letter:

3 It will be remembered that Italy was then actually menaced very seriously by Bolshevism and that it was saved from this calamity by the establishment of Fascism.

233

Budapest, 5th January 1920

From: American Military Representative in Hungary

To: American Red Cross

Subject: Conditions in Budapest and Hungary

1: The Roumanian military forces occupied practically all of Hungary from early in August until November 14, 1919, upon which latter date they evacuated the city of Budapest. Their requisitions and seizures, by which names they dignified their general looting, were about as systematic as the antics of a monkey in a cabinet of bric-a-brac. They took machinery and instruments that were ruined beyond repair the moment removed from their locations; they seized and removed practically all available food supplies, even to the last animal and the seed grain from many farms; and their general conduct and procedure were in violation of international law, the customs of war, and the requirements of decency and humanity.

2: The result of all this has been a sadly impoverished and destitute Hungary which, instead of being an indemnity asset for the Allies, is, owing to the act of one of them, Roumania, a sadly stricken poverty patient.

3: While in Bucharest in September I saw a Red Cross organization and equipment out of all proportion to existing or possible future needs in a country which, while already well supplied with food, was running in thousands of carloads of necessities from her prostrate neighbor. Despite the ultimatum of November 16 from the Supreme Council for Roumania to evacuate immediately all of Hungary, the Roumanians still occupy all of the country east of the Theiss and are continuing their barbarous methods even to the seizure of seed grain.

4: As we were apparently powerless to prevent our Roumanian associates from creating the conditions above described, it becomes in my opinion our imperative duty to alleviate them in every way possible.

5: I recommend that the American Red Cross organization in Budapest not only remain, but that it be enlarged to cover all of Hungary now free of invaders, and that it then gradually expand as long as necessary to meet the increased difficulties now being prepared by the Roumanians east of the Theiss.

H. H. Bandholtz

Brig. Gen., U.S. A.

These colds that one has in Europe seem to be caused by a different bug, which gives a good deal of the effect of the "flu" and leaves one like a dishrag for several days after the cold seems to have left. It does not leave one's nerves in the best condition. This condition is not improved by having a pleasant-faced valet like Lugubrious Luke, who comes in like a cloud of gloom every morning and disturbs my room. He speaks Hungarian, German, and I believe French, fluently and understands absolutely nothing. Yesterday a party came up into our offices and dumped down four hundred thousand dollars in American currency, with the request that I send it to Trieste to purchase lard from Swift and Co. As we have no means for sending such a small sum, and as we do not care to keep it in our possession, we had them lug it back, and we shall try to make arrangements through our Vienna Mission to handle the matter.

January 6, 1920

This morning I came to the office and got my work well under way, and then I went down to the old painter where I spent the whole forenoon.

In the afternoon Colonel Poillon and Colonel Yates came to the quarters, and we spent considerable time going over the situation, after which I came to my office and spent most of the time at my desk, except for a short conference with General Gorton and the new British High Commissioner, Mr. Hohler, to whom I have loaned temporarily the use of one of my office rooms.

January 7, 1920.

Last night Colonel Sheldon and I went to the opera, lured by the understanding that, in the Hungarian production of "Carmen," the prima donna in the last act pulls a corset string up out of her bosom and chokes herself to death. As this was rather a novel finale, we decided to go and see it, but were disappointed.

This morning, like yesterday morning, I came first to the office, got my work going and then went out and sat the whole forenoon for the old artist, who encouraged me by saying that he was sure the picture would not be dry enough to be taken inside of a month and ought not to be moved inside of a year. He admitted, however, that, although he was experienced in painting, he knew damned little about packing paintings, in which I agreed with him.

Upon returning to my quarters from the artist's, I found that Admiral Horthy had been over to see me and was desirous of making an appointment. Accordingly I went over to his Headquarters in the afternoon and spent about an hour and a half with him. He went into great detail in explaining the Bolshevist situation in this part of Europe. He repeated what I already knew, viz., that four Bolshevists who came over from Vienna had come for the purpose of blowing up his Headquarters, blowing up the Royal Palace with General Gorton and myself, the

Prime Minister's, the Government Building, the Coronation Cathedral and the Opera House.

The Admiral is satisfied that the Austrian government, as now existing, is almost in the hands of the Communists and that Béla Kun and many of his confreres, although supposed to be interned at Karlstein, are given every conceivable liberty, at least as regards correspondence. He is also sure that the first outbreak will be in Czecho-Slovakia, and he expects them to turn loose in Prague during the month of February. I explained to him that the United States had already deported 250 Bolshevists, and recently in one night's roundup had arrested 5,000 more who would be deported as soon as found implicated in the movement[4].

We then shifted to the other issues, and he told me that he considered that former Prime Minister Friedrich was a political adventurer, his speeches were incendiary and were of a type to which very ignorant hearers would be glad to listen, but which any sane man, not ill advised on the doctrines, would find impossible of execution. He wanted to know what the status of our government was as regards the Hapsburgs, and I told him that could best be determined by the message which the Supreme Council had sent to the Archduke Joseph when he was at the head of the Hungarian government. The Admiral further stated that he had been approached by men in all positions and advised that he take over dictatorship. This, he said, he did not personally want to do, but was wondering, in case it were necessary, how our government would look at it. I told him, of course, this would require an inquiry before I could answer.

He is positive that Friedrich will be elected by a large majority and made Prime Minister, and that one of his first acts will be to put in the Archduke as palatine, to be followed shortly afterwards, if possible, by his coronation. It is believed in some quarters that the Admiral is thinking of the King job for himself but whether he is or not, the Archduke Joseph certainly has the bee buzzing loudly in his own bonnet.

4 Without proper information, General Bandholtz refers here to the shameful persecution of radical-minded and liberal people in the United States by the Attorney General Mitchell Palmer. A scathing condemnation of it may be found in the book of the Undersecretary of Labor at that time, Louis F. Post, *Deportations' Delirium of 1920.* See also H.P. Fairchild's *Immigration*, p. 427.

January 8, 1920.

I am getting to be quite an opera fan and may as well keep it up as long as the Royal Box is available, because one cannot always disport oneself amidst such regal surroundings.

In the afternoon, after going through routine work, I had a long conference with Mr. Hohler and discussed with him the various propositions given me by Admiral Horthy, without letting him know from whom I had received them.

A courier arrived with a few letters today. Fortunately one of them was from my young friend and former chauffeur in the New York Division, Lieutenant Littwitz, who wrote me more in detail about Mrs. Bandholtz's condition than anything that I have had in months. It seems good to have somebody that can sympathize with me in my situation here and give me the kind of news that is most needed.

January 9, 1920.

Last night I went to see a snappy little opera called "Don Juan" which, not by actual count but from estimate, had forty-eight osculation scenes. A rooster-legged galoot with a face like a Wah-wah monkey and omniverous as regards females, was the main guy. All the girls looked alike to him; whenever he saw a skirt he would run her down, scratch his wing at her, claw the dirt and then bite her in the face. One female who was trying to be the bride of another ass, was repeatedly bitten and seemed to like it.

Things got so animated that even a statue came to life and coughed up a lullaby. In the final scene Don Juan got drunk, the singing statue came in à la Spook, coughed up another lullaby and things got so hot that the house caught fire and Don Juan was asphyxiated in his own gas, and responded to three encores.

This morning I went to old Stetka again with Count Teleki, my aide, for what I supposed to be my last sitting, and as I was feeling a little bit cranky, it kept the old fellow busy saying:

Exzellenz, bitte ein wenig freundlich.

When we finished for the morning, he told me that this last sitting was like a last ultimatum to the Roumanians; he would like to have me come again. So I agreed to come Sunday.

This being the day upon which our courier arrives from Vienna in the morning and goes back in the evening, I was kept busy all the afternoon in the office, getting out my memoranda to the State Department and shipping off the completed pages of my journal.

January 10, 1920.

After winding up last night all business connected with the courier, I saw that there was still time to go to the opera, so Colonel Sheldon and I left about 6 o'clock to see "La Bohéme."

The afternoon was all spent in my office and Count Széchényi[5], the husband of Gladys Vanderbilt, came in and spent about an hour with me.

January 11, 1920.

Last night we had as our guests the entire Szirmay family, including Count and Countess Szirmay, and the Countesses Juliska, "Electricity," Puszi and Mani.

This morning was to be my last day with the old artist, so I went down to his atelier accompanied by Count Teleki at 10.30 and stayed with him until about 1.30. He asked me to come again tomorrow, but I told him I'd be damned if I would. So he went on trying to put a little more intelligence into my forehead and touching up my hands, and finally said that he would not need me again.

After lunch I came right over to the office and had a conference with Colonel Poillon, who had just returned from Vienna, and then I had a long talk with Count Somssich.

The Count stated that he had received a telegram from Count Apponyi, the head of the Hungarian Peace Delegation, requesting information as to the kind of representation of the United States in the Supreme Council, and asking as to whether or not he should furnish copies of all papers, memoranda, etc., to the American Ambassador. I sent a code telegram embodying this information to the American Embassy in Paris.

---

5   Count László Széchényi, at present [1932 and for a long time after-wards] Hungarian Minister at Washington.

During the conversation, I catechized the Count in regard to his opinion as to the outcome of the election, and he is not so certain that Friedrich will be elected. He says that Friedrich has pulled off so many asinine stunts that the people are beginning to lose confidence in him and doubt if he is the type of man which they want at the head of the government.

The Count, like all other Hungarians, is of the firm opinion that sooner or later Hungary will have to be a kingdom, and he is in hopes that there will be something in the peace terms which will authorize the restoration of a monarchy, but which will forbid a Hapsburg from sitting on the throne of Hungary. He says there are three Hapsburgs who will be pretenders, the first being the present King Karl, the second the Archduke Joseph, and the third Prince Albrecht. Karl could say to the Hungarians that in case they recalled him, he would bring Croatia with him, because Croatia is fanatically loyal to him. Prince Albrecht, on the other hand, has large holdings in the north and could make a like promise in regard to Slovakia if he were elected. The Archduke Joseph, the count considers to be an honest, capable and brave man and well qualified for the regal honor; but he is afraid that should any one of the three be put in power, there would always remain too many pretenders as long as a Hapsburg dynasty reigned. Most of the Hungarians would like a King of the English royal blood, or some one selected by the English, in order to have British backing.

The Count also related portions of a conversation he had had with the French General Franchet d'Espérey[6], on the occasion of the latter's last visit to Budapest. The Count says, that assuming an attitude that Hungary placed her faith in the League of Nations, he had discussed the prospect of treaties, etc., when the Frenchman waxed furious and said that the League of Nations was worthless; that France, owing to Wilson, had received an execrable peace; that France needed, ought to have, and would have had, the left bank of the Rhine, but that Wilson prevented it. The Count is of the opinion that the peculiar French attitude of favoring Roumania and being invariably anti-Hungarian, is more or less on account of a desire to oppose England and make it difficult for the latter to gain headway in this section of Europe.

6 At the end of the world war, Commander in Chief of the Southern Army of the Allies. Cf. Introduction.

January 12, 1920.

Last night Colonel Sheldon and I went to the opera to see "The Masquerade," not expecting to see very much, but stayed through the last act and were simply delighted with it.

The plot is based on a governor who is in love with his secretary's wife. The Serbian attaché, who came into our box, assured us that it was purely a Platonic love affair, but as such there was surely a hell of a lot of squeezing and biting in it.

This afternoon I was called upon by a Colonel Vina, who said he was representing the Italian government in settling the frontier between Austria and Hungary. It took about ten minutes to air the room out after he left, and he will probably vote for whichever party turns out the most champagne.

Mr. Zerkowitz came in and I gave him instructions to go over to the Prime Minister and deliver to him the following letter, and to tell the Prime Minister that I was disgusted with some of the members of his cabinet:

Budapest, 12th January 1920

From: American Military Representative in Hungary

To: His Excellency the Hungarian Prime Minister

Subject: Attitude of Food Ministry on Importation of Supplies.

1: In order to alleviate in a slight degree the shortage of foodstuffs in Hungary I recently consented to aid in the importation of sugar from Czecho-Slovakia for the use of officials and employees of the posts, railways, telegraphs, telephones, and banks.

2: I considered it necessary, however, to require a guarantee that the sugar imported would be used for the purpose stated, that there would be no profiteering, and that the fixing of prices and distribution of the sugar would be under the supervision of the appropriate Ministry.

3: I am now informed that the required guarantee has been refused by the Food Ministry, and under the circumstances I am regretfully obliged to withdraw my support from the entire transaction in question which appeared to be at the time a most praiseworthy enterprise.

H. H. Bandholtz

Brig. General, U.S. A.

January 13, 1920.

It is a great comfort to have no more visits to pay to the old artist, and it enables me to catch up on all my back work.

In order to cinch the sugar deal, I sent for Mr. Zerkowitz and had him accompany me over to the Prime Minister's, and translate for me to the Prime Minister my opinion of the whole sugar deal, which was about as follows:

On account of the acute suffering in Hungary for lack of both sugar and fats, I had been approached by persons requesting that I aid them in importing into Hungary from Czecho-Slovakia, thirty carloads of sugar for officials and employees of the posts, telegraphs, railways, and banks, and requesting in particular that I assure the Czecho-Slovak authorities that empty cars would be returned, or others substituted for them on the border. This I had consented to do, but in view of the fact that the American Mission, neither collectively nor individually, was allowed to engage in any business transactions, I insisted that I receive a letter from the appropriate government Ministry to the effect that this importation was for the purpose stated and that no profiteering would be permitted.

I had received a proper communication from the Food Ministry in regard to twenty-four carloads intended for the banks and was assured that a satisfactory contract had been made by the importer with the Hungarian government, and I therefore notified the bank that the transaction could proceed.

I told the Prime Minister that, however, I was now informed that the contract with the government required the importers to deliver six carloads of this sugar to the Food Minister at about 33 1/3 per cent below cost to them, as a result of which they were authorized to sell, at about three times cost, the remaining eighteen cars; that I considered this a most reprehensible transaction and that I would not be a party to it; that the whole proceeding must be absolutely clear and above board, and uniform prices throughout. I told him also that in the case of the other six carloads of the thirty, the Food Minister had required a deposit of fifty thousand crowns as a guarantee that the sugar would be imported with the penalty of forfeiture of the same in case the sugar had not arrived within six weeks. I added that in view of the fact that the American Mission was protecting the enterprise, this was an insult to me, and in any event it had the appearance of graft, and I would not stand for it.

His Excellency explained that the present Food Minister, who had been forced upon him by Sir George Clerk, was of the peasant type, that he was utterly unqualified for the position, and that he had not the slightest idea of what his proper functions were. He assured me that there would be a new Minister by the twenty-fifth of the month and begged me to suspend action, and he could have the matter adjusted and bring it before the first meeting of the Cabinet.

January 14, 1920.

After clearing up what little desk work there was in the forenoon, I went down town with Colonel Sheldon to do some shopping and returned about noon. I got word from the Foreign Office that Mihály Károlyi, who had turned over the Hungarian government to Béla Kun and who is now in Czecho-Slovakia, was planning to go to America in disguise and under an assumed name for the purpose of spreading communism there, and that the Czecho-Slovak Minister of Foreign Affairs, Benes was going to arrange for the passports. I therefore sent a cipher telegram to the American Minister at Prague and also to ourState Department, to advise them of K.árolyi's intentions[7].

In the afternoon I was called upon by a delegation of bishops and others, consisting of Bishop William Burt, Bishop William 0. Shepard of Wichita, Kansas, Doctor John L. Nuelsen, Resident Bishop in Europe, Mr. A. J. Bucher, editor of the Christian Apologist from Cincinnati, and Mr. Hanford Crawford, all of the Methodist Episcopal Church.

I gave these gentlemen an idea of what had happened during the Roumanian occupation and arranged to do my best to send them on their way, and invited them to lunch tomorrow.

January 15, 1920.

After cleaning up the work at the office, Colonel Loree and I went to see the paintings which I had purchased, and to attend to one or two other down-town affairs. Then I came home for our lunch with the bishops.

7　It will be remembered that Károlyi has on later occasions been refused admission to the United States.

I had planned an interview for them with the Prime Minister at 12.15 and then sent Captain Gore to get them. As was to have been expected, when he arrived at the hotel there were difficulties. The bishops were having a meeting and had given orders that they were not to be disturbed. However, he disturbed them. When they came down to get started, one of their number was missing. They finally located him. When they landed up at the government building, they were between twenty minutes and half an hour late, and the Prime Minister had gone on with his other audiences. The result was that instead of showing up at the house for lunch at one o'clock, it was after two when they arrived. They were very contrite, but laid the delay all upon the fact that they had been detained by the Prime Minister, ignoring the fact that the initial guilt was theirs.

We gave them a square meal which they seemed to appreciate. Finally we sent them on their way rejoicing, arranging first to have the two ladies of the party come to lunch with us tomorrow.

The work is falling off so that if we do not get away from here soon, we shall all of us certainly get into mischief.

January 16, 1920.

Rumors of Bolshevist uprisings are persistent and seem to be fairly well founded. Although the Hungarians will not give us the details, we know that there was a so-called attempted Bolshevist uprising a few days ago near the Ganz-Danubius Works, and it is understood that about twenty Bolshevists were killed in its suppression. We have it pretty straight that recently Bolshevism reigned for about two hours in the town of Szolnok, which is on the Theiss River about thirty miles east of Budapest, but that it was vigorously and thoroughly suppressed by Horthy's troops, who killed several hundred Bolshevists and had only four of their officers killed.

A telegram was received from Mr. Grant-Smith, indicating that he will arrive in Vienna about the twentieth, and that he will there await his supplies and then come to Budapest. This again leaves us up in the air as to our plans, because it may take several days before his supplies reach him. Like the watched pot which never boils, the last days of our stay seem to be interminable.

January 17, 1920.

This morning I received pretty definite information that the Bolshevists in Vienna are planning an uprising to take place on Thursday the twenty-second, and that there will be a sympathetic one at the same time in Budapest. The authorities here are well prepared to suppress anything that may occur, but none of the people in Vienna seem to have the slightest idea of what is going on in their midst.

The Hungarians today received information in regard to the peace terms, and although they have known almost definitely for months just what these peace terms would be, the blow, when delivered, like the death of a long-suffering invalid, has come as a shock. All of the public buildings and many other buildings are draped in mourning and black flags are flying everywhere. It is understood that there are to be three days of this kind of mourning before normal life will be resumed. Incidentally, it gives another excuse for laying off work. If the Hungarians were a trifle more industrious and energetic, they would have less cause to complain of Jewish domination.

January 18, 1920

Last night Colonel Loree, Colonel Sheldon, Captain Gore and myself attended a dinner given by our old friend, Dr. Lazar Baitch, the Serbian Minister, and the Serbian Military Representative, Major Body, and Mrs. Body. The other guests present were General and Mrs. Gorton and Major and Mrs. Foster, of the British Service, Count and Countess de Troismonts, of the French, and some nondescript whom I could not locate.

As invariably happens on such occasions, Doctor Baitch, after one sip of champagne, got communicative; after two he became confidential; and after three, affectionate and cuddlesome. During the dinner he had much more than three sips, so when he rolled up to me I was prepared for all sorts of confidences, which came. He cussed the French in fluent and voluble French, could not do the Italians justice in any language, was warm in his praise of the British, and demonstrative as Hell when it came to America.

He said that Serbia and Hungary must get together and combine against Roumania[9], and that Greece and Serbia should likewise get together on account of Bulgaria. He told me that the Greek representative on the Reparation Commission, who arrived here a few days ago, had come and told him that his government had instructed him to follow the lead of the Serbians in everything on the Reparation Commission.

.About half past ten, with our tummies filled with food and our eyes filled with cigarette smoke, we pulled out for our quarters and played four different kinds of solitaire until bedtime.

The Danube is apparently on a rampage, and I understand it is the highest it has been since 1827. Of course these people, before they began to try to save any of their property, allowed the water to get up into their storehouses and flood them. Too bad they are such procrastinators.

This morning I had planned to go over and see Admiral Horthy and have a plain talk with him in regard to his soldiers again becoming active and assuming a strong anti-Semitic attitude. He also wants to buy my car when I leave, and I thought I would show it to him by daylight. I found, however, that he was away on a hunting expedition with Mr. Hohler. That left me with practically nothing to do.

In the evening Captain Gore and I went down to the telegraph office to get telegrams now coming over our lines for the Hungarian government, and then called on the Szirmay family.

January 19,1920.

The Danube today practically reached high-water mark, has flooded a good many houses, and is causing some damage. It is understood, however, that from now on it will begin to recede and that there is no serious danger.

January 20, 1920.

In the afternoon, by appointment, I called upon Admiral Horthy, told him that I wished to call his immediate attention to the case of the American citizen Black, who had received ill treatment at the hands of Hungarian officers on December 31; that I hoped that he would give this matter his immediate attention, as it would do a great deal to prejudice American feeling against Hungary should the incident be published. He promised that he would take it up immediately.

9 How differently international relations have developed. But it must be remembered that the relations between Roumania and Serbia were very strained on account of the situation in the Bánát.

I then told him that I was sure it would appeal to him as being advisable to be frank with me in regard to any Bolshevist uprising, or anything of the kind; that I had repeated and almost confirmed rumors of the killing of some Bolshevists at the Ganz-Danubius Works in Budapest, and of an incipient Bolshevist uprising at Szolnok. He appeared astonished at this information, and said positively that he had never heard anything of the kind; furthermore, that he had just come from Szolnok within the past twenty-four hours. He then called in his Chief of Staff, who substantiated everything that the Admiral had said.

The natural inference is that these persistent rumors of Bolshevist uprisings and killings in Hungary are due to unfriendly propaganda, but it is hard to tell just who starts it.

January 21, 1920.

As the days roll by and the end of our stay approaches, the monotony becomes more deadly and the work more uninteresting, and we are all anxious to get away.

Most of the day was spent in routine work, but I had a short talk with General Gorton, during which he told me that the worm, in the shape of the Inter-Allied Military Mission, had finally turned. They had decided to send a telegram to the Supreme Council informing that honorable body that it was the opinion of the members of the Inter-Allied Military Mission that the Mission had been treated with superciliousness and contempt almost from the beginning, and then to give the concrete cases of telegram after telegram containing inquiries, requests for decisions, etc., which had been addressed to the Council and which never had even been acknowledged. I told General Gorton I was glad to see that they were finally getting a little ginger, but it had taken them about six weeks after I left the Mission, practically for that same reason, for them to show any pep.

Hardly a day passes now but that I receive several letters offering me valuable collections of carved ivory, Gobelin tapestries, rare old paintings, antiquities, etc. The prices for the collections range all the way from five thousand dollars up. The ivory, I remember, could be purchased for the mere pittance of fifty thousand dollars, and they are sure to mention dollars, because at this writing it takes two hundred Hungarian crowns to equal one dollar, whereas before the War two hundred crowns equaled forty-three dollars.

I received a telegram this date from Mr. Halstead, stating that Mr. Grant-Smith had arrived there and would remain probably a few days.

Owing to the difficulties of railroad transportation present on account of the coal shortage, I had originally planned to secure a special car, have it run over Szeged and attached to the Simplon Express, and go rough that way. However, in view of the fact that the Hungarian Peace Delegation is to leave here about February 7 by special train directly to Paris, and because they have expressed not only a willingness but a sire to take my entire party on that train, we shall probably go that way and reach Paris earlier than we would the other way by starting on the fourth.

These poor simps, instead of tightening up their belts, gritting their teeth and bucking into things, spent tree days in idiotic mourning when they heard the Peace terms announced, having known for the past six or eight months just what these peace terms would be. No dancing, operas, or anything of the kind is permitted, and now that Count Apponyi has returned with e peace treaty to discuss the terms, they have decided have another day of useless mourning tomorrow, then all stores will be closed and all business suspended. This eternal crying over spilt milk does not appeal to an American. I guess, however, with the type of peasant they have in the country and the lower classes in the city, it is necessary to pull off these stunts, the same as was in the Philippines.

This afternoon Count Apponyi called upon me and spent about an hour in describing his experiences in Paris[10]. He seemed very much encouraged over the fact that he had actually been given a hearing and felt that to a certain extent he had impressed his listeners.

He said when they first arrived in Paris he was subjected to considerable rudeness from M. Clemenceau who, however, later on appeared to be very much mollified.

After having been at the Chateau de Madrid some days, the Count says that they had their own credentials returned to them as being satisfactory. They then received the credentials of the representatives of the other powers, among which, however, the credentials of the American representative were missing. The messenger informed them that they were to be ready to accept the peace terms on the following day. The Count, thereupon, wrote to Clemenceau that it would be most difficult for them to go over the credentials of the Entente Powers and to be prepared in such a short time to receive the peace terms. He requested that there be a delay of at least one day, incidentally calling attention to the fact that the

10 See Apponyi's *Memoirs* in the Appendix.

credentials of the American representative were missing and requesting information as to the manner in which they were to negotiate with the United States.

M. Clemenceau replied promptly and brusquely to the effect that he was astonished that the Hungarian Delegation should resort to any such puerile excuse; that the peace terms would be ready to be delivered at the time prescribed and that if the Hungarian Delegation was not then ready, it would be construed as a refusal to receive the peace terms, in which case there would no longer be any reason for their remaining in Paris; that the fact that an American representative was not present at the conclusion of the terms with Germany, did not prevent the conclusion of the terms with Germany and did not prevent the conclusion of a treaty with that power. The Count called my attention to the fact that nothing had been said in his communication to M. Clemenceau as regards Germany.

To this communication, Count Apponyi replied, in effect, that the specific object of the journey of the Hungarian Peace Delegation to Paris had been to receive the peace terms and that, therefore, they would receive them, whenever given to them; that in the meantime he had received the credentials of the American Ambassador, which relieved the situation in that respect, and that he would be very glad indeed to do his utmost to facilitate matters.

He then wrote, through M. Clemenceau, to the representative of each power, stating that he felt, in justice to his country, he should request that he be allowed to present his case properly before the Supreme Council, but, should this not be possible, he would respectfully request each individual representative to give him a personal hearing. The Count thought that the result of this was the compromise granting him permission to address the Supreme Council, with the understanding that there would be no discussion. He said, however, that when he was through speaking, Mr. Lloyd George asked him for several additional explanations, which really amounted to a discussion, and that during these explanations he was able to present many things in a different light from that in which they had formerly appeared to the Supreme Council.

I asked what effect he thought the withdrawal of M. Clemenceau[11] would have upon the Hungarian case, and he said he was afraid that it might make matters worse; that Clemenceau, true to his name of "The Tiger," and being very much embittered, would probably do his utmost to even up scores; and that whoever succeeded him would be afraid of his attacks. I asked if on the other hand, in view of the fact that Clemenceau had been defeated, this did not show that his opponents were no longer afraid of him and that they would now show like independence of action toward the Supreme Council. He said that he had not thought of this point of view, but hoped that it was so, and that he felt sanguine of at least a modification in the severe terms to Hungary in case Mr. Lloyd George should become President of the Supreme Council and the sessions should be adjourned to London.

January 22, 1920.

This date I was in telephonic communication with Mr. Grant-Smith in Vienna. He expects to arrive in Budapest on the morning of January 27, awaiting his supplies here instead of in Vienna. As I had arranged to remain one or two weeks with Mr. Smith in order that he might absorb the situation instead of endeavoring to swallow it at a mouthful by one interview, and as the return of the Peace Delegates to Paris early in February will synchronize with my departure, Count Apponyi invited my party and myself to return on their train. There will also be a British representative and a French representative on the train, and, as it will assure our staying here a sufficient length of time to turn affairs over to Mr. Grant-Smith and to arrive in Paris without difficulty, I accepted the invitation with cordial thanks.

January 23, 1920.

Last night was the five-hundredth presentation of the popular Hungarian light opera, "János Vitéz," and about the four-hundredth appearance in it of their favorite actress, Fedák Sári. I received a complimentary box with an urgent invitation to attend, so I took the damned thing in.

January 24, 1920.

Yesterday all the stores were closed as threatened, and a general day of mourning was again observed.

In the forenoon General Soós, accompanied by Count Anton Apponyi, a nephew of the statesman, came to see me about arranging for the purchase by the

11 On January 17, Paul Deschanel had been elected President of France, defeating Clemenceau, who thereupon resigned with his Cabinet on the following day.

Hungarian government of a large quantity of supplies which had been sold by the United States to the Ukrainian government and which the latter, being practically already defunct, could not pay for. They brought in a telegram from a commercial representative of the United States Liquidation Commission, recommending that negotiations be entered into with Hungary for the purchase of the supplies which Ukrainia could not take. I sent the telegram and added likewise the information as to the quantities and where they were. It appears that there is enough hospital equipment for five large hospitals at Marseilles; that there is over five million dollars' worth of clothing and supplies at Bordeaux; and about two hundred and fifty thousand dollars' worth of automobiles and motorcycles at Langres.

As Count Apponyi has been in America and talks English fluently, I lit into him about the slowness of the Hungarian government in acting upon complaints of abuses of American citizens. He became very much interested, took down all the data and said he would personally push the matter through with both the Hungarian Commander in Chief and the Prime Minister.

Last evening I called on the Szirmays, but I sent Colonel Sheldon to the opera with them to see the "Troubadour," in the last act of which there is much crude and brutal slaughtering, to which, being a soldier, I am naturally opposed.

This morning I was called upon by a delegation of Slovaks, who protested earnestly against the treatment they have been receiving at the hands of the Czechs. They voiced an appeal from the various minorities in the countries now lost to Hungary, stating that they had been condemned unheard at Paris[12]; that they had been separated from a country to which they had been joined for a thousand years; that they had been annexed to nations of lower culture and despotic and violent characteristics; that they had been treated, not as human beings, but rather as chattels or currency, and had been given as such to the Roumanians, the Czechs, and the Serbs.

They implored the Supreme Council to give them a plebiscite, and gave warning that in case the present plans were carried out, the treaty of peace would not result in peace, but in war.

12 See related information from Stephen Bonsal: *Suitors and Suppliants, The Little Nations at Versailles* [Prentice Hall, 1946], included in the Appendix.

The gentlemen who called upon me were representatives of two thousand who met in Budapest, practically spontaneously, without any encouragement or assistance from the Hungarian government.

They also brought up the question of the separation in Czecho-Slovakia of the church from the Church of Rome[13], and wished to go to America so that the Czecho-Slovak government and people could not spread unfavorable propaganda among the Slovaks in the United States.

After these gentlemen departed, accompanied by Count Teleki, my aide, I visited first the Museum of Posts, Telegraphs, and Transportation, which is very interesting; and then the Agricultural Museum, which is one of the most celebrated of its kind in the world.

January 25, 1920.

Today is the election, which is going to last two days[14]. All women over twenty-four years of age are required to vote, under penalty of four thousand crowns' fine and imprisonment for three months and loss of franchise for the ensuing year. The weather today, as during the past three days, is beautiful, which would seem to indicate a Republican victory, although there are no such things in Hungary.

The river has gone down appreciably and all danger of a flood has been removed.

January 26, 1920.

This morning, accompanied by my aide, Count Teleki, I went down to the Parliament Building, where I was met by a guide and a governmental representative who took me all through the building. It is not quite as ornate as capitol buildings usually are, but it is most appropriate and is really a magnificent edifice. That these people can get excited is shown by the fact that they showed me the bullet holes in the Speaker's desk, where a member of the opposition, in

13 One of the chief causes of discontent on the part of the Slovaks is the fact that many Czechs are freethinkers and agnostics, and offend the devout Roman Catholic Slovaks by passing laws unfavorable to the free exercise of their religion.

1913, shot at Count Tisza who was then presiding. For the past year there has been no assembly, and the building has not been utilized for its ordinary purposes.

January 27, 1920.

Mr. U.S. Grant-Smith, Colonel C. B. Smith, Colonel Nutt, Lieutenant- Colonel Causey and Consul Hatheway, who accompanied Mr. Grant-Smith, all arrived in Budapest this morning and came up to the office about 11 o'clock. After a long talk, I took them to the house, where we had lunch. After lunch, they were shown over the Royal Palace and then scattered to keep various appointments.

This is the second day of the Hungarian election and everything is proceeding as quietly as could be expected. The Christian Nationalist party, of which Friedrich is the head, is apparently in the lead and will win a majority throughout the country without the necessity of fusion with the next stronger party, called the "Small Farmers."

14 As a result of these elections and by-elections of February so, the following parties were elected:

National Christian Union 68; Christian Socialists 5 ; Economic Christian Socialists 4; National Christian Party of Small Landowners 3; Christian Party of Small Landowners 4; National Party of Small Landowners 71 ; National Democratic Party 6 ; Non-Partisans 3; Total: 164. The Social Democrats refrained from voting. The Károlyists did not elect a single candidate. An interesting chart of the Hungarian parties may be found in Malbone W. Graham's *New Governments of Central Europe,* New York, 1924 (p. 242).

January 28, 1920.

Last night, as there was a first presentation of a short opera, I decided to attend, and it turned out to be a sort of a three-ring circus, starting in first with an opera called "The Last Dream," then a ballet, and then another opera, the translation of the title of which was "The Harlequin."

This morning Mr. Grant-Smith came over about ii o'clock, and at 1 1.15 we went to see the Prime Minister, Mr. Huszár, who started by giving me a hell of a big send-off, explaining what a debt of gratitude all Hungary owed me and a lot of similar rot. Mr. Grant-Smith, not to be outdone, said that this was realized by our State Department, who had looked upon my administration here with admiration and respect. The Prime Minister then started to ask a few favors and Mr. Grant-Smith immediately told him that any such things must be given to General Bandholtz, who would be absolutely in charge until his departure; that he, Mr. Grant-Smith, was here to learn the situation and absorb what he could in the interim between the present and my departure.

After quite a little session we departed, and Colonel Loree, Colonel Sheldon, Captain Gore, Colonel C. B. Smith, Colonel Nutt, Lieutenant-Colonel Causey and myself went down to the Hotel Pannonia, where we were the guests at lunch of the Burgermeister Bódy. It was really a very good lunch and very little talking. The Burgermeister toasted "His Excellency, General Bandholtz, and the other Americans," to which I responded with a toast to "The future of Hungary, and may it be prosperous, successful and tranquil."

I arrived back at the office at three-thirty and was called upon by a staff officer from the War Ministry to ascertain whether or not there had been any reply received from the telegram sent in regard to purchase by the Hungarian government of supplies that the Ukrainians had not been able to pay for.

January 29, 1920.

Last night Colonel Sheldon, Colonel Loree, Captain Gore and myself took dinner with Count and Countess Szirmay and my adopted family. Three or four young Hungarian counts, who are scratching their wings at the girls, were also there as guests.

In the afternoon Mr. Grant-Smith was in the office for some time, going over my memoranda and getting posted on the situation. He asked me if I knew that, since early in December, instead of being just the American Military Representative in

Hungary, I was the United States Commissioner in Hungary. I told him I did not, that they had never told me what the devil I was. So I had simply wired that, if no objections were offered, I would designate myself as American Military Representative in Hungary; that no objections had been received, and, therefore, I had so designated myself

I received a cablegram from Washington, stating that through some clerical error my recommendation for Distinguished Service Medals for Generals Graziani, Mombelli and Gorton had not been immediately forwarded, but was coming now and they trusted that action would be taken on the same in the very near future.

I also received a telegram from Colonel Harry Howland in Paris, stating that the sailing date of the "Adriatic" had been postponed from February 25 until March 3; that he had reserved a suite of two rooms for four passengers, at a total cost of three hundred thirty-eight pounds, eight shillings; that no first class single rooms were available; and that he desired confirmation of the reservation at once. We decided to make the reservations on the "Adriatic," so at this writing we should sail from France March 3, which, I suppose, will land us in New York somewhere around the tenth. It would probably be much cheaper to remain here in Budapest for some weeks, but on the other hand there is no telling what railroad difficulties we may be up against. Therefore we decided to go to Paris, get our stuff together, and be robbed by the French once more.

If there is time, and the expense involved is not too great, I may take a trip to Spain, as I have never yet been there and am anxious to see the Spaniard at home, having known him so well in other countries.

January 30, 1920.

Last night I went to see the opera "Aïda," but it was another of those endurance tests, and I left after staying three hours. The stage effects were magnificent and the little cockeyed gazelle who took the part of Aida, in a red chemise, had a beautiful voice. As I understand the last act is devoted to a suffocation scene, in which they keep on howling even after they should have been properly gassed, it was probably just as well that I missed it.

This noon I gave a luncheon to Mr. Grant-Smith, having as other guests General Gorton and Major Foster, of the British Service, Mr. Hohler, Count Széchényi, and Consul Hatheway.

Our last few days here are practically a struggle for existence in the way of getting gasoline. It is now costing us only a small matter of $1.50 per gallon. As a result, practically everybody is walking.

January 31, 1920.

Count Somssich called upon me this morning to discuss the situation. He said that a clash is imminent between Friedrich and Huszár, owing the fact that the former maintained that when he quit the Premiership at the request of Sir George Clerk, was understood that he would return to office after the elections. The elections now being through, he maintains that he should again be the head of the state. Huszár is determined to combat this, and it is believed at Admiral Horthy will support Huszár.

I pointed out to Count Somssich, as I did to Huszár the other day, that Friedrich's political utterances during his political campaign had done the country incalculable harm. He had given his constituents what he ought would please them, rather than what they ought to have. He invariably referred to the Hungarian Army as being the best army at present in Europe, well disciplined, well trained, well armed and well equipped, capable of expelling the Roumanians and thrashing the Czechs and Serbs combined; whereas we all know that, in its present condition, the Hungarian National Army could not lick a chicken with the pips. These speeches, however, were practically the only ones that were repeated in the French and other foreign papers and naturally interested foreigners accepted the utterances of a former Prime Minister as being authentic, which gave them the feeling that there was no necessity for doing anything for Hungary except to crush her still more.

I had Mr. Grant-Smith come in and meet Count Somssich, who shortly afterwards departed.

This noon Colonel Loree, Colonel Sheldon, Captain Gore, and myself were entertained at luncheon at the Ritz Hotel by Mr. Grant-Smith, after which we returned to the Palace.

Yesterday there were being distributed handbills, of which the following is a translation:

Hungarian Brother!

Join our party, because our country will be strong only if we have a National King.

There is only one royalist party, which wants a National Kingdom, vidz.:

The Hungarian National Royalist Party.

Every real Hungarian who is not ashamed to be Hungarian, should join us. If you do not want to fall into darkness, join our party, which fights for the one ideal.

Long live the candidate of the Hungarian National Royalist Party:

His Royal Highness Archduke Joseph,

the future King of Hungary!

Hurry into our camp, because the time to act has arrived.

The Hungarian National Royalist Party.

February, 1920

February 1, 1920.

This being Sunday, it afforded us an opportunity to go over to the office and clear up on back work.

February 2, 1920.

Last night I went to the Royal Opera House to see a light opera, called "The Bat."[1] It was supposed to have received its title from a gentleman in masquerade costume, dressed up to represent a bat. He had to spend all night outdoors, returning in broad daylight in his costume. As a matter of fact, it deserved the title, because every actor and actress was certainly on one Hell of a bat. Such a mélange of intoxication would be difficult to beat. Ladies and gentlemen were indiscriminately soused, which, however, did not interfere with their lung power. There is this much to be said for it, there is no stabbing or kicking the bucket as is usual at the Grand Opera House.

This morning Count Albert Apponyi called upon me, and we spent about an hour talking over the situation and what the Hungarian Peace Delegation proposed to do. The Count said that there were four distinct points which they wished to insist upon:

(1) That no territory be separated from old Hungary until after a plebiscite; that this plebiscite should be held only three months after the present Roumanian, Serb and Czech troops of occupation had withdrawn from the occupied territory and after this territory had been occupied by neutral troops. In this connection, he stated that he had no objection to American or British troops occupying territory supposed to be given to the Czechs, but that he did not want them [the Czechs] in territory, on account of Latin brotherhood. As to the French, he did not want them in any territory[2]. He stated that only by such procedure would a plebiscite express the free will of the people, and that, with such a plebiscite, the Hungarians would pledge themselves to abide by its decision, whether favorable or unfavorable.

---

1 "Die Fledermaus," by Joseph Strauss.

(2) That there be geographical continuity of new Hungary to include the two million Magyars who had been torn from Hungary and thrust under other domination, although the country they inhabited was contiguous to and continuous with Hungary.

(3) That whenever any territory was annexed to the other small nations created by the Peace Conference, there be absolute minority protection, because he well knew that neither the Roumanians, the Serbs, nor the Czechs were paying the slightest attention to the minority clauses in the present treaties of peace.

(4) That in order to insure a gradual adjustment of conditions, there be economic unity for two years of the various sections, affected by the Peace Treaty, which had formerly been under one government. He explained that the sudden rupture of all economic and other relations could not result otherwise than in confusion.

The Count then repeated his invitation for us to accompany him on his train and stated that the train would leave Budapest at 8.40 on Monday morning February 9, arriving in Paris at the same hour on February 11, exactly six months to a day from the time of our arrival in Budapest.

2   It was, of course, well known to the Hungarians that the French were extremely sympathetic to all the enemies of Hungary and that no fairness could be expected from them. The attempt of the French brothers Tharaud to whitewash their government in its actions against the Hungarians is futile and will not deceive anyone familiar with the facts, no matter how cleverly and how charmingly the book is written. (Jerome and Jean Tharaud, *When Israel is King*. English translation, New York, 1924.)

Compare the reference in Ray Stannard Baker's book. Baker shows that the affairs of Eastern Europe were in the hands of the French militarists and that they should he mainly held responsible for conditions in Hungary. He says that "every evidence in these secret documents [i.e., contained in his book] goes to prove clearly that the French military and diplomatic authorities not only welcomed but stimulated this outcome with the idea of forcing military action and military settlements" (Vol. II, p.30). General Bliss recommended that it should he made clear to the French that the United States did not approve of it (Vol. III, p.244). Herbert Hoover was in favor of establishing the hunger blockade, for the

Owing to our departure, we have all our dates filled from now until next Saturday, the seventh. Tomorrow I shall give a luncheon to all of my former colleagues of the Inter-Allied Military Mission. On the fourth we shall be the guests at luncheon of General Graziani of the French Mission. On the fifth we shall be guests at luncheon of General Mombelli, on the sixth we shall lunch with Mr. Hohler and on the seventh with General Gorton.

February 3, 1920.

This morning I spent until 10 o'clock at ordinary office work and then, accompanied by Mr. Grant-Smith, I called upon Admiral Horthy at his Headquarters at the Hotel Gellért. Admiral Horthy in his talk practically covered the same points that he had covered with me on my last interview with him, calling particular attention to the inadvisability of allowing the Hapsburgs back on the throne of Hungary[3] and to the charlatan methods of Friedrich.

Before leaving, I told him that I wanted a report of the investigation of the alleged mistreatment of the American citizen, Mr. George G. Black, on a steamer in Budapest, December 31. I called particular attention to the fact that if something were not done about this promptly there would undoubtedly be distorted versions of it in the papers of the United States, and that serious harm would be done the Hungarian cause.

purpose of overthrowing Bolshevism in Hungary and encouraging a counterrevolution (Vol. II, pp.351, 352).

When the brothers Tharaud write that "it was to be foreseen that the Roumanians would not comport themselves with the forebearance of the soldiers from Touraine or Burgundy" (p.217), it sounds like a bitter joke to the people who had to suffer from the French troops of occupation.

Count Apponyi knew very well why he did not want the French in any Hungarian territory.

3 On February 2 the Allies had issued a formal declaration against the return of the Hapsburgs. Huszár had openly declared for a restoration of the monarchy on January 29, the Archduke on January 30.

February 4, 1920.

This morning, accompanied by Mr. Grant-Smith, I returned Count Apponyi's call. As the papers had contained the statement that the Archduke Joseph had renounced his candidacy to the Hungarian throne and that Admiral Horthy would become the head of the state[4], this question was naturally brought up and was confirmed by the Count. He said that the result would be an indefinite continuation of the *status quo*[5], that very few people understood the Hungarian mentality, and that it would be impossible for them to have any king in Hungary as long as Karl was alive, owing to the fact that he had been crowned. The Hungarians, he said, held in reverence and placed a halo about the head of any anointed king, and that, whether Karl reigned or not, he would always be considered by hem as their king[6].

He explained that although there were many reasons why it would have been advantageous for him to have remained in Budapest and presided at the first session of the National Assembly, nevertheless he felt it to be his duty as head of the Peace Commission to be present in Paris and conclude the labors of that body. The Count in his previous conference with me had stated hat he was afraid that Mr. Grant-Smith was anti-Hungarian and I had assured him at that time that I was sure he was mistaken.

Colonel Sheldon, Mr. Grant-Smith and myself had Lunch this noon with General Graziani at the Széchényi Palace.

The afternoon was spent at the office winding up my affairs, including the drafting of letters to the Prime Minister and Admiral Horthy, announcing that the American Military Mission as such would terminate its labors and leave Budapest on February 9, giving up my offices in the Royal Palace, and the Royal Box at the Opera House.

4 Admiral Horthy was elected Regent on March 1, 1920, with 131 out of 138 votes cast. Huszár resigned as Prime Minister.

5 Marginal comment by General Bandholtz: "And there has been!"

6 Count Apponyi has been and is today [1932] the leader of the Legitimist Royalists who desire to see the old line of Hapsburgs on the Hungarian throne F-K K.).

February 5, 1920.

Our departure is scheduled to take place at 8.40 A.M. on the ninth. We shall be about three hours in Vienna that evening and should arrive in Paris about 8.30 on the morning of the eleventh. A suite has already been engaged for me on the SS. "Adriatic," which is to sail from Cherbourg on March 3. What we shall do in Paris for three weeks is a question which is mainly a financial one. It will probably cost me less to take a trip to Spain and return than to pay Paris hotel bills. I might also take a run back to Coblenz and stay a few days with my old friend, General Allen, who was my predecessor as Chief of the Philippine Constabulary and who now commands the American Forces in Germany.

While we shall all be glad to be homeward bound, yet we cannot but feel some regrets at leaving Hungary. Personally I came here rather inclined to condone or extenuate much of the Roumanian procedure, but their outrageous conduct in violation of all international law, decency, and humane considerations, has made me become an advocate of the Hungarian cause. Turning over portions of Hungary with its civilized and refined population will be like turning over Texas and California to the Mexicans. The great Powers of the Allies should hang their heads in shame for what they allowed to take place in this country after an armistice. It would be just as sensible to insist also that Switzerland, on account of her mixed French, German, and Italian population, be subdivided into three states, as to insist upon the illogical ethnographic subdivision and distribution of the territory and people of old Hungary. It is simply another case of the application of long-range theory as against actual conditions.

The Hungarians certainly have many defects, at least from an American point of view, but they are so far superior to any of their neighbors that it is a crime against civilization to continue with the proposed dismemberment of this country.

February 6, 1920.

Yesterday afternoon I was urgently requested to come some evening to the Otthon Club, which is the gathering place of all the Budapest journalists, and corresponds here to the Lamb's Club in New York City. I told them that the only evening I could show up would be tonight, and I agreed to go between 10 o'clock and midnight. Early in the evening Colonel Sheldon and myself, with a party, saw "Madame Butterfly" at the Opera House. Then we went home for dinner and afterwards to the Clubhouse, where we found a big gathering. They were most vociferous in their applause and planted us immediately at large banquet table despite the fact that we had just risen from our own dinner. During the afternoon, hey had telephoned around to the best-known actors and actresses and musicians in town and the whole bunch was there. It was one A.M. before we could get way. We had all sorts of dances, songs, vaudeville performances, speeches, etc. I was obliged to respond, with Mr. Zerkowitz as interpreter, but warned them that nothing that was said could be allowed to be published.

February 7, 1920.

All my officers and myself were entertained at dinner by Prime Minister Huszár. All of the prominent Cabinet Ministers and many of their wives were present, as were also Count and Countess Apponyi, and Admiral and Madame Horthy. During the dinner, Count Apponyi made a most eloquent address in beautiful English. The main point was thanking me for what I had done for Hungary and requesting my continued assistance. I was obliged to respond in like strain, concluding with the hope that I might sometime return to Hungary under such conditions that I could say all that I felt. The Count prefaced his remarks by referring to the fact that I was among technical enemies, but that that made no difference. To this I responded that the Bible had instructed us to love our enemies, and that I was endeavoring to carry out the Biblical injunction.

Today will be spent in closing and vacating our offices at the Royal Palace, tomorrow we shall close up and vacate the house, and at 8.40 o'clock Monday morning we are due to leave on the train of the Hungarian Peace Delegation.

....

The Rattigan Correspondence

Confidential Memorandum from Mr. Rattigan British Charge d'Affaires in Roumania to British Foreign Minister Earl Curzon, Followed by a Critique on the Same by General Bandholtz

South-Eastern Europe.

Confidential

Mr. Rattigan to Earl Curzon - [Received October 15.]

Bucharest, October 8, 1919.

My Lord,

The relations between this country and the Allies appear to me to be reaching so serious a stage that I venture to draw the attention of your Lordship to certain aspects of the situation which are perhaps easier to comprehend here than abroad.

I cannot help thinking that an atmosphere has been created by a chain of extraneous circumstances which is obscuring the main issue. It would seem that the first question we should ask ourselves in deciding upon our policy in the Near East is "What are the chief elements of order upon which we can rely to carry out that policy?" Roumania is, in my opinion, the first of such elements, if not the only real one. The fact that the country has for some time past been exploited by a gang of unscrupulous politicians is apt to blind the eyes of the average foreign observer to the real qualities of this people. The mass of the population, and especially the peasant classes, are simple primitive people, with many of the virtues one would expect to find in such conditions as exist here. They are, for example, sober, hard-working, easily contented, fairly honest, and above all orderly. These characteristics make Roumania very unfruitful soil for the propagation of the new communo-socialism. In fact, the peasants are fiercely hostile to the idea of communism. They are, on the whole, contented with what they have got, but are determined to retain it, and will oppose with all their any attempt to pool their small properties. In these circumstances there is little doubt that Roumania may be relied on to resist any Bolshevist wave which may advance

263

either from the east or west. A glance at the map will show that she stands a rock in a sea of actual or potential Bolshevism.

If; therefore, it is once admitted that Roumania may be regarded as the most reliable weapon to our hand for the carrying out of the policy of law and order, based on such ideas as the League of Nations, as opposed to the Bolshevist tendencies the surrounding Slav, and possibly Magyar races, then it seems to me that we should attempt to do all in our power to conciliate her and bring her back into the fold from which she in danger of being severed. She will then inevitably develop to the outpost of Western civilization against the disruptive tendencies of Bolshevism.

I do not for a moment suggest that Roumania has not brought on herself much of the treatment with which she has met. Her choice of representatives at the Paris Conference was undoubtedly unfortunate. M. Bratiano is certainly a patriot, but his character lacks the pliancy necessary for such work, and he apparently succeeded in exasperating all those with whom he came in contact by the excessive nature of his claims and the somewhat arrogant and unbending manner in which they were presented. Naturally this state of things reacted very unfavorably upon the Roumanian case. Moreover, it created an atmosphere of suspicion, in the light of which the actions Roumania, even when possibly of an innocent character, were looked upon, not unnaturally, with a grave mistrust.

To take a case in point, presumably no reasonable man would now maintain that her action in resisting the Hungarian Bolshevists' wanton attack upon her, defeating it, and pursuing the remnants of the beaten enemy to Budapest, was anything but justifiable. Yet it must be admitted that at first, at any rate, Conference was inclined to take the view that she was entirely at fault, and that she was openly flaunting the Allies. Surely nothing could have been further from the truth. She was in fact accused of disregarding an armistice in which she had taken no part, which had not protected her from attack, and which the Allies themselves could not have regarded as still in existence by the fact that they had asked for Roumanian co-operation in the event of an Allied advance on Budapest. This is, of course, past history, and I only venture to bring it before your Lordship in illustration of the atmosphere of suspicion to which I have referred above.

From the moment of the Roumanian entry into Hungary proper the question entered on a new phase. Anyone with a knowledge of the Roumanian character could not but be aware of the fact that there would be abuses. As I had the honour to report to your Lordship, I lost no time in endeavouring to impress both on M. Bratiano and the King the vital importance of doing nothing further to shake the confidence of the Allies. I implored them to show all possible moderation in the way of requisitions, &c. I strongly advised M. Bratiano to tell the Conference frankly that, though he accepted the principle of the common property of the Allies in respect to goods taken from the enemy, yet that the critical situation of Roumania obliged him to remove certain quantities of railway material, &c., without waiting for its eventual distribution amongst the Allies. He should at the same time make a full return of all that he had been obliged to take, and ask that it should be set off against the share to be apportioned eventually to Roumania. This M. Bratiano would not agree to do. The real reason for his refusal was that he was well aware of the disfavour with which Roumania was regarded at Paris, and was consequently afraid that any such proposal would be rejected.

Thus the elements of discord and suspicion were sown at the very outset. It must be remembered that there is much of the naughty child in the Roumanian character. Conscious that he is doing wrong, and frightened at the impending punishment, he becomes almost impossible to deal with. In such conditions there is need of the greatest tact to prevent the situation developing along fatal lines. Unfortunately this tact has been throughout conspicuous by its absence. The Allied generals, with all their many qualities, are necessarily inexperienced in diplomacy or statecraft. I venture to state, upon the fullest reaction, that they entered upon their duties in a wrong atmosphere, and that their focus became more and more distorted through the progress of events. They are necessarily dependent to a very large extent for their views on elements frankly inimical the Roumanians. Most of their agents are of course Hungarians. The more the latter perceived that reports hostile to Roumanians were acceptable, the more violent were the reports they made. There was of course sufficient material of a true nature to serve as a basis for these stories. Large numbers the governing classes of Roumania are corrupt, and it was not to be expected that there would not be many abuses. But I cannot help thinking that more could have been done to combat these abuses by a spirit of friendly advice and co-operation than by the methods employed.

I had the honour to recommend in my dispatch No. 168, that, in view of the above circumstances, it might be advisable replace the four Allied Generals by one high civil functionary representing the Conference. This would have the advantage of making the Roumanians understand that the Allies have one single policy. At present it cannot be said that the Allied Generals are entirely "solidaires," and the Roumanians are consequently inclined to try to play off one group against the other. As your Lordship is aware, the French by their attitude here give the Roumanians the impression that are really on their side, but are obliged to yield to Anglo-American pressure. Presumably the same impression is given at Budapest. If one civil representative of the Conference were appointed, and he combined the requisite qualities of tact and firmness, there would be every hope of a speedy and satisfactory solution of the present difficulties. Possibly it might be advisable to appoint a mixed commission, under the presidency of the representative of the Conference, to enquire into the whole question of requisitions. The Roumanian authorities profess themselves ready to place at the disposal of an Allied delegate full information in regard to everything requisitioned or removed by them. They indignantly deny that they are responsible for the starvation of Budapest. On the contrary, in response to the representations made by me on receipt of your telegram No.410, they informed me that they had sent 3,000 wagon loads of cereals to Budapest and two trains of wood fuel to Kes Kemet[7]. The 3,000 wagon loads of cereals had been requisitioned from the district between the Theiss and the new Roumanian frontier —a district which, it is alleged, is overflowing with food— and had been promised to the Transylvanians and paid for by them. In spite of the protests of the latter, these cereals had been sent to Budapest. With regard to the wood they informed me with some truth that Bucharest itself is almost completely destitute of wood fuel, but that in spite of this they had handed over the two trainloads in question to the Hungarian authorities.

There appears to be almost a deadlock in regard to certain questions at Budapest. For example, the Roumanian Government claim that they have an absolute right to co-operation in the formation of a Hungarian Government in so far as to ensure that no Government hostile to themselves is installed. Again, with regard to the evacuation of Hungary by their forces, they maintain that what is asked of them is entirely unreasonable. They assert that they themselves are anxious to leave. The Friedrich Government has also expressed a wish for their withdrawal. The Allies, however, they allege, desire them to remain until a Government which is hostile to Roumania is firmly established in the saddle. They maintain that they are most anxious to co-operate loyally with the Allies in settling the Hungarian imbroglio, and that they are ready to extend their support to any Government chosen by the Hungarian people and acceptable to the Allies, provided this Government is calculated to restore order and is not imbued with hostile sentiments towards Roumania. But the Allies can, they say, hardly them to assist a Government which is openly hostile to themselves. With regard to the demand of the Allied Generals the handing over of 10,000 rifles for the use of the Hungarian police force, they say that they had a right to ascertain, before handing over these rifles, what were the numbers of the armed forces in Hungary over and above these 10,000 police

7   The proper spelling is Kecskemét.

troops. To meet the wishes of the Allies they have, however, now waived their objections and delivered the required quantity of rifles.

Whatever the real rights and wrongs of all these questions may be, they would appear capable of adjustment if handled with tact and goodwill on both sides. In Budapest, however, at present these qualities are, as I have said above, conspicuous by their absence. I do not suggest that firmness is not also needed in our relations with the Roumanians. On the contrary, I consider that in dealing with them it is essential to exercise great firmness so as to make them understand that no nonsense will be tolerated. But it should be possible to combine firmness with an attitude of friendliness and goodwill.

In view, therefore, of the considerations which I have ventured to emphasize, I would respectfully suggest that some such solution as that proposed above is necessary, and that the whole question of our policy towards Roumania may be examined from the standpoint of her importance to us as the representative of law and order in this part of the world.

I have, etc.,

F. Rattigan.

Critique by General Bandholtz on Mr. Rattigan's Letter

Confidential Memorandum to Earl Curzon

Budapest, Hungary

13th November 1919

There must be something besides mixed metaphor in the Roumanian "atmosphere created by a chain of extraneous circumstances" that obfuscates even strong mentalities. Mr. Rattigan is of the opinion that we should "do all in our power to conciliate" Roumania, but unfortunately he does not go into details as to what further conciliatory offerings should be made, in addition to the great gobs of soft-soap conciliation already thrown at our Ally, and which, to continue mixing metaphors, it has been almost impossible to deliver telegraphically.

Next he accuses M. Bratiano of being a patriot, one who truly loves and serves his fatherland. "Nuff sed." Then in Bratiano's own words, we have a sophistical explanation of the occupation of Budapest, followed by an ingenious defense of the principle of Roumanian seizures, and the condensation of the whole situation into the statement, "It must be remembered that there is much of the naughty child in the Roumanian character. Conscious that he is doing wrong and frightened at the impending punishment, he becomes impossible to deal with." Beautifully euphemistic but decidedly un-John Bull-like. What today would have been the situation in India, Egypt and South Africa if other naughty children had been coddled and cuddled as has been naughty little Roumania with her hands and clothes all daubed with grease from locomotives and machinery stolen from the assets of her Allies, her face smeared with loot jam and her belly distended from gorging on supplies that her Allies will have to replace? What she needed was to have the shingle of common sense vigorously applied to her.

"The Allied Generals, with all their many qualities [fortunately not enumerated and blushes thereby spared] are necessarily inexperienced in diplomacy or statecraft." To which charge, considering the international fame of their accuser, they must plead "guilty" and throw themselves on the mercy of the court. However, when Mr. Rattigan "upon the fullest reflection" locates the Generals' distorted "focus," makes definite statements as to their sources of information, and begins to think, all bets are off, he in effect confesses that he knows as much about the Budapest situation as does an Ygorrot dog-eater about manicuring.

"The Roumanian authorities profess themselves ready to place at the disposal of an Allied delegate full information in regard to everything requisitioned or removed by them. They indignantly deny that they are responsible for the starvation of Budapest. . . . The Allies, however, they allege, desire them to remain until a Government which is hostile to Roumania is firmly established in the saddle," etc., etc., "Can you beat it? 'Nem, nem sabat!'"[8] Verily a personification of Roumanian veracity would make Baron Münchhausen or St. Ananias look like a glorified George Washington.

"It cannot be said that the four Allied Generals are entirely 'solidaires.'" Nevertheless fifty per cent of them, "not mentioning names," have displayed a fine example of solid cohesion. "One high civil functionary," especially one experienced

---

8 Bandholtz attempts here the Hungarian "No, Not Allowed:" (nem, nemszabad". - ALS)

like Mr. Rattigan in diplomacy or statecraft, would have been the solution and he would have had a carnival of effervescence trying to precipitate in himself the closely allied interests of the Allies in the land of Hunyadi János.

Passing from the Rattigan solution, which should have been received with paeans of joy, and adopted with alacrity by a brain-fagged Supreme Council, we then come to a well-rounded and fitting climax: "Whatever the real rights and wrongs of all these questions may be, they would appear capable of adjustment if handled with tact and goodwill on both sides. In Budapest, however, at present these qualities are, as I have said above, conspicuous by their absence." The Gospel truth! Every effort humanly possible has been made by an Inter-Allied Military Mission, with the patience of a setting hen on a nest of china eggs, to coax Roumanian Headquarters into carrying out the expressed wishes of the Supreme Council or into keeping any of its solemn promises. The goodwill was one-sided with a vengeance.

Judging from the Roumanian occupation of Hungary, our little Latin Allies have the refined loot appetite of a Mississippi River catfish, the chivalrous instincts of a young cuckoo, and the same hankering for truth that a seasick passenger has for pork and beans.

Referring to the first sentence hereof it would seem that the writer of the original monograph on South-Eastern Europe had become a Rattigianu instead of remaining a British chargé d'affaires.

Chronology of Events

August 6, 1919 Julius Peidl government overthrown by a coup d'état. Archduke Joseph assumes power as Regent with Stephen Friedrich as Prime Minister.

August 7 King Ferdinand of Roumania arrives in Budapest. The Roumanians ignore the demands of the Inter-Allied Peace Council that they withdraw.

August 14 Mr. Lovászy forms a new cabinet in Hungary.

August 15 The Peace Conference informs the Roumanians that it, not the government of Roumania or its Army, will take care of the Hungarian readjustment.

August 22 The Supreme Council informs the Archduke Joseph that he must resign his position of leadership.

August 23 Archduke Joseph abdicates and Friedrich resigns.

August 27 Friedrich forms a new cabinet.

September 10 Peace Treaty of St. Germain with Austria signed. The Roumanian delegates refuse to accept the treaty.

September 13 The Roumanian Cabinet under Premier Bratiano resigns because of complications in foreign affairs.

September 13 Gabriele d'Annunzio assumes control of Fiume, in defiance of Allies.

October 11 Roumanian troops withdraw from territory west of the Danube.

October 25 Sir George Clerk arrives in Budapest as special delegate of the Supreme Council. He forms a new coalition government, which includes some Socialists.

November 4 D'Annunzio seizes Zara.

November 7   The Supreme Council demands for the fourth time the withdrawal of Roumanian troops from Hungary.

November 13   Roumanian troops evacuate Budapest. Admiral Horthy enters Budapest with Hungarian troops.

November 19   The Senate of the United States, after months of debate, rejects the Treaty of Versailles.

November 23   Karl Huszár becomes Minister President after Friedrich's resignation.

November 24   The Jugo-Slavs demand of the Supreme Council that it should take action against d'Annunzio.

November 27   Treaty of Neuilly with Bulgaria. Roumania and Jugo-Slavia are not permitted to sign until they have signed the treaty of St. Germain.

December 9   American delegates join in signing an agreement of the Allies with Roumania concerning the withdrawal of Roumanian troops from Hungary.

December 9   Members of the American Peace Delegation depart from Paris.

January 5, 1920   The Hungarian Peace Delegation leaves to receive the peace terms from the Allies.

January 15   Peace terms handed to the Hungarians.

January 17   Paul Deschanel elected President of France, defeating Clemenceau.

January 18   Clemenceau resigns with his cabinet.

January 25   Millerand forms new cabinet in France.

January 25   First elections for a National Assembly in Hungary.

January 27   Jugo-Slavia accepts the Allied Fiume settlement.

February 23 Hungary responds to treaty proposal; demands   plebiscites in territories to be ceded to Austria and Roumania; protests against economic terms.

February 28   Provisional Constitution accepted by National Assembly (convened February 16).

March 1 Horthy chosen Governor. Huszár resigns, and Alexander Simonyi-Semadam forms an Agrarian-Christian Nationalist cabinet, with Count Paul Teleki as Foreign Minister.

March 23 Horthy proclaims Hungary a kingdom and assumes the title of Administrator of the Realm, or Governor [kormányzó].

June 4   Treaty of Trianon signed.

November 13, 1920   Treaty of Trianon ratified by Hungary.

....

Newspaper Articles on Bandholtz

The following article appeared in the Pester Lloyd *of January 31, 1919, written by Emil Zerkowitz.*

Having fulfilled his Mission, Harry Hill Bandholtz, Brigadier General of the United States Army, the leader of the American Military Mission, will shortly leave Budapest and return to his country and to his home after an absence of nearly two years. The noble-minded and brave General leaves us after having done his work, and we must say that he could not have won a nobler, a more uplifting and happier victory than the one he achieved in Budapest. He conquered the hearts of millions, the love and gratitude and appreciation of the Hungarian nation accompany him on his journey, and we tie a wreath of victory for him out of the flowers of love.

When he arrived in our midst, in the dreary days of the month of August, the country had hardly had time to regain consciousness from a stupor caused by a period of terror when the darkness of renewed horrors covered our souls; the Hungarian capital, occupied by foreign troops, was turned into a death chamber. Armed guards were watching over the downtrodden and tortured national conscience, on the eve of a frightful ordeal. We could not raise cries loud enough, we could not speak openly, for even the winking of our eyes was regarded with suspicion. How could the wide world, the foreign nations and the few friends that we had left and who still retained some humane feeling after a war of five years, a chaotic compound made up from mutual hatred, get to know in what plight we were and what fate was in store for us?

But lo! the world was moved and with it the conscience of triumphant victors. The great powers of the Entente delegated mission of Generals to Budapest; American, British, Italian and French Military Missions with a general at the head of each of them, who met every day to discuss the position of the occupied country. This was an essentially military function, but it could not maintain its rigidly military character for long. In order to investigate into the damages caused by Roumanian occupation, a Claim Office was set up by the council of the four Generals and placed under the control of the American Mission. In such manner, the American Mission developed into a Mecca, as it were, of the suffering Hungarian pilgrims. It must be admitted that this was a practice that had been

275

adopted by the sufferers long before the Claim Office was brought into being. They hurried to the American Mission hoping for assistance.

Their hopes were not in vain. General Bandholtz, the hardy and brave soldier, was a warm-hearted guardian of the sufferers, the impartial and inexorable judge of injustice, whom nothing could keep from acting, if something was to be done in the interest of a just cause. He persecuted all excesses with unbounded energy and investigated all complaints with inexorable impartiality. He rigorously combated injustice and relieved all innocent sufferers with happy contentment.

He carried into practice all the principles of the much advertised modern diplomacy. He made no secret of what was in his mind, but openly stated his opinion. He was ever ready to discuss matters of importance, but, what is more, he acted. His door was open to all; he received everyone and heard all who wanted to speak to him. This is how he gained a deep insight into the Hungarian soul. He did not limit himself to the study of books or of historical documents, but he turned for information to the data supplied by real life. He made the acquaintance of Count Albert Apponyi, the greatest of our political leaders and often, after discussing with him for hours such questions as were most intimately connected with our very existence, he heard the complaints of some poor farmer, turned out of his property by the troops of occupation. Having been at work all day, he hurried on one occasion late at night to the National Museum to seal its doors with his own hands, thus saving the most valuable treasures of the nation, the precious memorials of its culture and civilization.

He knew us in our suffering and so became the true friend of our nation. It is not mere pity that made him our friend. He proved, by persevering at our side even in our direst catastrophe, a true friend who did not abandon us, but who exhorted our nation to work, our only salvation and the only means to forget. When doing so, he called to our memory our glorious past, and taught us that this nation could not fall a victim to destruction, filled as it is with a keen desire of life, this being the lesson taught by our national history of a thousand years. This is what he said to many of our statesmen and to many journalists who interviewed him, and whoever had an opportunity to get in touch with General Bandholtz could see that his words were prompted by sincere conviction. He will herald these ideas of his, even when he has left the Hungarian capital and when he returns to independent America, his country and the land of George Washington, its Father, of Abraham Lincoln, the liberator of the slaves, and of Thomas Jefferson, the advocate of true democracy. He returns to America, the country where Louis Kossuth, the greatest son of oppressed Hungary, was received in 1851 more warmly and more enthusiastically than any other foreign statesman before or since. America is he country where nearly two million fellow countrymen of ours have found work and a warm reception, the majority of whom have been granted citizens' rights, and where the Magyar is being appreciated, not only for his physical work, but also because of the true virtues of every Hungarian. In America, where there is such a fertile soil for the love of our country and for sympathy, General Bandholtz is sure to become an advocate of our true cause, of our desire to live, and of our faith in the future. His brave collaborators will assist him in his pioneer work. Colonel Loree, who is an incredibly hard worker, an indefatigable, excellent man, who was working for us day and night with love, willingness and self-denial, will be at their head, and so will Colonel Sheldon, this soldier inspired by truly humane ideals, the supporter of all needy people.

The Chief of the Military Mission surrenders his post to the Representative of the American Foreign Department, the Chief of the American Mission, who has just arrived, Mr. U. Grant-Smith. This excellent diplomatist, who worked at Vienna in the service of diplomacy for a number of years, knows our position thoroughly. While taking leave of General Bandholtz with feelings of appreciation and of respect, the public of the country warmly welcomes Mr. Grant- Smith, to whose future work the nation looks with fullest confidence.

And yet our hearts are pained in parting from the General. It is with painful feelings that we see him depart, him, the noble-hearted, excellent gentleman, who, although a soldier, was the first man to make us forget that nations faced each other with arms in hand, nations who used to be united by the traditional feelings of brotherly love, by a community of souls, and by the most glorious human ideals. We want to forget and we are going to forget. But we cannot possibly forget all that we owe to the glorious and noble work of General Bandholtz. On all his ways, our gratitude and undying love will accompany him.

....

The following is a translation of an article that appeared in the National Journal, *Budapest, January 28, 1920:*

"This forenoon the American High Commissioner, Mr. Grant-Smith, and General Bandholtz, called on Prime Minister Huszár, who described to them the political and economic situation of the country.

"At 1.30 o'clock General Bandholtz and his officers lunched at the Hotel Pannonia as the guests of the Mayor of the City, Mr. Bódy.

"General Bandholtz and the American Military Mission will leave Budapest at the will always gratefully remember General Bandholtz, because we have so much to thank him for. During the Roumanian occupation, he protected us against the Roumanians' injustice, nd it is mainly due to him that they evacuated the country between the Danube and Tisza and also that they did not rob our museums. The General himself sealed the National Museum and it was the American Mission that prevented the Roumanians from delivering the Bolshevists.

"It is General Bandholtz also who revived interest in charity work in Hungary."

....

The following is a translation of an article which appeared in the Hungarian newspaper Uj Nemzedék, *January 29, 1920.*

"The members of the American Military Mission and their chief, General Bandholtz, are soon leaving our capital, probably about the fifteenth of February. The affairs of the Mission

are now being handed over to the American High Commissioner. The Magyars will always remember General Bandholtz with the feelings of deepest gratitude, as there is such a lot we must be thankful for to him and to the Mission. In the days of our profound sorrow, during the occupation of our country by the Roumanians, it was he who stood up for our righteous cause, and we don't know of any instance when he did not defend us. General Bandholtz persuaded the Roumanians to evacuate Transdanubia and the territories between the Danube and the Tisza, and it is owing to him that the Roumanians did not pillage our museums. The General personally sealed the entrance of our National Museum. Also we owe it to the energetic intervention of the Mission, that the Roumanians' endless efforts to liberate arrested Communists were frustrated. was General Bandholtz who initiated the American actions of benevolence and hereby dried a sea of tears on the Hungarian faces."

Principal Persons Mentioned in the Diary

Americans:

Members of the American Military Mission in Hungary:

Gen. Harry Hill Bandholtz
Col. Halsey E. Yates, Chairman of the Commission on Police and Gendarmerie
Col. Raymond Sheldon
Col. James Taber Loree
Col. Nathan Horowitz
Lieut. Col. Charles Beatty Moore
Captain Edwin Bulkley Gore
Captain Will Shafroth
Captain Weiss
Lieutenant Laurens M. Hamilton

Other Americans:

Colonel Causey, Advisor to the Austrian Government
Major Moffat, Head of the American Red Cross in Hungary
Colonel Anderson, Head of the American Red Cross in the Balkans
Mr. Frank Lyon Polk, Assistant Secretary of State, with the American Peace Commission
Mr. U. Grant-Smith, American diplomatic representative to Hungary
Mr. Schoenfeld, American chargé d'affaires at Bucharest
Mr. Halstead, American Commissioner in Austria

English:

Gen. Reginald St. George Gorton, Head of the English Military Mission
Major Foster, Chief Assistant in the Military Mission
Admiral Sir Ernest T. Troubridge, Head of the Inter-Allied Control of the Danube Navigation
Lieut. Gen. Tom Molesworth Bridges, of the English Army
Sir George Russel Clerk, special representative of the Inter-Allied Peace Commission, charged with the investigation of the situation in Hungary
Mr. Th. B. Hohler, British High Commissioner to Hungary
Mr. W. F. A. Rattigan, British chargé d'affaires at Bucharest

French:

General G. Graziani, Head of the French Military Mission

General Franchet d'Espérey, Commander in Chief of the Inter-Allied Balkan Army during the World War

Gen. Max Weygand, Chief of the Staff of the French Army during the World War

Italians:

General Mombelli, Head of the Italian Military Mission

Colonel Romanelli, chief assistant to Mombelli

Jugo-Slavs:

Dr. Lazar Baitch, diplomatic representative in Hungary

Major Body, military representative in Hungary

Roumanians:

Ferdinand I, King of Roumania

Maria, Queen of Roumania

Carol, then Crown Prince of Roumania (later, in 1933] King Carol II)

General Mardarescu, Commander in Chief of the Roumanian Army in Hungary

General Holban, Commander of Budapest

General Mosoiu, succeeding General Holban as Commander of Budapest

General Serbescu, in charge of Roumanian requisitioning

General Rudeanu, liaison officer

Colonel Vasilescu, Roumanian Chief of Staff

General Panaitescu, Vasilescu's successor

Colonel Dimistrescu, Assistant Chief of Staff

Lionel I. C. Bratiano, Roumanian Prime Minister

Constantine Diamandi, chief diplomatic representative in Hungary

Ardeli, diplomatic agent in Hungary, Diamandi's go-between

Hungarians:

Archduke Joseph of Hapsburg

The Archduchess Augusta, his wife

Stephen Friedrich, leader of the Christian Socialists, Prime Minister

Heinrich, Minister of Commerce in the Friedrich government

Count Somssich, Minister of Foreign Affairs under Friedrich

Karl Huszár, Prime Minister succeeding Friedrich

Count Albert Apponyi, Head of the Peace Delegation

Michael Károlyi, leader of the Democratic-Socialist revolution; President of the Hungarian Republic

Admiral Nicholas Horthy, Commander in Chief of the Hungarian Army; later Regent of Hungary

General Soós, Chief of Staff

Lieutenant Count [Paul] Teleki, liaison officer, attached to the American Mission [as Minister President of Hungary, he committed suicide on the eve of the German attack against Yugoslavia in 1941.]

M. Emil Zerkowitz, civilian liaison official

M. de Pekár, civilian liaison official, preceding Mr. Zerkowitz

Dr. Bódy, Mayor of Budapest

Count Edelsheim, host of General Bandholtz in Budapest.

Appendices

CZECHS, SLOVAKS, AND FATHER HLINKA

by Stephen Bonsal[1]

Excerpted from *SUITORS AND SUPPLIANTS - The Little Nations at Versailles*, Englewood Cliffs, NJ: Prentice Hall, Inc.; 1946.

September 19, 1919

The day after our return to Paris from London and the Conference on mandates, Jean, the bright-eyed veteran who ran one of the elevators in the Crillon, famous for his nimble wooden leg and his breast covered with the decorations he had won in the gallant defense of Verdun told me that several Slovaks had arrived in Paris and were to see the Colonel. I advised him of the coming of this belated delegation, but House decided that at this late day he should not intervene in the matter.

"I will, however, ask Frank Polk, who now presides over the delegation, to see them. As you know, I have many misgivings as to the justice of the settlement that has been reached in this thorny Czechoslovak problem. However, there is comfort in the thought that at least we have, under the provisions of the Covenant, called into being international machinery which in the end should effect a just settlement. You can tell them if you see the Slovaks that this is my hope."

---

1 Stephen Bonsal was a celebrated foreign correspondent of New York papers. He served as Colonel House's assistant in the American Peace delegation in Paris at the end of W.W.I. In the early 20's he was persuaded by President Wilson to publish his Diary. Here we include Bonsal's experience with the clandestine Slovak delegation.

On time evening following their first call, Jean appeared at my room, acting in an unusually secretive manner.

"The Slovaks are here again," he whispered. "I have them on the back stairs. Shall I bring them up?"

"No, put them in touch with Mr. Polk's office."

"But they have a letter to you personally from General Stefanik[2]. I knew the General was your friend; otherwise I would not have admitted them."

This was indeed mystifying. I knew all the world knew that Stefanik had met with a tragic death on a flying field near Bratislava three months before. My curiosity was now fully aroused and I asked Jean to show them in. One was a Catholic priest evidently, although he had discarded his clerical garb. The other was a small farmer with a very engaging face. They produced the letter, I recognized that it was authentic and I saw that it had been written only a few days before the Slovak soldier-leader embarked on his last flight. It read:

"Do what you can for my friends. I hope to join them in Paris soon. If possible, secure for them a hearing by time President or by Colonel House. I can vouch for the absolute truth of the statements they are authorized to make."

Both of the Slovaks spoke a strange Magyar-German to which every now and then the priest would attach a Latin tag, but they made their purpose perfectly plain.

"Many obstacles have been placed in our way," they explained. All permits to travel were denied us. It has taken us three months to reach Paris with our protest, and as our presence here is illegal, we have taken refuge in a monastery where the good fathers do not have to make reports to the police or announce the arrival of guests. Our General has been foully dealt with [at the time I did not understand the full significance of these words] but with us we have brought our leader, Father Hlinka. He is ill, worn out by the hardships and the uncertainties of our clandestine journey, but he hopes you can come to him. He would like to explain the hopes and the fears of our people."

2   Milan Rastislav Stefanik (July 21,1880 - April 4, 1919) Slovak astrono-
    mer and general who, with Tomas Masaryk and Edward Benes, helped
    found the new nation of Czechoslovakia in 1918-19.

"Come at this hour tomorrow night," I replied, "and then I will go with you or tell you why I cannot do so."

In the morning I explained to the Colonel what had happened and he gave his permission for me to go. "If," he said, "you have no doubt about the Stefanik letter."

I had none and was eager for an adventure which smacked of E. Phillips Oppenheim. Late on the following evening we left the hotel by the baggage entrance, coming out on the rue Boissy d'Anglais. We walked along in the pelting rain for several minutes before my mysterious escort would allow me to hail a cab. Then, to my amazement, they said, "Drive to the Luxembourg." For a split second I hesitated, but after all the letter they had brought was authentic and I was clearly in the hands of Stefanik's friends. Once at the Gardens, which were closed for the night, they dismissed the cab and we wandered about for ten minutes or so in narrow, unfamiliar streets. Twice we turned sharply and reversed our course. Only when convinced that we were not being followed did my escort lead me into what seemed to be a blind alley at the end of which we came to a halt before an iron-bound gate which, after three carefully measured knocks, was opened to us. The guardian seemed to be a priest, but as he remained in the shadows, only throwing the feeble light of his flickering lamp upon us, I could not be certain. We went on now through a gloomy garden to another gate which was open and unguarded and along a narrow corridor for about twenty yards. At the end was an alcove cell, damp and dark, where by the light of a tallow dip I saw a man fully clothed lying on a narrow iron bed reading, in low tones, his breviary. The disguised priest, my escort, said:

"This is Father Hlinka, the leader of the Slovak Peasant Party," and with that he and his companions withdrew into the darkness of the corridor.

I assured Father Hlinka that I would listen to what he had to say and report it carefully to Colonel House; but, I said: "You have come late, and for the moment I fear nothing can be done. You see, on the tenth the Treaty of St. Germain was signed. There can be no further change in the structure of the Succession States of the former Austro-Hungarian Empire until the meeting of the Council of the League some months hence."

"I feared as much," said the Father, with a sigh. "And that accounts for the extraordinary steps which the Czechs have taken to delay our arrival here. Ten years ago Slovakia was but a two-days journey from Paris. Today in the New Europe, which the Czechs control, it has taken us three months to reach the City of Light, and only to find then that the light has been extinguished. I have come to protest against the falsehoods of Beneš and Kramar, and they have, not without reason, hampered me on my journey in every way. Even so, they would not have triumphed had they not silenced the voice of General Stefanik. To him, our great leader, all the assembled envoys would have listened because he worked not only for his own people, but for the Allies in the Siberian campaign and on the Italian front. Well, they silenced him in a most dastardly manner."

"What do you mean by this?" I inquired.

"You have been told - the whole world has been told - that General Stefanik came to his tragic end in an airplane accident. There is not a word of truth in that story. The plane that brought him from Italy made a successful landing, but as he stepped out he was shot down by Czech soldiers placed there for this diabolical purpose by Beneš . Many know the details of this crime and by whom it was plotted, but in the present state of affairs, what can they do? The truth is also known to the general's brother; but he is a prisoner in his village, and should he dare to say a word he would be brought before a firing squad."

[I did not believe this story at the time, or for that matter later, when several of Stefanik's adherents, having escaped over the mountains into Russia, told it to the world; but Hlinka believed it, as did many of his partisans, and it was this belief that made all the efforts toward a reconciliation with the Czechs hopeless.]

January, 1933.

I have recorded in my diary the terrible charge which Father Hlinka brought against Beneš as to the manner in which General Stefanik met his death. I had neither the opportunity nor the authority to investigate his indictment, but I would not feel justified in suppressing it. The fact that he believed in it explains much that followed. I greatly admired Beneš's behavior at the Conference, and it was certainly extremely fortunate for the Czech people to have such a resourceful leader.]

"One of the difficulties that will confront you when the time comes to reopen the question will be the documents you have filed with the Conference," I suggested as delicately as I could. "Voicing the wishes of your national committee, both you and Stefanik are on record as asking for union with Prague for many and cogent reasons—the ever-increasing disorders, the encroachments of the Bolsheviki. . ."

Poor Hlinka groaned. "I know, know. We did that very thing. May God forgive us. The Czechs spoke us fair. They said that in union there was strength, that many, very many Slovaks had fought with them on many fronts. We had been brothers in war, and now that peace was at hand, a troubled peace to be sure, why not stand together? 'It is only a temporary measure at best—or at worst—they explained. 'It should be regarded as a trial marriage, and then should the union prove irksome, we could each go our several ways without let or hindrance. But in three months, indeed, after only three weeks, the veil was lifted. In this short time we have suffered more from the high-handed Czechs than we did from the Magyars in a thousand years. Now we know *extra Hungariam non est vita* (outside of Hungary there is no life for us). Remember these words, time will prove their truth. Beneš is an ambitious knave. He even wants to absorb Polish Teschen." [And as a matter of fact, rightly or wrongly, he did.]

"But your union with the Magyars—that sins against the principle of ethnic solidarity which is in such high favor now," I suggested.

"I know, I know," interrupted Hlinka. "It runs counter to the popular current. We cannot mix with the Magyars and we do not want to, but economically, and above all religiously, we can get along with them better, much better, than we can with the irreligious free-thinking Czechs who, as we now know, have no respect for God or man. We have lived alongside the Magyars for a thousand years and the traditional tie is strengthened by the lay of our respective lands. All the Slovak rivers flow toward the Hungarian plain, and all our roads lead toward Budapest, their great city, while from Prague we are separated by the barrier of the Carpathians. But the physical obstacles are not as insurmountable as are the religious barriers, which shall, I trust, always keep us Catholics apart from those who were Hussites and now are infidels."

Although I tried to turn his thoughts away from the unfortunate move he and some of his adherents had made in the hour of victory, I was not successful, and he returned to it time and again.

"Yes, I did sign the declaration which went to the Powers a few days after the Armistice. I did say, may God and my unhappy people forgive me, that we Slovaks were a part of the Czechoslovak race and that we wished to live with them with equal rights in an independent state. Why did I do it? I cannot explain—not even to myself—but I will tell you some of the reasons that swayed me then unfortunately. In the Pittsburgh declaration of our independence which the American Slovaks sent on to us, I read that Masaryk had guaranteed the independence of Slovakia and had further agreed that we should be represented at the Peace Conference by our own delegation. Even then I had my doubts as to the wisdom of the step I was taking, but what else was I to do? When the people in

Prague saw that I was hesitating and the reason why, they reassured me by saying, 'This is merely an emergency move, and you can make it with mental reservations. When Europe settles down you can make your own final decision.

"And of course I saw the plight of Hungary. Having accepted the role of cat's-paw for the Germans, she was powerless, while the Czechs were in a strong position. Some said to me: 'We must spread our sails to the prevailing winds,' and I agreed. God has punished me, but I shall continue to plead before God and man for my people who are innocent and without stain. For long and fateful years we fought for our religion and our freedom shoulder to shoulder against the Magyars. Our relations with them were nor what they should have been, but during all those years we did not suffer one tenth of the wrongs that we have had to bear at the hands of the Czech soldiers and the Prague politicians in the last few months."

"The Czechs regard Slovakia as a colony, and they treat us as though we were African savages. Abroad they shout that we belong to the same race, and yet at every opportunity they treat us as helots. Within the borders of what they are pleased to call Czechoslovakia, they only treat us as hewers of wood and drawers of water for their High Mightiness of Prague."

(The fact that the people of Prague speak of the newborn state as *Czechoslovakia* and not as *Czecho-Slovakia*, is a grievance which also rankles.)

Three days later, still under escort, I was back at the mysterious monastery bringing to Father Hlinka a copy of the Covenant in Slovak, with the article indicated through which, upon the assembling of the League, he would be entitled to ask for a review of the decision and, indeed, of the treaty. The Father was now sitting up amid, to explain his physical condition and his delay in reaching Paris, he told me many details of the hardships he had experienced on his three-months journey. It was a checkered land-Odyssey, but unlike the second Korean Mission headed by my old friend of Seoul days, General Pak, which never got beyond Lake Baikal, the Slovaks, though battered, and limping, and above all, late, had now arrived.

"We had the best of reasons for knowing," explained the Father, "that the new people in Prague would not assist us with passports; in fact, we were confident they would throw every possible obstacle in our way; so we sneaked out of our villages by night, and wandering across country, often on foot, through Teschen, we came to Warsaw. Here we were well received by Marshal Pilsudski. He had many troubles of his own. His people were, as you know, in a desperate plight, and so he was only able to give us words of encouragement. Even the French traveling passports which he asked of the French Embassy were refused. His parting words, however, sustained us in many a trying hour of our journey. 'You are entitled to your independence as much as we are, he said. 'I shall instruct our delegation in Paris to assist you all they can.' "

"We also received kind words from another great man, Achille Ratti, the Papal Nuncio in Poland. He gave us his Apostolic blessing. He, too, deplored that Christendom had placed the devout Slovak congregations under the tyrannical rule of the enemies of the true Church. But he begged us to give up our journey, at least for the moment. He asserted that conditions were too unfavorable; that for the present they could nor be overcome. He urged us to stay with him, to watch and pray, to pray for the peace of Jerusalem. This we regarded as a counsel of despair, and so we pushed on, without credentials and with little or no money. Often our poverty-stricken countrymen, exiles in strange lands, saved us from starvation and by their contributions enabled us to travel many stages of the journey at least in fourth-class cars; but progress was slow and often, very often, we had to stop and retrace our steps because of the political conditions by which we were confronted. Germany we knew was unsettled. We were warned there was not one chance in a hundred of getting through there. The longest way around gave better promise, and so we wandered on through Yugoslavia to Italy and at last to Switzerland. Once there we did not have to sleep out under the stars or go supperless to bed, as had become our habit. A committee of good people from our unfortunate country took us in charge, arranged for our stay with our brothers in Christ, and brought us to Paris in that relative comfort - which we had not enjoyed for so long..."

Five days later I called again on Father Hlinka, for no reason in the world but that I wanted to have one more, and what I feared would be a last, look at what they would call in Maryland his "honest affidavit face." And now I needed no guide and could reach the monastery unescorted. It was the Paris home of the Pères du Saint-Esprit, with whom evidently the Catholic Slovaks had close affiliations. The gatekeeper wanted to send me away in short order. "The Slovaks are gone,"

Later Pope Pius XI. He gave us his he said. But I insisted on seeing the Abbot, and from him, between his lamentations and self-reproaches, I learned what had happened.

"A week after our dear brothers arrived," he explained, "we had to make room under our roof for those who came to take part in the annual assembly of our Order. We secured rooms for our Slovak visitors in a little hotel a few steps down the street. There we hoped they would remain as our valued guests until once again there would be available space for them under our roof. They were loath to leave, and now too late we recognize how right they were. Apparently their presence was immediately announced to the police by the keeper of the hotel and they were called upon to show their papers at the prefecture. These were not in order; in fact they had none, and so, twenty-four hours later, in spite of our protest, they were escorted to the station and placed on an eastbound train.

"It was a great triumph for Beneš and his infidels," lamented the Abbot, "and we shall never forgive ourselves for unwittingly assisting them. Father Hlinka was sure that Beneš brought about his expulsion and so am I. But how could a country, how could France, that at least until recently was the eldest daughter of the true Church, lend itself to such a dastardly act?"

I chose to think that neither the government, except in a perfunctory, routine way, or for that matter Beneš, had anything to do with the expulsion. Perhaps Hlinka and his friends were simply victims of the newspaper crusade against unregistered aliens and others that the Paris press had preached, with the warm approval of the delegates to the Peace Conference, as a result of the murderous attacks upon Clemenceau, Venizelos, and other delegates. Reproached for their criminal laxity, the police with many indiscriminate *rafles* now made a clean sweep of the lodging houses of Paris. I trust this is the explanation of the unhappy and most untimely expulsion of the Slovak Mission, but I must admit that the good Abbot would not accept it and as long as I stayed with him kept repeating, "Beneš and Tardieu, Tardieu and Beneš, they are the villains."

Tardieu, at least, I think was guiltless and had not the remotest idea that the Mission had been in Paris, for when some days later House broached the subject of their dissatisfaction with the St. Germain settlement, he thought it was based entirely on protests that had reached us from the American Slovaks, residents for the most part of western Pennsylvania.

Colonel House was impressed by Father Hlinka's story and deeply touched by some of the details of his hazardous and necessitous journey which I gave him. "I had thought," he said, "that all roads led to Paris and that the Conference was easy, perhaps too easy, of access - but at least in this instance I'm mistaken."

When the Colonel recovered his health, the Slovaks had been expelled, but he brought the memorandum which I drew up for them to the notice of our delegation and also called the matter to the attention of Tardieu when he came to the Crillon on one of his frequent calls. Tardieu admitted that he had heard of the schism between the Czechs and the Slovaks, which was increasingly apparent, but had consoled himself with the thought it was due merely to a misunderstanding which could and should be cleared up.

"At times," suggested the Colonel, "I fear you are not going about the foundation of a strong Czechoslovak state in the best way," and Tardieu promised to study the matter very carefully, indeed "prayerfully." he admitted that lie had been startled and impressed by the plea of the Slovaks.

"Of course we knew," he went on, "that a plebiscite would disclose a number of minorities inn the new state. There are the Germans and Hungarians, and those strange Carpatho-Russians, all very difficult to understand, much less to assimilate. But what could we do other than we have done? It would be absurd to turn this section of Europe into a hodge-podge of governments, a crazy quilt of little nations. On the other hand, the government in Prague is a liberal one. It was and is our staunch ally and we have every reason to believe that in an autocratic world it will prove a bulwark of democracy. It seems to me that we have the right, even the duty, to make that government as strong as we can."

....

[1938. On their arrival in Vienna, the expelled delegates separated, Hlinka going to his native village of Ruzomberek to work with his people, while one member of the delegation was sent to Budapest to keep in touch with the Magyars. Hlinka decided to enter parliament and there, in what he was told would be an open forum, fight for the liberties of his people. Some weeks before the election, however, Czech soldiers broke into his house at midnight and, before his adoring peasants had any idea of what was happening, carried him off to a distant prison. This high-handed act provoked an insurrection that was only suppressed after much bloodshed. Hlinka remained in prison for many months and was treated with such cruelty that he never recovered his health.

He fought on, however, and in 1938 came his hour of triumph. Some American Slovaks brought to Europe the long-concealed original draft of the Pittsburgh

Pact between the Slovaks and the Czechs, reached in 1918. It demonstrated the fact that, although he had taken some part in drawing it up, Masaryk was honestly mistaken as to its terms and that Hlinka was fully justified in maintaining that complete autonomy had been promised his people and further that they were assured that on a basis of equality they would sit with the Czechs at the Peace Conference. Andred Hlinka died a few days later. With his last words he again demanded the plebiscite too long denied. Even had it been granted it would now have proved too late. The discord between these two branches of the Western Slav family, which would have taken years of fair and friendly dealings to remove, made the conquest of their common country by the Germans in 1939 a matter of but a few days.

I retain pleasant memories of my intercourse with the Slovak priest. At times I think of him as the most sympathetic of the many agents of the scattered and disinherited ethnic fragments with whom I was brought in touch. He had dark luminous eyes of rare beauty; they were indeed the windows of a soul that was transparently sincere. His speech was straightforward and convincing, but here was the rub. It was not words alone that could set his people, free, and apparently his bitter memories made it impossible for him to listen to, much less accept, the compromises and the adjustments the situation demanded and which might have saved it to the ultimate advantage of all.

July, 1943. Thanks to the way in which Hlinka's teachings swayed them, although he, their apostle, was now dead, the Slovaks escaped the inhuman, barbarous treatment by which the Austrians, the Czechs, and, above all others, the unbending Poles, have been crucified. But they cannot be congratulated on their "escape." Some, blinded by their unbrotherly strife with Prague over Teschen, believed that Hitler would live up to his promises and that their dear country would be comfortable, well fed, and happy - even as a satellite state.

But today the Slovaks know the truth; even the puppet president, Tiso, admits that their situation is hopeless, that they have lost faith in themselves and their leaders. All their food and movable property have been looted, and those who survive are treated as serfs. The divisions they were forced to send to the Eastern Front have been annihilated except for a few fortunate units which, honoring their ancient Pan-Slavic creed, deserted to the Russians whenever the opportunity presented itself.

Today [1946] it can be said that 90 per cent of these unfortunate people are praying, and as far as it is in their power, are working, to reestablish their country as a free part of an independent Czechoslovak state. Poor Father Hlinka has really deserved a better fate than the crown of thorns that is his today. He and his teachings have helped destroy the people he loved so well and so tragically misled.]

....

In 1965 publisher Malcolm Forbes wrote: "What's became of a used-to-be country Called Czechoslovakia? I remember studying, reading and hearing some four decades ago so much about that relatively new nation. Its people were vibrant, vigorous, hard-working, and its Democracy was genuinely democratic. Industry flourished along with a healthy agriculture. Then came Munich and Chamberlain and the Sudetenland and betrayal. Now? Nothing. In most of the other lands behind the Iron Curtain, there have been rays of hope. But Czechoslovakia? Whatever has became of that beacon which shone so brightly between the two great wars?"

We all know now what happened. The Czech propaganda machine came to a halt. Then, three years later came the Prague Spring, lead by Alexander Dubcek a Slovak. The hope of Slovak nationalism was put out by the Soviets. But in 1989 Czechoslovakia's Velvet Revolution ended the communist rule. On January 1, 1993 Slovakia became a free nation.

Father Hlinka would be proud.

....

HOW PEACE WAS MADE AFTER THE GREAT WAR

by Count Albert Apponyi[4]:

Excerpted from *The Memoirs of Count Apponyi*, New York: Macmillan,

1935.

I do not intend to criticise the contents of the peace treaties, but to describe the events which took place when they were drawn up. In so far as the treaty with Hungary is concerned, I took a personal, though, of course, a passive, part in its making. All the same, I was present, and the experience remains a fragment of history. It should be of some value to describe this event from what I would call the anecdotal point of view.

---

4   Albert Apponyi (1846 - 1933) was a scion of one of the oldest aristocratic families of Hungary. He served sixty years as a member of Hungary's parliament. A friend of concert pianist Ferenc Liszt, Apponyi's maiden speech at Parliament initiated the establishment of the Budapest Conservatory of Music, alma mater of many great musicians known in America such as Bartók, Kodály, Dohnányi, Doráti, Szell, Solti and others. In 1888 he was a founding member of the Inter-Parliamentary Union, an organization of members of parliament of many countries devoted to world peace. He has known five American presidents and was a personal friend of Theodore Roosevelt. In 1913, he was the third foreigner invited to address the United States Congress, an honor granted only to Marquis de Lafayette and Hungary's Louis Kossuth before him. After World War I he was Hungary's representative in the League of Nations.

By the late autumn of 1919, after my country had overthrown Bolshevism and had been swamped by a Rumanian invasion, a government was set up whose authority was recognised throughout the country, though it lacked any legal basis, and with which the Allied Powers were prepared to negotiate officially for the signing of peace. This government consisted of representatives of all parties, under the leadership of Károly Huszár, who belonged to the Christian People's party. It had two principal objects, one of which was concerned with internal and the other with external affairs. The first was to summon, by means of a universal franchise, a national assembly to decide upon the internal management of the country, which was in a state of complete disorder. The other task was to send a peace delegation to Paris, whose duty there would be to receive the decisions of the victors, represented by the Supreme Allied Council, and to draw them up in treaty form. I was chosen to be the leader of this peace delegation, and, as public opinion in my country supported the choice made by the provisional government, I could not refuse this saddest of duties, though I had no illusions as to there being any possibility of my securing some mitigation of our lot. This fate had been realised already through the occupation by our ex-enemies of great areas of Hungarian soil. The spirit which I was up against declared itself at the first step I had to take on that thorny path.

I was then living with my family at our former estate of Eberhard, near Pozsony, which has been taken from me by the Treaty of Trianon. I had come to Budapest for a short time only, to assist in the negotiations which led to setting up the Huszár Cabinet. The part of Hungary in which my estate was situated had already been occupied by the Czechs, and was actually under Czech control. Through the local Czech authorities, I received in the middle of December an urgent request from the Hungarian government to come to Budapest. The Czech authorities had no objection to my travelling. In Budapest I learnt for the first time that it was suggested I should take over the mission to Paris. After I had accepted, some days were spent in negotiations concerning the personnel of the peace delegation, and in fixing the date of its departure. January jth, 1920, was selected, by arrangement with the delegates. When all this had been settled, I naturally wanted to return to Eberhard, and spend Christmas there with my family. To my great surprise, I met with an abrupt refusal from the Czech government, whose motive was expressed as follows in the original French: "Il est inadmissible qu'un personnage désigné pour soutenir les intérêts de la Hongrie contre ceux de l'Etat tchéchoslovaque puisse séjourner sur le territoire de ce dernier." In vain I appealed to the representatives of the Entente against this decree, which was absurd from the point of view of international law. They probably sympathised with me, but they did not help me. The decree stood, and I was not allowed to go home. As soon as this was decided, my family applied to the

Pozsony authorities for permission to spend Christmas with me in Budapest. This also was bluntly refused —as we were told, on direct instructions from Prague. I withhold comment. If anyone can find a satisfactory explanation for such wilful interference with family life during the favourite Christian festival, it is not for me to disabuse him; for my part I have found none. I had, therefore, to remain in Budapest, the only consolation for my loneliness being the presence of my son, who could not leave Budapest, because he was a liaison officer at the English Military Mission.

January 5th arrived. The Hungarian peace delegation was fairly numerous, for we foresaw that a written answer would have to be prepared to the so-called offer of peace, and this would require, in addition to the chief delegates, a number of experts and adequate technical advisers. Among the chief delegates, I will mention Sándor Popovic, afterwards President of the National Bank of Hungary, and formerly President of the Austro-Hungarian Bank, Count István Bethlen, Pál Teleki, Imre Csáky, Tibor Kállay and Lajos Walkó, who have all subsequently taken a leading part in Hungarian politics, but most of whom were already well-known politicians. Excellent legal and military help was allotted to us. Both the Hungarian government and I myself had been at the greatest pains to secure for us as representatives the best intellects in the country, with regard to political, financial, economic, legal and general technical matters. However slight was the prospect of successful negotiations, in fact of negotiations at all, the honour of the country had to be preserved under all circumstances. Our delegation travelled to Paris in a special train, whose formation was no small task for the plundered Hungarian railways, since the work of reconstruction had not even begun. They succeeded, however, and our train looked as if normal conditions had obtained. All the passengers were comfortably provided for, and they even found a Pullman car which served for discussions on the journey.

These discussions were interrupted at every large station along the Hungarian line in a way that was very touching, but at the same time, painful. Everywhere there were large or small deputations, and sometimes crowds of poor people, who filled the waiting rooms at the stations, and whose spokesmen wished us God-speed, declaring the confidence of the Hungarian people that we would undoubtedly succeed in winning acceptable terms of peace for our country. It cut us to the quick to see this trust and confidence, and to realise the enthusiasm with which their words were uttered. We knew only too well that there was not the slightest reason for such hopes, that we were faced already with an accomplished fact and that we went on our forlorn mission out of no more than a painful sense of duty. Occasionally, doubts assailed us as to whether it would be better, after all, to do as had been seriously suggested to me, namely, sign the conditions presented to us in

Paris without negotiating, and in this way make still more obvious the coercion that was being put upon us. After careful consideration, we decided that we would not follow this advice, because one can never be absolutely sure in such matters, and even a minute hope carried with it the duty at least of attempting to obtain something. What a painful contrast there was between our mood of hopeless duty and the enthusiastic confidence which cheered us on! In replying to the speeches addressed to me, I could only speak the truth, saying that I neither promised nor expected a success, and could do no more than give my assurance, once and for all, that the honour of our country would not suffer.

On the journey, we were accompanied by one or two officers of the English and Italian Military Mission in Budapest. We were on the friendliest terms with these officers, who had lived in Budapest for some time, as we were with all the members of the Military Mission, who had come to Budapest full of prejudices and antipathy, only to undergo a complete change of opinion after spending a little while in our country. This was especially so with the Italian General Graziani, who had assumed a very abrupt demeanor at the beginning of his official duties, but, after a few weeks of personal experience, formed such an attachment to our country that everyone was sorry to see him go when his mission was over. The etiquette observed by the French was very different from that of the military delegates of other countries. Their principle was that they would be dealing with an enemy until the peace treaty had been signed, and hence all friendliness beyond the demands of common courtesy was undesirable. No sooner had we reached Paris than we realised that this rule was to be maintained.

A French officer had been sent to meet us at the frontier, and from him we received the order —I forget in what form, but certainly as politely expressed as possible— that we could not yet shake hands, but must limit our greeting to the curt bow usual between utter strangers. And that was what actually happened. Our arrival in Paris took place after a railway journey of forty-eight hours, in the early morning of January 7, and was so arranged that our special train came into a deserted station. A small Military Commission —we called them our warders— was there to meet us, at whose head was Colonel Henry, who afterwards turned out to be a most kindly and benevolent man, though he received us as we got out of the carriage with merely ceremonial military salute, which we returned in a like manner. As the leader of the delegation, I entered an official car with him, and the officers were divided accordingly among the remaining members of the delegation. Quarters had been prepared for us at Neuilly, a suburb of Paris lying in the middle of the Bois de Boulogne, where we were to stay at the Hotel "Château de Madrid," which is accustomed in the summer-time to shelter much less serious guests. During the drive from the station, I told Colonel Henry, somewhat naïvely, that I would like to visit certain people in Paris who were old French friends of mine, and he answered that he regretted this would be impossible. We had, so he told me, complete freedom of movement in Neuilly and the Bois de Boulogne, but were asked never to visit Paris itself without informing him. If a member of the delegation expressed this wish he would see that a car was placed at our disposal, and that we were provided with an adequate escort, *"afin qu'on ne manque pas de respect!"* We would not be allowed to pay visits in Paris, or to meet anyone, without his authority. In other words, we were interned in Neuilly. We could only enter Paris under the eye of a detective and with special permission, and we were allowed no visitors. All this was strictly carried out, though with the maintenance of formal politeness. Once a young journalist who belonged to our delegation, trusting to his obscurity, attempted to travel unnoticed to Paris by tram; at the last stopping-place before the Barrière de l'Etoile, he was peremptorily ordered by an unknown man to leave the tramcar. This man announced himself as a police agent, and, without more ado, ordered the culprit back to Neuilly. I received from the military authorities who were in charge of the foreign peace delegations an order to send the young man home at once, for the incident would otherwise lead to regrettable explanations. I would emphasise the fact that we had no complaint to make of any violation of the rules of courtesy by the French officers entrusted with our supervision. On the contrary, when we had been there some time, our relations became less tense, but the rules of the internment system to which we were subjected remained the same. We grew accustomed to them, thanks to the very cordial feeling between the members of our delegation. The same intense grief for the fate of our country, and for our inability to help her, dominated us all in a similar way.

Anything that might otherwise have divided us yielded to this supreme sensation. The area within which we were free was sufficiently large, and at that season sufficiently deserted, to allow us a variety of walks, during which no one so much as looked askance at us; although after a fortnight in the streets and coffee-houses and little restaurants in and about Neuilly, which we visited from time to time, every child knew us. I would almost say that we were accorded exceptional treatment in that locality. It happened only once that three members of the delegation, who were taking a walk in the Bois de Boulogne and had reached a deserted part of the forest, were insulted by the cry "Les sales Boches!" shouted at them from behind by a pedestrian. This pedestrian was no other than myself. I had caught sight of my friends, though they had not seen me, and I wanted to amuse myself by watching how they would react to this friendly greeting. They behaved in the proper way, namely by ignoring it, but that evening at dinner, to my great amusement, they related what had happened to them, saying that we could not be sure of our peace after all. Amusement became general when I revealed myself as the cause of this solitary insult suffered by our delegation during their long stay at Neuilly.

Our visit began with the performance of certain formalities, among others the mutual presentation of credentials, and this led at once to a characteristic incident. When our opponents credentials were handed to us, I noticed that those of the American representative were missing. I naturally addressed a letter to the President of the Supreme Council, who was no other than Clemenceau, drawing attention to this omission. In answer to this I received —which was less natural— an almost rude reply: "If we wanted to make trouble," ran Clemenceau's answer, "we had better say that we would not negotiate at all," and in that case they would know how to deal with us. This letter aroused consternation in our circle because of its unusual tone, and I tried to dissipate the bad feeling with an anecdote. I told a story about a Tyrolese peasant whom an artist wished to paint, while on a visit among his mountains, because he had a "head full of character." The peasant related this to his old wife, and added, "I'm blowed if I know what an 'ead of character is, but whatever it means, I took good care to box 'is ears for 'im." This was apparently Clemenceau's method as well, whenever he did not understand anything. My answer to his charming "whatever it means" communication was very definite. I could not imagine how Monsieur le Président had ever formed the idea that we wished to delay the fulfilment of our task. If we had not had a sincere desire to negotiate, we would never have come to Paris. Since we had also to make peace with America, it was natural that we should wish to ensure the presence of an American representative. The incident was in any case at an end, for the American credentials had been handed to us meanwhile. I was anxious to make Clemenceau understand that his letter had met with no success, if he thought to intimidate us by it. In a situation such as ours, to hold one's head proudly is a rule from which there must be no flinching. Later on in this introductory correspondence, I wrote to Clemenceau asking if we might be granted the opportunity of personal negotiation, instead of receiving a written statement of the peace conditions, such as was sent to defeated States whose delegations had been in contact with the Supreme Council before our own. In answer to this letter, the only reply I received was an invitation to present ourselves at the Quai d'Orsay one morning in the course of the next few days, to receive the terms of peace. It was explained to me that I might be accompanied, as far as I remember, by ten members of the Hungarian delegation. We, of course, presented ourselves punctually at the hour mentioned, and were shown into a large waiting room, from which a door led directly into the room where the Supreme Council was already sitting, and where the remaining events were to take place.

This was a lengthy room, down one long side of which, with their backs turned to the five or six windows that lighted it, the members of the Supreme Council were sitting on a platform, in the following order: England, represented by Lloyd George, Lord Curzon and Bonar Law; Italy, represented by Nitti; then Japan. America had already withdrawn from the general peace negotiations, and had also refused to deal directly with us. At the head of the room, Clemenceau was sitting in front of a table, surrounded by several members of the French Cabinet and a crowd of senior officials of the French Ministries concerned. Here also were crowded the by no means large number of official reporters and stenographers. At a little distance from Clemenceau's Presidential seat, armchairs were set out for me and other members of the Hungarian delegation taking part in the ceremony, while in front of mine stood a table. This arrangement had the very considerable disadvantage for me that I could not see the faces of the Allied representatives, apart from Clemenceau's, for all of them had their backs turned to the light, and only their outlines were recognisable. We bowed to one another without speaking, and when we had all taken our places, Clemenceau spoke a few words to me, which amounted to no more than an announcement of the handing over to Hungary of the suggested peace terms. ("Le traité de paix propose a la Hongrie.") The terms were handed over at once by a senior official. It was not without inward bitterness that I noticed the euphemism employed by Clemenceau when he spoke of an offer of peace "proposed to Hungary," for we knew only too well that he was dictating his terms. Of course, I could only receive the "offer" with a silent bow, for Clemenceau at once proceeded to make us the following announcement, which I must quote from memory, but which I can trust myself to repeat almost word for word: "Monsieur le Président" —this was how he always addressed me— "you have asked the Supreme Council for permission to make a speech about the situation of Hungary. The Supreme Council has unanimously decided to grant your request. There can, of course, be no question of a discussion. I shall, therefore, ask you, Monsieur le Président, to mention the day on which it would be convenient to you to make this statement."

I replied as follows: "I thank you, Monsieur le Président, for your information and the Supreme Council for their compliance, but I must observe that there has been a misunderstanding, for what I desired was not so much to make a speech as to take part in a discussion. Since the wishes of the Supreme Council in this matter appear to be final, I gratefully accept your offer. As regards the time of the meeting at which you will be so kind as to listen to me, I have no other request to make than that we should be allowed at least two days, in order to acquaint ourselves thoroughly with the contents of the terms of peace. After this interval, I shall be at the service of the Supreme Council on any day they may choose to suit their own convenience."

To this Monsieur Clemenceau, observing that the other members of the Council were nodding their heads in agreement, informed us that we would be expected at the same time in the morning three days hence.

Our first meeting with the Supreme Council was at an end. It had not really disappointed me, for I had never seriously hoped that we would be granted a real oral discussion, and, in fact, I had only requested it *"pour l'acquit de ma conscience."* What I had actually obtained was of no great practical value, but I could not refuse it, and, rather than worry over the inadequacy of a speech without a discussion, it was my duty to prepare this statement of our case with the greatest care. It was no less important to insure that on the day, and at the hour, appointed for my speech, I should be in the best possible frame of mind, and have my nerves under control. This last is easier said than done, but I felt I could depend upon what I had learnt by experience, that I never speak in public without emotion —even to-day, after sixty years' practice— although after the first few minutes of my speech, my nervous system would become completely calm, and a feeling of absolute confidence would come over me. I prayed to God that it would be so this time, for the audience before whom I had to speak, my relations with them, and my position before the assembly whom I had to impress, were all so completely new to me and attended with such difficulties, that no certain conclusion could be drawn from past experience. I devoted extreme care to the preparation of my statements, for in them I had to explain how utterly grotesque were the terms of peace which had been drawn up for us. I tried to express the great amount which I had to say as concisely and clearly as possible, but I did not compose an outline either in French or English, in both of which languages I expected to be called upon to speak. I could not achieve the necessary calm of mind to write or to dictate. Only the skeleton of my speech was prepared. As for the text, it would have to develop as I went along from the inspiration of the moment, and from any magnetic contact with the audience which I might succeed in establishing. I decided upon the tone which should dominate my speech. There was to be no sentimentality, no lamentations, no appeal to the charity of the victorious Powers, and especially no emotionalism of any kind, but a dry and, as far as possible, a lucid statement of facts, whose natural pathos would work its effect.

As I stepped into the room at the appointed hour, I felt again very strongly the unique character of the situation. I was to address an audience among whom there was not the slightest sympathetic element, an audience of enemies in the technical sense of the word, and for the most part of men ill-disposed towards us, with a slight admixture of indifferent listeners. I was saved from a feeling of complete isolation only by the fragment of our Hungarian delegation which was allowed to accompany me. In them, at any rate, I had ten or twelve companions who were possessed by entirely the same feelings as were uppermost in my mind. To me, they were a symbol of the Hungarian nation for whom I was about to speak.

This thought steeled my nerves for the trial which they would have to undergo.

I have already mentioned that the arrangement of the room made it impossible for me to see the faces of that particular section of the audience from whom I expected less hostile prejudice, namely the English, the Italians, and the Japanese. I stood face to face only with Clemenceau and his staff, and this part of the audience could not or would not hide their far from friendly attitude when I began my speech. In front of me were some malevolently serious faces, and others that wore a mocking smile. I could not be in any doubt as to the kind of prejudice with which my words would be received.

When Clemenceau invited me to begin my speech, I rose to do as he requested, whereupon he asked me very courteously to remain seated. I declined his offer by appealing to my Parliamentary habits. As a matter of fact, I prefer to stand, rather than sit, when addressing any considerable audience.

I began without any introduction by stating that the terms of peace proposed to us were completely unacceptable, and that I would demonstrate this with regard to their principal demands. I at once noticed that this dry tone, avoiding all sentimentality, came as a surprise to my listeners, or at least those of them whose impressions I could observe, and that it reacted not unfavourably on their mood. Very soon, I felt that I was amply compensated for my inability to watch the expressions of most of my audience by being enabled to read in Clemenceau's face even the slightest reactions which my speech provoked. On the whole, I was able to perceive a change taking place in his attitude. He was apparently not displeased with me as a speaker, and consequently his face soon lost the expression of mockery which at first he had not been able to suppress, despite an affectation of politeness. His features took on, little by little, almost a benevolent look. At all events, his eyes left me as seldom as mine left him. I had been speaking for about ten minutes when Clemenceau interrupted me with the remark that my speech would now be translated into English. The interruption had been made at an opportune moment, but it affected me unpleasantly by disturbing the organic structure of my observations. I said that if Monsieur le Président had no objection, I would myself undertake the English translation, for I preferred to carry on in French to the end, and then, after a pause, to deliver my speech as a whole in English. Clemenceau did not accept this. It would be rather too long, he said, for the gentlemen who did not understand French to listen to the whole speech without knowing what it contained. What could I do except bow to the President's decision and obey his wishes? It was left to me to decide at what points I should break off and in the course of my address I had to change over four or five times from the rhythm of the French language to that of the English, and from English back to French, which proved a very troublesome addition to the mental strain I already had to endure. Fortunately, I was able to overcome this obstacle without allowing the carefully prepared unity in the construction of my observations to suffer, or any failing of power to be apparent in my speech. It was only in the afternoon of that memorable day, when the nervous excitement of the event had worn off, that I experienced a feeling of weariness such as I have never known before or since.

A great part of my speech was devoted to proving how completely mistaken were the territorial clauses of the Treaty of Trianon from an ethnographical standpoint. It showed how some of the proposals were a direct blow in the face for the principle of nationality which was their slogan. While I was explaining this in English, Lloyd George sent a note to Clemenceau, which the latter was obviously annoyed to receive, though he answered it by a nod of the head to Lloyd George. I was curious as to what this incident meant, and I was not informed until my speech was over. When I had finished, Clemenceau called on Lloyd George to speak, and the latter invited me to supply more detailed explanations of what I had said in the course of my speech concerning the distribution of races, and especially of the Magyars, in the territories detached from Hungary.

I now understood why Clemenceau had seemed put out when Lloyd George's note was handed to him. The principle by which no discussion should be allowed had been broken to some extent by this request for more exact explanations. Fortunately, I was prepared for such questions. I had brought with me Pal Teleki's excellent ethnographical map of Hungary, and with this I went up to where Lloyd George was sitting. The national leaders crowded there in a body, and with their heads together over a map heard my explanations. These obviously caused them to have some doubts about the wisdom of the vivisection which they had proposed to carry out on my poor country without sufficient anatomical knowledge. Lloyd George whispered to me, "You were very eloquent." I replied, "If there was any eloquence, it was not mine, but the eloquence of facts."

I was told, in fact, that after this meeting some quite strong protests were made by England and Italy, who complained that they had been/led into the unpleasant situation of being made a party to such gross errors. Nitti even made a serious attempt to bring about certain changes in the more absurd clauses of the treaty, but he was at length overruled by the argument that the entire map arranged by their peace treaties would collapse if an alteration were permitted in any part.

When I had come safely to the end of my French and English addresses, and, out of politeness, had spoken a few words to the Italian delegation in their own language, Clemenceau made me a little speech, whose almost friendly tone was in striking contrast to that which he had adopted at the beginning of the meeting.

"Monsieur le Président," —he said in effect— "you have seen with what keen attention the whole Supreme Council has followed your statements. You will certainly not expect that we should at once make up our minds about what you have told us. You may rest assured, however, that we will give the most careful and close consideration to this matter. Meanwhile, we are awaiting the written answer of the Hungarian delegation to the terms of peace which have been submitted to them, and we would ask you to tell us how long you will require to complete your reply." I asked for an interval of four weeks, which was immediately granted.

And so ended the morning which had brought me the most difficult hours of my public life.

There can be no doubt that, on the whole, a somewhat more favourable atmosphere was created among those with whom the decision rested. It was clearly perceptible wherever we had direct contact with Allied circles. On the other hand, there was no sign of it in the Paris press. The reports which appeared there on the meeting I have described were obviously from an official source. In these, some tribute was paid to my linguistic achievement, while the truth of my statements was brushed aside with a few derisive observations of a general kind.

No words need be wasted in explaining why the French press was hostile to our mission, for this hostility was a natural consequence of the situation. How carefully this hostile attitude had been worked up may be seen from the following almost incredible details. Thirteen years earlier, in 1907, on the occasion of an Inter-Parliamentary meeting held in Berlin, I had delivered a humorous speech at a dinner-party. In the course of this, I remarked that, if the man in the moon came down for a short time to the earth and asked me which of our so-called world languages he should learn for the sake of his general education, I would unquestionably recommend German, because the assimilative power of the German intellect would open the way for him through excellent translations to the greatest number of cultural achievements in other lands. This was brought up against me in the Paris press —I repeat, after thirteen years— as a proof of excessive pro-German feeling! Still more amazing was a reference in the Paris press to an equally humorous after-dinner speech which I had made in Budapest many years before the outbreak of war, in honour of Dr. Gyula Vargha, then head of the Bureau of Statistics. On the occasion of some jubilee or other, his friends arranged an agreeable little dinner-party, at which I remarked that Vargha, who was also a lyrical poet of some standing, would be capable of transfiguring even the driest figures into poetry by the ardour of his patriotism. I had completely forgotten about this speech, and was astounded to see it reprinted by the Paris press in 1920 as evidence that Hungarian statistics were no more than poetical falsification. This resuscitation of long-forgotten remarks, which even in their time had had no significance, typifies the atmosphere in which we lived.

For the moment, we had nothing further to do in France. The detailed statement in which we were to reply to the terms of peace that had been handed us could be prepared just as well, and even better, in Budapest than in Paris. After a stay of ten days, we therefore set out for home on January 18.

In Budapest we were received, on our arrival at the station, by all the members of the government, as well as by Admiral Horthy, who was not yet Regent, but Commander-in-Chief of the Hungarian forces, and an immense crowd of people. The entire city had been decked out with black flags on receiving official news of the terms of peace. In the addresses of welcome one felt, besides their warm acknowledgment of our efforts, a painful sense of hopelessness, which was only the logical reaction after the mood of unwarranted confidence that they had felt a short time before. It was our duty now to protest against this other extreme, and, in my reply to the official welcome, I asked the authorities to have these black flags removed, and to support the work of the peace delegation, which was only now entering upon its decisive stage, by preserving their self-control like men.

We began our work immediately. The situation was thrashed out with eminent politicians of all parties, and, with the assistance of leading experts in all branches of public life, a complete, detailed statement was prepared of the injustices and shortcomings in the draft treaty. On February i 2, we returned to Paris, and, on our arrival, at once handed over our voluminous answer to the Supreme Council. Once this had been accomplished, we had nothing further to do but to wait in Neuilly for the final decision which the Supreme Council would make, after they had considered our reply.

We waited until March 31.

The events of that month and a half belong to the preliminary history of the Treaty of Trianon, and are to a great extent still unsuitable for publication. Here I intend to speak only of matters which can be treated in an anecdotal way, and which throw some light on the psychological situation.

As I have said, the Hungarian peace delegation had returned to Paris, or more correctly to Neuilly, provided with an immense amount of material which had been worked up for them on ethnography, geography, history, finance, trade, hydrography and other technical subjects. We occupied our place of internment again, under the same conditions as during our first stay. All contact with Paris was forbidden. It happened once that a French lady, who had been governess in the house of one of our delegates —Vilmos Lers, State Secretary in the Ministry of Trade— and was now living with her children in Paris, read in the newspaper the name which she knew so well. She came to Neuilly to welcome the father of her former pupils, but she was not allowed to see him. This is only one instance to show how inflexibly the principle of our isolation from the outer world was maintained. After the short interval of relief which we experienced when the general atmosphere had seemed brighter, we relapsed into the dark pessimism which we had brought with us on our first arrival in Paris. This was increased by the inactivity which our situation forced upon us. We had nothing to do but to wait and see what decision we would receive concerning the critical statement we had handed in. We could not even hope that we might soon be enlightened on this point, but on the contrary were obliged to look upon this postponement of the answer as a good sign, for it allowed us to assume that the arguments we had advanced were being made the subject of serious discussion. In daily consultations, we racked our brains to know what we might still do for the advancement of our cause. We made use of every possible occasion to address notes on this or that special point to the Supreme Council, in most cases without receiving an answer. An exception to this was one lengthy memorandum which I personally addressed to the newly-elected President of the Republic, Monsieur Deschanel, with whom I had formerly been on very good terms, in which I endeavoured to make clear certain consequences of the partition of Hungary which would affect the special interests of France. This memorandum was at least thought worthy of an acknowledgment.

From a human point of view, another incident is perhaps not without interest, as it is certainly gratifying. I received private information that one of my oldest friends, who was living at Temesvár —a town seized by the Rumanians— was the victim of particularly virulent persecution which might even lead to his being sentenced by a military court. I wrote personally to Clemenceau appealing to his humanity, in the hope that he would intervene on my friend's behalf. I received no answer, but I assume the intervention took place, because the persecution suddenly ceased.

Some members of our delegation who had friends in Paris got in touch with them by letter, and arranged to meet them at certain parts of the Bois de Boulogne. They were not a little proud of having thus broken through the internment cordon, although these secret meetings could be of no great help, except in so far as they gave us more information about events in French politics than we could derive from the newspapers. I would add that these skillfully plotted meetings of conspirators ended humorously. At the end of March, when our duties in Paris were over, we returned definitely to Budapest, leaving only Mr. Prasnowsky, afterwards Hungarian Minister in Paris, to settle any remaining details. One day our chief military supervisor, the same Colonel Henry whom I have already mentioned, came and smilingly handed him a sheet of paper with these words: "You will find here, my dear Monsieur Prasnowsky, a list of all the people whom you have met in the Bois de Boulogne. I am not criticising you, far from it. But I would not like you to think us fools." We had therefore been under much closer observation than we had suspected.

Great was our surprise when one day two countrymen of ours living in Paris, Dr. Károly Halmos and Andor Semsey, who afterwards entered the Hungarian diplomatic service, were led into our conference room by Colonel Henry, and we were informed that these gentlemen had free access to us at any time. What could have happened? In high French financial circles, a movement had started for a large scale trade agreement with Hungary. That this was considered very seriously is proved by the fact that the firm of Schneider-Creusot was taking the lead. This firm enjoyed the favour of influential political circles in France, and met with such support at the Quai d Orsay that, at their request, the gates of our internment house were opened. Mr. Halmos had business connections with these financial circles, and it was taken for granted that they would use all their influence to secure a modification of the conditions of peace imposed upon Hungary.

From now on, our presence within the radius of Paris acquired an entirely new character. Members of our delegation could often go to Paris, and even deal directly with the Quai d Orsay. I designated for this purpose, with the subsequent approval of the Government, Count Imre Csáky, and afterwards, on the advice of our financial experts, Counts István Bethlen and Pál Teleki. I thought it best not to take part myself in the negotiations. They lasted well on into the summer, long after the Hungarian peace delegation had ceased to exist. It does not belong to these recollections to describe the hopes which they aroused, or the reason why they came to nothing. Throughout most of our second stay, they created for us a better, and almost hopeful, atmosphere, which we breathed as eagerly as a man breathes the pure air when be comes suddenly into the open from some stuffy room. I well remember how we won back our sense of humour, and how certain members of the delegation went into Paris to hear some of the frequent concerts of the season, without being prevented by the authorities. The inevitable detective travelled with them to a certain point in the city, where our friends were given complete liberty of movement until the hour arranged for their return to Neuilly.

I myself only made use of this chance to visit the city under police supervision when an acute toothache made it necessary. This happened in the early part of our stay, perhaps about the beginning of March. The detective travelled with me to the dentist, and remained in the waiting room until I had been treated, when he again took me under his protection. As it was then almost spring, and I had only brought with me a warm winter overcoat, I availed myself of one of these dental expeditions to buy a spring coat in one of the big Paris shops, I think the Bon Marché. The detective of course accompanied me there, and he could not rest until he had whispered my identity right and left to the entire personnel of the departments we crossed. The consequence was that, on reaching the overcoat department, I was surrounded by a whole group of inquisitive people, who obviously wanted to see if a Boche looked human and had civilised manners. This flattering curiosity was not to the advantage of my business transaction. It caused me to finish it as quickly as possible, and the result was that I came to possess an overcoat which did not suit me at all. I gave it the name of the Danaïd coat, because, instead of the pocket in which I usually carry my handkerchief, it had only an opening, whose purpose was not made clear, on either side, through which I lost many handkerchiefs, before I got used to the situation. This overcoat, and the losses which it caused me, were the subject of much merriment in our delegation, and it remained the only material souvenir which I carried away with me from this otherwise very serious visit. Seen from that point of view, my acquisition of it is an example of the frequent mingling of the grotesque with the serious, or even tragic, of which anyone who has been through serious events in his life can relate instances.

We left Paris at the end of March, because the negotiations which were taking place did not require the presence of our whole delegation and had also to be carried on partly in Budapest. We were in a comparatively joyful frame of mind. The answer of the Allied Powers to our observations on the proposed treaty had not been received at the time of our departure. It had been postponed until it was known if, how far and in what manner the peace treaty might be modified as a result of the negotiations, though these were admittedly only of a business kind. The Hungarian government never concealed the fact that they could only make business concessions in return for others of a political nature.

It will make an interesting chapter in the history of our times when it is possible to describe why and when the whole attempt finally collapsed.

When this failure had once been ascertained, there was nothing left for it but to accept the fate which was ordained for us. The day at last broke on which was held that tragic session of Parliament at which the Treaty of Trianon was to be ratified. No one who took part in this ceremony in Parliament will ever forget it. The dry, business-like way in which the event was carried out heightened its terrible effectiveness. A minority protested against the ratification, and left the chamber. The majority stayed behind, and remained silent when the President asked if the assembly agreed to ratification. Thereupon, the President assumed that no opposition was being made, and hence that the ratification must be taken as voted. Under the impulse of an irresistible instinct, the whole assembly rose and broke out into the Hungarian national anthem, the voices of the gallery mingling with those of the members. No eye remained dry. Since that day, the flags on the Parliament House and on all other public buildings are flown continually at half-mast.

Thus was the seal set upon the vanity of our efforts. It redounds greatly to the honour of my people that they have borne no grudge against the members of the peace delegation, and in particular against me, its leader, for the failure we incurred but, on the contrary, have valued our valiant attempt as highly as if success had crowned it. This nation has indeed its faults, but meanness of disposition is not among them. It is noble and generous through and through in its sentiments. I would almost say that its soul is too great for the wasted body into which it has been crushed, though it gives to that body a power of achievement far greater than its population would seem to support. To have served this nation faithfully, as I believe, for sixty years, and perhaps to be able to serve her longer, is my pride and joy in the evening of my life.

My first visit to Paris after the events which I have here described took place the following year. The atmosphere which I found there was so similar to the one I had known as leader of the peace delegation that it may still be described in this chapter under the heading of "How Peace was made after the Great War." I use the word "atmosphere" because all external circumstances which would have indicated a continuance of the state of war, such as, for example, the limitation of one's freedom of movement and so on, had, of course, disappeared. Immediately after the signing of the Treaty of Trianon, we had shaken hands, and this was now permitted to everyone, but not everyone took to it kindly, as I was soon to discover. I had come to Paris to take part in a meeting of the League of Nations Union, which was then being formed, and from which we could not absent ourselves. I made use of the opportunity to get in touch with some leading politicians, which I was easily able to do. The most interesting conversations I had were with the new President of the Republic, Alexandre Millerand, and with

Monsieur Poincaré, who was then looked upon as the head of the extreme nationalists. I also called on Paleologue's successor, Berthelot, who was the actual head of French foreign policy, and not so well disposed towards us as his predecessor. The welcome I received from him was most courteous, but the conversations which I had with him were calculated to destroy any illusions I might still be cherishing. He was always stressing the fact that the peace treaties which had just been signed must never be altered, and that Hungary would have to reconcile herself to this situation. This was no surprise to me, and for that reason I was not greatly impressed. It was Raymond Poincaré who spoke out more clearly than any. The conversation with him lasted for about an hour, and as he had no official post at the moment, he put off his reserve and allowed me to have a frank conversation on all matters. We carried on a discussion about the problem of war guilt, and our talk terminated in a sentence which he delivered with his customary sharp intonation. I remember it word for word. "The whole question comes to this: Is Hungary definitely prepared to accept the situation made for her by the Treaty, without any intention of bringing about a change? If so, we can get on very well together." As he was obviously waiting for an answer, I spoke as follows, —I can quote my reply almost word for word: "Monsieur Poincaré, am I to tell you a lie? In that case, you would not believe me, so I will answer 'No.' Hungary cannot accept the injustice which has been inflicted on her. One thing of which I am certain, though, is that we are not thinking of violent methods to restore our rights." Poincaré's reply was not quite audible, but I thought I heard something like "It's always like that." With this, I took my leave of a statesman for whom I have the greatest respect, in spite of his rough manner. These semi-official conversations were quite calm and orderly. I was still looked upon as the President of the Hungarian peace delegation, and therefore a person who enjoyed to some extent diplomatic immunity.

Of quite another kind was my first meeting with unofficial people who took part, like myself, in the sessions of the League of Nations Union. Some of these I had met more than once in the course of the year at Inter-Parliamentary Conferences, and I was on friendly terms with them. Chief among these was the late Senator, d'Estournelles de Constant, who had been my guest at Eberhard, and who had given me the warmest welcome whenever I came to Paris in the last years before the War. At his hospitable house, he had always arranged for me to meet such politicians as I was particularly interested in. All unsuspecting, I went up to him and offered my hand, but his attitude was icy. Reluctantly and with a bad grace, he accepted my handshake, and, in answer to my friendly words, said just as much as was necessary in order not to be actually rude. I saw quite clearly how another of my old friends manoeuvred to avoid meeting me, which made me feel very uncomfortable. On the same afternoon d'Estournelles de Constant felt obliged to offer an explanation. It was clear that it hurt this good and kind man to be forced, as he thought, to adopt this attitude with an old friend. He came up to me, and said that he felt he owed it to our former friendship to explain the distant manner which he must now assume towards me.

It was his duty to behave in this way, because I had been one of those who caused the War and among the most eager promoters of it. To this amazing accusation I could only retort: "As regards the origin of the War, I can prove an alibi, for when the ultimatum was sent to Serbia I was on the coast of Belgium, the very last place where I would have chosen to be if I had had any idea of what was going to happen. As regards my having urged the continuance of the War, I do not hesitate to admit that, once the die was cast and the clash could not be avoided, I put forth all my efforts, in word and writing, at home and abroad, to sustain the energy and enthusiasm of my people in their decisive struggle."

I do not know if d'Estournelles regarded this attitude as an incitement to war, but I do know that, had he been in the same position, he would have behaved as I did. D'Estournelles was obviously touched, but he did not submit at once and it was not for me to take any further steps towards reconciliation. This was to happen at our next meeting, in the course of a Council session of the Inter-Parliamentary Union, when he overwhelmed me with signs of esteem and friendship. Whenever an opportunity presented itself, he tried to support my suggestions and, in fact, to make up for the rudeness of his behaviour at our first meeting, without actually having to offer an explanation. I willingly responded to this method of silent compromise, but I knew all the time how deeply embedded was the war psychosis, and I realised the necessity, both from a political and from a personal point of view, of re-establishing our former contacts. . .

I have thought it worth while to record these personal memories because they throw considerable light on the war psychology which was still uppermost when the treaties were signed in 1919 - 20, and thus enable one to understand the nature of that peace-making. At the same time, I wish to put on record that I have been able in subsequent years to observe the progressive subsidence of these emotional antagonisms. This has been clear to me at various international assemblies, such as Inter-Parliamentary Conferences, meetings of the League of Nations Union, and the periodical sessions of the League of Nations itself which I have attended regularly for eight years as the representative of my country. I am prepared to state my opinion that the political differences which are still outstanding will no longer be embittered by enmities of a personal kind. Ties have been established which should assist the peaceful settlement of difficulties that are objective in character. Whatever may be said against the League of

Nations —and I do not deny that its activities leave much to be desired— the opportunity which it provides for international discussion is a service of incalculable importance to the cause of international reconciliation. However great the antagonisms and difficulties may still be, I hope that a continuation of this chapter will appear within a reasonable time under the title of "How real peace was made in the year x."

....

Milton Keynes UK
Ingram Content Group UK Ltd.
UKHW010033290923
429602UK00014B/208/J